OFFICIALLY DISCARDED

Eastern Europe
in the 1970s

edited by
**Sylva Sinanian
Istvan Deak
Peter C. Ludz**

Published under the joint sponsorship of the Center for Continuing Education and The Institute on East Central Europe, Columbia University

The Praeger Special Studies program—utilizing the most modern and efficient book production techniques and a selective worldwide distribution network—makes available to the academic, government, and business communities significant, timely research in U.S. and international economic, social, and political development.

Eastern Europe in the 1970s

PRAEGER SPECIAL STUDIES IN INTERNATIONAL POLITICS AND GOVERNMENT

Praeger Publishers New York Washington London

PRAEGER PUBLISHERS
111 Fourth Avenue, New York, N.Y. 10003, U.S.A.
5, Cromwell Place, London S.W.7, England

Published in the United States of America in 1972
by Praeger Publishers, Inc.

Second printing, 1974

All rights reserved

© 1972 by Praeger Publishers, Inc.

Library of Congress Catalog Card Number: 72-85988

Printed in the United States of America

PREFACE

This volume represents a compilation of papers prepared for a conference held at Columbia University, December 3-5, 1971, entitled "New Perspectives in Understanding East Central Europe." It is designed to promote a better understanding of Eastern Europe through scholarly work on the area.

Any volume such as this of course has more specific objectives also. One is to emphasize the need for a reorientation of Eastern European studies by pointing to the advantages of cross-national academic cooperation. Hence the inclusion of papers by experts from the United States, Canada, France, England, and the Federal Republic of Germany, and of contributions by scholars from Eastern and Southeastern Europe—Hungary, Poland, and Yugoslavia especially. Another is to point out the advantages of an interdisciplinary approach in Eastern European studies; thus the incorporation of works in history, political science, sociology, economics, and philosophy. Yet, the emphasis here is not on an "inventory" of present knowledge and research. No effort has been made to make as complete a list as possible of what is known and is worthwhile studying in the Eastern European field. Rather an attempt has been made to identify some significant and topical subjects of Eastern European research.

The cross-national cooperative and interdisciplinary approach advanced here is very different in its conception from those found in studies conducted during the cold war period. The individual states of Eastern Europe are not regarded as Moscow's satellites; the assumption is that each country is a separate entity with its own historical, political, and social conditions that warrant careful study. The methodological framework is therefore broader than that of most Communist studies of cold war vintage. This means that the articles in this volume deal with Eastern European countries by treating specific topics related to their recent history and describing their actual political, social, and economic situations; while also identifying trends for the immediate future in order to improve the scholarly understanding of these countries and reevaluate the influence of Communist ideology upon them.

The examination of the impact of Fascism and National Socialism on Eastern Europe in the period 1930-45 and after World War II illustrates the need for such a broad and interdisciplinary approach, as does the question of Soviet war aims and their effect on political, social, and economic developments in Eastern Europe. The compass of our concerns inevitably leads to an examination of the "national question" or, more precisely, the problems of national self-determination involving issues of both social policy and power politics. In all Eastern and Southeastern European countries national integration and political identity are at stake. And these problems can hardly be considered without some understanding of the legitimacy of power. This, in turn, is a difficult and highly controversial matter, further complicated by political crises in the West.

An evaluation of historical and political problems is further facilitated by taking into consideration data on economic integration. COMECON, providing its member states with an integrative economic and political framework, has a decisive influence upon all matters of national self-determination in Eastern Europe.

Finally, the approach of this volume is characterized by the assumption that Eastern Europe as a whole should be a field of study in its own right and not be an annex to or extension of so-called Soviet studies. In light of the role the Eastern European states are playing in international politics today, and of our increasing awareness of and interest in these countries, the separation of the Eastern European field from that of Soviet studies seems to be justified. This approach of necessity assumes that the German Democratic Republic should be included in the realm of Eastern European studies and regarded as equal to other countries in the area insofar as its political status is concerned.

The conference from which this volume emerged was sponsored jointly by the Institute on East Central Europe and the Center for Continuing Education at Columbia University. It was organized by Prof. Peter C. Ludz of the University of Bielefeld in the Federal Republic of Germany and Professor Vojtech Mastny of Columbia University. Mrs. Sylva Sinanian was the administrator. Prof. Istvan Deak, Director of the Institute on East Central Europe, provided valuable advice and counsel. The editors are also grateful to Mr. Paul Shapiro who gave the manuscript a final reading. The conference was attended by about 300 scholars.

CONTENTS

		Page
PREFACE		v

Chapter

1 IS THERE AN EAST CENTRAL EUROPE?
    Hugh Seton-Watson — 3

2 FASCISM IN INTERWAR EASTERN EUROPE: THE DICHOTOMY OF POWER AND INFLUENCE
    Peter F. Sugar — 13
    Analyses — 32
        Martin Broszat — 32
        Istvan Deak — 36
        Gyorgy Ránki — 40
        Piotr S. Wandycz — 42

3 LEGITIMACY OF POWER IN EAST CENTRAL EUROPE
    Alfred Meyer — 45
    Analyses — 68
        Oskar Anweiler — 68
        W. Harriet Critchley — 71
        George L. Kline — 76
        Rudolf Tökes — 79

4 SPHERES OF INFLUENCE AND SOVIET WAR AIMS IN 1943
    Vojtech Mastny — 87
    Analyses — 107
        John C. Campbell — 107
        Herbert S. Dinerstein — 111
        Richard Löwenthal — 113
        Jovan Marjanovic — 116
        Henry L. Roberts — 118

Chapter		Page
5	THE NATIONAL QUESTION AND THE POLITICAL SYSTEMS OF EASTERN EUROPE	
	Paul Shoup	121
	Analyses	171
	Stephen Fischer-Galati	171
	Paul Shapiro	173
	Georg W. Strobel	176
	Kenneth Jowitt	180
	Paul E. Zinner	184
6	TOWARD A SOCIALIST ECONOMIC INTEGRATION OF EASTERN EUROPE	
	Heinrich Machowski	189
	Analyses	200
	Ivan Berend	200
	William Diebold, Jr.	202
	John M. Montias	205
7	EAST CENTRAL EUROPEAN STUDIES: THEIR PRESENT AND FUTURE	209
	The Role of the Social Sciences, by Peter C. Ludz	209
	Research Opportunities, by George W. Hoffman	220
8	NORMALIZATION OF RELATIONS BETWEEN THE FEDERAL REPUBLIC OF GERMANY AND EASTERN EUROPE	228
	Roundtable Discussion Number 1: Moderated by Zbigniew Brzezinski	228
	Participants	228
	Richard Löwenthal	228
	Pierre Hassner	233
	Claus Soenksen	235
	P. Andrzej Wojtowicz	237
	Harry Schwartz	238
	Robert Bowie	240

Chapter		Page
9	THE ROLE OF THE GERMAN DEMOCRATIC REPUBLIC WITHIN EASTERN EUROPE	242
	Roundtable Discussion Number 2: Moderated by Robert G. Livingston	242
	Participants	242
	Melvin Croan	242
	William E. Griffith	246
	Henry Krisch	248
	Peter C. Ludz	251
	Phillip Schmidt-Schlegel	254
10	SUMMATION	
	Marshall Shulman	258
ABOUT THE EDITORS		261

Eastern Europe
in the 1970s

CHAPTER 1

IS THERE AN EAST CENTRAL EUROPE?

Hugh Seton-Watson

Obviously East Central Europe does exist in the sense that those countries exist. But the question that the rather frivolous title is intended to raise concerns the position of those countries in Europe today.

Various names have been used at different times: Central Europe, Southeastern Europe, the Balkans, Eastern Europe, and others too. At the end of World War II, in English-speaking countries, the term "Eastern Europe" came into fairly general use. Then there was the expression "East Central Europe," devised by Prof. Halecki. I have recently been rereading his book The Limits and Divisions of European History,* and after more than 20 years its insights and its brilliant presentation have lost none of their power to fascinate me. But today we must ask what has changed in these 20 years. Which of the names that have been used to describe the countries are most appropriate for today? Is any of them appropriate or is there indeed the possibility of finding a new name?

Let us briefly consider the different views that have been held of the divisions of Europe and the different names that have been used for them only since the beginning of the twentieth century. Perhaps

---

*Oskar Halecki, The Limits and Divisions of European History (London and New York: Sheed and Ward, 1950).

Hugh Seton-Watson is Professor of Russian History at the University of London.

by recalling the name and the period we may be able to take a fresh look at today's reality.

At the beginning of this century, Western, Central, and Eastern Europe could fairly easily be distinguished. Western Europe consisted of the German Empire and the Habsburg monarchy; and Eastern Europe of the Russian Empire. In the southern part of the continent it was difficult to apply these divisions; Spain and Portugal were marginal to Western Europe: only Catalonia belonged wholly to the West. Italy had elements of both West and Central Europe. Southeastern Europe was a separate region known as the Balkans, consisting of a remnant of the Ottoman Empire in Europe and the small independent states that had emerged from that Empire.

I think it was the historian Nicolae Iorga who remarked that there was, in fact, only one Balkan state, Bulgaria. Romania was a Carpathian state, Greece was a Mediterranean state, and as for Yugoslavia, whatever it was, it was not, in Iorga's terminology, a Balkan state. He had a point, but the name stuck nevertheless.

If, for a moment, we leave out the three southern peninsulas, we can think of Continental Europe as divided at that time (around 1900) into three great cultural regions: the French, the German, and the Russian. One can also speak of three main types of political systems: the Parliamentary, with Britain and France as two divergent and yet basically related examples of one type; secondly, the semiliberal and semiauthoritarian Rechtsstaat, of which Prussia and Austria again provide different variants; and finally, the Russian autocracy, which, even in its diluted form in the age of Stolypin in the first decade of the century, was still very different from the regimes of Central Europe.

Another great distinction between Central and Eastern, but not at that time between Central and Western Europe, concerned the nature of public administration. In Russia, the unpredictable despotism of the gendarme and the provincial governor, and the corruption and procrastination of lower officials were of the very essence of the system. In Germany and Austria, officials may at times have been rather pompous or arrogant, but they were honest, efficient, punctual; they knew and observed their own laws. One might perhaps modify this by saying that these characteristics were a little less prevalent when you crossed the Leitha into Hungary.

Other important divisions cut across and made nonsense of the lines separating Western, Central, and Eastern Europe mentioned above. The Russian Empire proclaimed the supremacy of the Orthodox Church, but those of Orthodox faith could be found outside Russia, not only in the Balkans but also in the Habsburg monarchy, and there were Catholics in the Russian Empire. Frontiers ran right through the middle of certain nations, through the middle of the lands inhabited by Poles, Romanians and Serbs. There was another important dividing line that was independent of state frontiers. This was the division between predominantly urban, industrial, and educated communities and predominantly rural, agricultural, and illiterate or semiliterate communities. This line ran from north to south well to the west of the Russian border, and left to the east of it Galicia, Transylvania, Bosnia and a large part of Hungary proper and of Croatia. If we think of the division between Central and Eastern Europe in primarily social and economic terms, then our line must pass through the Habsburg monarchy itself. There were, in fact, two lines, both significant: a political line, the frontier of Germany and Austro-Hungary with Russia; and a socioeconomic line, running much further west. There were, of course, important urban islands in the middle of backward regions. Budapest, Cracow and Zagreb were socially and economically Central European islands. It might be argued that Bucharest, where more French was spoken than German, was to some extent a socially and economically Western island. Incidentally, the social and economic dividing line did not come to an end when it reached the Adriatic. It cut across middle Italy westward and across Spain, roughly from Barcelona to Bilbao.

After the World War I, the frontiers were shifted to the west and the north. Now the Poles, Romanians, and Serbs were united in larger states. To some extent the political line between west and east had now been brought up to coincide with the socioeconomic line, but not entirely, of course. Then, further to the east lay the Soviet Union, whose leaders claimed to be building a new world aimed at realizing the brotherhood of man, including but transcending all of Europe through the world revolution. Nevertheless, the old frontier that had separated the old Central Europe from the old Eastern Europe and the Balkans had left a deep imprint. The frontiers now corresponded more nearly with the socioeconomic dividing line, but the dividing line of political traditions and administrative practices was left further east, passing through the middle of some of the new states. In four of the new states, Poland, Czechoslovakia, Romania, and Yugoslavia, a fusion took place of Central and Eastern elements. In Czechoslovakia, the economically and culturally more advanced Czechs prevailed, through their greater numerical strength, over the Slovaks who had previously been in the Central-East border zone. But in the other countries it was the Easterners who were the stronger. In Poland and Romania the Easterners' methods were resented, but, nevertheless, national unity of all Poles and all Romanians was never in doubt and was greatly reinforced between the wars and survived the later cataclysm. In Czechoslovakia and Yugoslavia the major social and cultural divisions also coincided with national divisions. The Slovaks disliked being bossed by the Czechs even if, in fact, the Czechs were leading them to a better material and cultural life. The Croats not only disliked being bossed by Serbs, but lost no opportunity to brandish their thousand-year-old culture and to proclaim their contempt for the oriental, corrupt Serbs. It must be admitted that those Croatian businessmen and officials who made use of the opportunity to compete on their own ground with the Serbs often more than held their own.

However, even if we leave out the moralizing rhetoric, the fact remains that the creation of the new states had not obliterated the old division between Central and Eastern Europe. When I first got to know some of these regions and peoples in the 1930s, I found the existence of the distinction widely recognized. Yet all attempts to reduce it to simple formulas failed.

Then came the war, conquest by Hitler, conquest by the Soviet Army, the barbed wire and search lights most of the way from the Baltic to the Adriatic. Everything was shifted westward. The Soviet Union advanced nearly to the western border of the Russian Empire; Poland advanced to the Oder; and Western Europe was pushed into dependence on the United States. In the center of Europe, Germany and Austria were prostrate and Italy was not in much better shape. This is the situation that Professor Halecki had in mind when he wrote his book. He saw Europe still intact, merging itself into a new Atlantic community. And so he made, in that book of his, a rather striking comparison. He compared the period toward the end of the first Christian millenium when the loss to Islam of Spain and of the southern and eastern shores of the Mediterranean was compensated by the gain for Christendom of Poland and Scandinavia—in brief the period when the transition from the Roman Empire to Christian Europe was completed—with the pushing of Western Europe into dependence on the Atlantic. The compensation for the loss of so much of Europe to the Soviet Empire consisted of bringing the Atlantic world into Europe. It was, in those days, an interesting and rather well-argued theory. At that time, to the east of the European Atlantic periphery, Halecki distinguished two zones: West Central Europe, consisting of the German speaking lands in ruins, and East Central Europe made up of the lands between Germany and Russia. This division by Halecki was far subtler and intellectually more challenging than the view that was on the whole prevalent at that time: namely, that Europe was divided into West and East by an iron curtain, that everything to the East was going to be swallowed up in a single monolithic, ideological empire, stretching from Weimar to Shanghai, and that everything to the west was doomed to a much more agreeable vassalage, but still vassalage.

Even so, it must be admitted that at the time there was a certain amount of evidence that pointed that way. Twenty years later, neither view seems to fit that reality. First, the distinction between Western and West-Central Europe had virtually disappeared. This is not to say that there still are not enormous differences between the French, German, Italian, and English national cultures. Nevertheless, the common features of Atlantic neocapitalism have become more and more obvious from Glasgow to Graz and from Stockholm to Palermo. The Atlantic way of life, the values of a consumer society for better or worse, extend all the way to the Lübeck-Maribor line. Indeed, they make themselves felt very much beyond the Pyrenees and, I should add, beyond the Karawanken.

During these 20 years, also, the differences between the culture, art, and way of life of the peoples of Halecki's East Central Europe and, on the other hand, those of the peoples of the Soviet Union seem to me to have grown deeper and deeper, while the differences among the peoples of the region have diminished. By differences, of course, I do not mean disagreements. All too many disagreements remain; hardy plants that no amount of gales of history seem able to blow away—in Transylvania or in Macedonia to take the most obvious cases. What I mean is that the differences between the cultural level, the social structure, and the degree of national consciousness of these peoples have enormously diminished, even in the case of the Czechs and Romanians, who a generation ago were at opposite poles of development and backwardness in the area.

Let me explain my point by referring to Romania, which I knew in the late 1930s and have revisited a number of times in recent years. In the late 1930s the Romanian intellectual and social elite were unquestionably European, with a culture largely derived from the French. This European culture extended below the elite, and perhaps strongly influenced at least a third of the population: small businessmen, minor officials, peasants in the more advanced regions. But below this level the bulk of the Romanian people consisted of very poor, unskilled, illiterate or semiliterate, exploited, and brutally misruled peasants and workers. The European elite and the Romanian masses lived in two different worlds. I would not go so far as to say that they were two different nations; in one sense they did definitely belong to the same nation. The masses certainly had some degree of national consciousness—they knew that their country was called Romania or, if they were Transylvanians, then they knew they were Romanians and not Hungarians. Romanian peasant soldiers fought with great bravery, and with greater success than historians have usually realized, for their country at the battle of Marasesht in 1917 in World War I, and in the Ukraine and, for that matter, after changing sides, in Hungary and Slovakia in World War II. The word "Europe" was also known to them as something to be applauded. It can hardly be said, however, that Romanian peasants and workers belonged in

any real sense to European culture. Between the wars, the river
Dniester was the boundary between an allegedly socialist state and a
semicapitalist, semifeudal bureaucratic state. But the peasants working on each side of it were far more like one another than were the
Romanian peasants to the polished Europeans who ruled in Bucharest.
Romanian peasants in the Dobrudja plain and the Kolkhozniki on the
Ukrainian steppe were both only a short stage removed from the
mujiks of nineteenth-century Russian literature. Now, in 1971,
Romania is not a land of mujiks. The peasants still form not much
less than half the population; they go to school for efficient, if perhaps ideological teaching. Their material standard of living is
greatly improved and their life has been transformed by the values
of urban culture. This is not to deny that a terrible price was paid
in human misery, injustice, and cruelty in the 1950s; that poverty and
backwardness still exist in many Romanian villages; or that there
is still among the peasantry some smoldering resentment against
the rulers in the towns. It would be surprising if these things were
not so. Nevertheless, the changes mentioned have taken place. As
for the children of peasants who have left the village to work in industry or administration, they have been even more transformed.
Today, Romanian national culture is coextensive with the Romanian
population. This process of penetration of a national culture from
an elite down into the masses, accompanied, of course, also by an
opposite process of influence by the masses on the elite, is familiar
to the social historian from the experience of many other nations
in many parts of the world.

The interesting thing about the Romanian case is that the process is taking place under the government of a Communist Party.
The national culture into which the masses have now been absorbed
is predominantly the same national culture, including a good proportion of national historical mythology, that was formed by the old
cultural elite during the nineteenth and early twentieth century. That
cultural elite was not destroyed by the postwar convulsion; it suffered
but it survived, and it passed on a large part of its values to its
children. The new regime, determined to develop both the economy
and the system of education, has had to rely largely on these people.
Some of the old mythology has been abandoned, and this is perhaps
not a cause for regret. A certain amount of Marxism and Leninism,
diluted with Romanian patriotic rhetoric, has been inserted. Yet in
the formation of a national outlook today, the continuity seems to me
to be more important by far than the breach. A spokesman of the
Romanian government might disagree or would say that this was an
exaggeration, but he would probably concur in good part with me.
And it must be said that the Romanian authorities for some time
past have given handsome recognition to the achievements of the

nineteenth-century upper class and bourgeoisie on behalf of the Romanian national cause. Thus continuity of the past is something that Romanian Communists have noted and of which they are not ashamed.

Similar processes have taken place among the Poles, Slovaks, Hungarians, Croats, and Serbs. These have become modern European nations, conscious of their national identity and of their membership in the European culture; and this is true of the great bulk of the population, not just of a cultural elite. The Czechs and the Slovenes, already before the war, were Europeans in the fullest sense of the word and they have continued to be such since.

This change may perhaps be summed up by saying that the process of Europeanization has affected all the nations of this region. Those that were more backward a generation ago were affected even more than those that were more advanced. The differences between them in terms of social and economic structure and general way of life have grown ever smaller. However, they have not come to know each other better. When I first came to know the region more than 30 years ago, one of the things that struck me most was how the educated class in each country looked only to the advanced countries of the West and ignored, indeed were rather proud to ignore, their neighbors. For example, the Hungarians had their eyes fixed on Paris, London, Berlin, or Vienna while showing no interest in the cultural life of the Slovaks, Romanians, Croats, or Serbs. Hungarians I mention purely at random; exactly the same could be said of each of the other countries. Today, this lack of knowledge of neighbors seems very largely to persist, although in a very different setting. For obvious reasons, all these nations are aware of the culture and the power of Russia, which did not bulk large in their minds between the wars. But Western culture still appears to be more attractive than neighboring cultures. As for the political aspect, alas, Serbs and Croats, Hungarians and Romanians, Bulgarians and Greeks, Czechs and Slovaks have not yet found a fraternal relationship to each other.

To return to the main theme, it seems to me that today Western Europe means the countries north of the Baltic and west of the line running from Lübeck to Trieste. The lands lying between this line and the western border of the Soviet Union constitute Central Europe. And the words Eastern Europe, if used at all, should be applied to the Soviet Union, or perhaps to the western parts of the Soviet Union.

West Central Europe has ceased to differ significantly from Western Europe, and that leaves East Central Europe as the only Central Europe. I would therefore suggest calling it Central Europe with no need for modification.

Of course, there are obvious objections to all this. As in past history, the countries in the south of Europe defy any attempt at categorization. Spain and Portugal, Greece and Turkey have this much in common that they have been considerably affected by the Atlantic neocapitalistic way of life, although lagging far behind in economic development. And all four remain strongly resistant to the political doctrines and institutions prevalent in the regions I call Western Europe.

Yugoslavia seems clearly to belong to Central Europe, Bulgaria probably too. The only reservation in my mind is that perhaps one might be tempted to regard Bulgaria, the only country in which there has been no sort of revolt of any kind against Soviet Russian domination, as a southwestern extension of the Soviet Union, as a sort of Black Sea gubernia. But my knowledge of modern Bulgaria is limited and so I leave that question open.

As for Albania, one can only say it is a law unto itself. And, of course, the notion of Southeastern Europe or the Balkan Peninsula as a significant unit is very much alive, and its cultural identity is real. Indeed, many of us here have been connected in some way with the international association for the cultures of Southeastern Europe, which leads a very vigorous life and brings people of Southeastern Europe and foreigners interested in it together.

To return to the region of Central Europe, I was not trying to argue that there is much uniformity in this region. When I said that Czechs and Romanians were much more similar to each other than they were 30 years ago, and than they are to Russians today, I was referring to their social structure, their way of life, the intensity of national consciousness to be found at each level of the social pyramid. The Czechs, of course, are still Czechs, and the Romanians are still Romanians; and very different they are. Indeed, not only the languages but also the historical heritage and national culture of Romanians, Hungarians, and Serbs, to take only three examples, differ probably more from each other than do those of French, Germans, and English. All the nations of what I call Central Europe have preserved and developed their own national identity. This is particularly evident in my specific discipline, historical writing, which is also that of many of you. Taking the past 26 years as a whole, there can be no doubt of the progress in historical studies throughout the region. However, this has not been smooth or uniform. In Romania, there was an attempt to cut off cultural ties with the Latin peoples in order to de-Latinize the Romanian language and to Russify Romanian culture. This attempt was resisted both by the Romanian nation and by the Romanian government, and was abandoned.

To take another example, in Czechoslovakia national history was falsified in the 1950s; then the truth slowly and increasingly

IS THERE AN EAST CENTRAL EUROPE?

prevailed in the 1960s; but now refalsification by order has set in. I must mention this somber fact: whatever our hopes for the future may be, however much we may want to be in an optimistic, cheerful mood, we should not forget our Czech and Slovak colleagues—those who are still able to practice, of course.

The biggest difficulty arises when one attempts to place Germany on the map of Europe. It is clear that there is one German nation, but also that there are at present two German states. My terminology would place the Democratic Republic in Central Europe and the Federal Republic in Western Europe. This seems rather absurd, but absurdities are sometimes true. Before 1914 the recognized boundary between Central and Eastern Europe ran through the middle of Poland; today the boundary between Central and Eastern Europe runs through the middle of Germany. Obviously, most citizens of the Federal Republic are aware that the people of the Democratic Republic are part of the same nation as themselves. Again, probably most Germans in both states, if they ask themselves these questions, would say that they belong to Central Europe. Indeed, the greater part of geographical and historical Central Europe consists of German-speaking lands, of course including Austria. This was the sense of Halecki's words when he spoke of West Central Europe, and his distinction made good sense for the past. Central Europe as a German cultural area in 1900 was a reality. My argument today is that this is changed; the frontier between the Federal Republic of Germany and France is not meaningless, because it is a borderline between two of the greatest and the richest cultures of Europe. It is an important line, but it was something different in 1900. The border between Western and Central Europe today is not the Rhine; it is the frontier between the two German republics.

It should now be clear that I have not succeeded in putting the whole of Europe in neat little compartments, nor did I try to. One obvious point is that historians, in dealing with different historical periods, must use the terminology and must be concerned with the historical units that existed at those times. For several centuries— very culturally formative centuries—the area under consideration was divided into three great political units: the Polish-Lithuanian Commonwealth, the Habsburg monarchy and the Ottoman Empire. Each of these constituted a cultural world apart and each left behind influences that are still real today. I did not treat these great empires because my subject was the twentieth century; but I am not unaware of their heritages and I strongly believe that we should all be aware of them.

Historians are perhaps apt to exaggerate the importance of history. However, I think you will agree that history, or perhaps I should say historical mythology, is something about which almost everybody in Central Europe feels strongly, workers as well as professors. Attacks on the national historical mythology are taken as national humiliation and they create bitter, even explosive resentment.

Whether we call it East Central Europe or Central Europe or something else, the peoples of this region will continue to be of great interest and importance in world affairs, and for some of us, at least, objects of great affection. That they will play their own part in future history I have no doubt at all.

CHAPTER

2

**FASCISM IN INTERWAR
EASTERN EUROPE:
THE DICHOTOMY
OF POWER AND INFLUENCE**
Peter F. Sugar

The interwar decades, the years 1919-39, have often been called the period of the "long armistice." It makes good sense to look at the period covered by this paper in this light not only because World War I raised more questions that it solved, not only because several states—notably Germany, Hungary, and Bulgaria—were consciously looking ahead to the "next round" practically from the moment the shooting stopped, but mainly because, for well-known reasons, a feeling of dissatisfaction, uncertainty, and even fear pervaded the thinking of victors and losers alike. The Italians and even some French believed that their governments sold them short and did not secure for them the advantages to which the great sacrifices made during the war entitled them. The losers blamed their governments either for the defeat or for signing peace settlements that were unacceptable. In spite of the creation of the League of Nations, no effective international organization or mechanism was established that could have alleviated frustration and fear and served as the broad framework for the solution of the numerous social and economic problems that proved too big for the individual states to tackle successfully.

Besides the above-mentioned international difficulties and the growing dissatisfaction of their populations, governments also had to face such problems as the conversion of economies from war to peacetime production; the integration of demobilized soldiers into the economy; inflation; the need for social, educational and land reforms; the social and communication problems created by new borders; and,

---

Peter F. Sugar is Professor of History at the University of Washington, Seattle.

finally, the less tangible but extremely important need to understand and adjust to a profoundly changed self-image of workers and peasants.

If these conditions convinced more and more people all over Europe that the known political systems were bankrupt, turning them away from the traditional political parties, one cannot be too surprised. Nor should it be cause for amazement to discover that when the people looked for ways to solve the many problems they faced, the new means that they devised to achieve their goals placed unprecedented powers in the hands of the authorities. The war had reinforced two trends already extant: the long-term historical one toward centralization and reliance on the all-powerful state, and the shorter but equally well-established trend of judgment on the basis of integral nationalism. Even the Marxists of various shades who ostensibly rejected nationalism followed, in a sense, these same tendencies. The state was replaced by the party or by the dictatorship of the proletariat, and the class took the place of the nation. Nationally or internationally oriented, this "politics of despair" produced the totalitarian movements of which Bolshevism and Fascism are the best known examples.

The best short definition of totalitarianism in my opinion was given in 1956 by Zbigniew Brzezinski:

> a system where technologically advanced instruments of political power are wielded without restraint by the centralized leadership of an elite movement for the purpose of effecting a total social revolution, including the condition of man, on the basis of certain arbitrary ideological assumptions proclaimed by the leadership in an atmosphere of coerced unanimity of the entire population.[1]

Together with Carl J. Friedrich, Brzezinski also enumerated six features that every regime must possess simultaneously to qualify as totalitarian.[2] Fascism qualifies as a totalitarian regime both under the definition just presented and in accordance with the six Friedrich-Brzezinski criteria.

Before we turn from totalitarianism in general to Fascism in particular, a few words must be said about Eastern Europe. This region—from Poland in the north to Greece in the south—is that part of Europe that lies between Germany, Switzerland and Italy in the west and the U.S.S.R. and Turkey in the east. It includes the Austro-Germans and those Bielorussians and Ukrainians who lived in interwar Poland. I know of no perfect definition of Eastern Europe. The one just presented delimits the area surveyed in this paper.

Everything that was said of the situation in Europe at the end of World War I existed in still sharper form in Eastern Europe.

The political, economic, and social dislocations produced by the war in Eastern Europe were much more fundamental and thorough than they were in the West. National antagonisms were sharp, affecting numerous people with disparate ethnic origins whose habitats overlapped and whose identity was not always easy to establish. Among the Eastern European workers and peasants the war produced an even deeper break with their prewar self-image than it did in the West, and the need for basic reforms was much greater here than in any other part of Europe, with the exception of Russia. Democratic political traditions were weak if they existed at all, and societies in general lacked the strong middle class that in the West was a political force in its own right while also serving as a bridge between the so-called upper and lower classes. Eastern Europeans in power understood even less well than those in power in the West the profound changes wrought by the war, and were unable to deal with them. They mastered the first wave of revolutionary fervor that was socialist or communist inspired, outlawed its leaders, parties, and ideologies, leaving only one direction open to those who wanted change at any price. For reasons that will be discussed later, they were unable to deal with these people, making Eastern Europe the ideal region for fascist agitation.

Brzezinski gave us a good short definition of totalitarianism, and he is not the only one who was able to do this. It is much more difficult to find an equally satisfactory short definition of Fascism. Francis L. Carsten takes more than seven pages at the end of his excellent book to define this movement;[3] Ernst Nolte gives various definitions on different levels in his well-known Three Faces of Fascism, winding up with a complicated, three paragraphs-long definition;[4] and numerous other authors are equally unsuccessful in defining succinctly this form of totalitarianism. The difficulty they faced is well summed up by S. J. Woolf, who begins the Introduction to the volume European Fascism that he edited with the following sentences:

> Perhaps the word fascism should be banned, at least temporarily, from our political vocabulary. For like other large words—democracy, reactionary, radical, anarchy—it has been so misused that it has lost its original meaning; or, at least, it has been so overlaid with newer and broader connotations that the narrower, historical sense almost seems to require apologetic inverted commas.[5]

Later on the same page he adds, "the word, unfortunately, has certain commode-like tendencies—the more you stuff into it, the more it takes."[6]

This commode stuffing began almost as soon as Mussolini gained power in Italy and certainly became a popular pastime among would-be Führers after Hitler's Machtergreifung. The definition became hopelessly blurred during World War II when so-called antifascist liberation movements or antifascist fronts were established everywhere, mainly by the communist resistance movements, to bring all those they fought under a common label. Finally scholars have added to the confusion by inventing such additional expressions as clerico-Fascism and monarcho-Fascism.

Fortunately it is not my task to succeed where others much better qualified than I have failed. While I do not have to define Fascism, I must indicate which Eastern European movements are considered fascist when the contrast between their power and importance is investigated in these pages. The movements considered were all "totalitarian" in the sense previously given. They were revolutionary in their desire to change the socioeconomic structure of the countries in which they flourished. Yet, primarily nationalistic, their planned revolutions were considered more of a return to the old national values than a new departure. This apparently contradictory goal of conservative revolution is somewhat clarified when one thinks of other men who in earlier days tried to do the same thing. For example, the nineteenth-century Ottoman reformers, whose goal was a thoroughgoing change in their state, called their movement Tanzimat (purification) to indicate their loyalty to the national past and traditions. Another approach to this curious contradiction is to call fascists the representatives of the "new" Right in the sense in which Eugen Weber used this term.[7] In this chapter the label Fascism will be applied to those political movements that were aiming at the establishment of totalitarian regimes (as defined by Brzezinski) with a chauvinistic, anti-internationalist, conservative-revolutionary program in mind. Although Eastern European movements fitting this working definition followed either the "German" or the "Italian" model, that difference must be disregarded in this chapter that, by its very nature, must concentrate on common features and attempts to generalize.

Limiting Fascism in this manner, men like Dollfuss, Pilsudski, Horthy, Carol II, Alexander, or Plastiras cannot be considered fascists while Seyss-Inquart, Piasecki, Szalasi, Codreanu, Pavelic, and Metaxas—to give only a few examples—qualify as representatives of Eastern European Fascism. With a very few honorable exceptions there has been nothing written since 1945 by those who have access to the documentation, the Eastern European scholars, about the movements led by these and other men.[8] Western scholars, on the other hand, have published enough to allow specialized investigations of several aspects of Eastern European Fascism on the basis of the material that they have presented.[9] One of these aspects—the contrast between the power and the great importance of the Eastern European fascist movements—is of great importance for the understanding of political developments in this region during the "long armistice."

The fascists of Eastern Europe proudly stressed that modern political anti-Semitism was born in their lands, that the Nazi movement had its origins in Georg von Schönerer's prewar movement, and that their post-1918 movements were "homegrown," not needing Italian or German examples. While there can be no doubt that native Fascism existed in Eastern European lands, it is also true that these movements were politically insignificant prior to the second half of the 1930s, when "foreign" developments helped their growth,[10] and that, with the exception of the short-lived government headed by Octavian Goga in Romania from December 28, 1937, to February 10 of the next year, no fascist party achieved power in Eastern Europe prior to the years of World War II when Hitler placed several fascist leaders at the head of satellite governments.*

This lack of success does not mean that the fascists of Eastern Europe represented only the "lunatic fringe" that nobody but themselves took seriously, nor, more importantly, that they were not extremely influential in shaping the policies of those in power to whom they were officially opposed and by whom they were often imprisoned. The influence of these native, politically unsuccessful, often suppressed movements becomes even more amazing in view of their lack of unity. In each country several fascist parties competed for the allegiance of a relatively small segment of the population. They were led by "Führers" whose activities were often exhausted by ridiculous posturing and who presented disjointed and badly formulated programs.

In his excellent short comparative study presented at Moscow in the summer of 1970, Lacko pointed out that in our region there was no strong middle class, no strong and politically conscious

---

*This government included among its members Professor Alexander C. Cuza and the future master of Romania, General Ion Antonescu. While I consider General John Metaxas, the archigos (Führer) of Greece from 1936 to 1941, a fascist, I see him as a fascist without a movement (he tried to organize one after he came to power) and for this reason look at his regime as authoritarian only, although dressed up in a fascist garb. This leaves Goga's regime as the only fascist regime in Eastern Europe prior to World War II.

working class—with the exceptions of Czechoslovakia and Austria, no democratic tradition, and no true political pluralism to limit the appeal and expansion of Fascism in the way they limited it in "highly developed" Western societies with the exception of Germany. Nor was Eastern Europe, with the exception of Albania, a truly "backward" region where traditional, basically patriarchal peasant societies presented a similar barrier to Fascism. In Eastern Europe "conditions conducive to fascism and its manifestations made their appearance soon and with great force to the point where both on the ideological level and in the domain of political methodology it exercised a considerable influence on the reactionary tendencies of Central and Eastern Europe."[11] According to Lacko, three main reasons accounted for the ease with which Fascism functioned here. The social structure and the general historical evolution was the first, nationalism the second, and the third was the traditions concerning power, institutions, and the views concerning the proper functions of the state.[12]

Society as a whole, although it had some classes (workers, tradesmen, professional people) that depended on trade and industry, was still dominated by a landholding upper class in close alliance with the impoverished gentry and civil servants and supported vaguely by a group of small shopkeepers and artisans. These people, in Weber's terms the "old Right," held power, were deathly afraid of losing it, together with their wealth and social position, and, while incapable of adjusting to the demands of the other social strata, were far from being homogeneous themselves.

Historically speaking, our states were all "new" states in 1919-20, despite their long histories and traditions. They faced within their new borders new social and economic problems and tried to solve them either by political integration of previously disparate lands (Regat and Transylvania, Czech lands and Slovakia, the three parts of partitioned Poland, the various provinces of the Kingdom of Serbs, Croats, and Slovenes) or by revisionism (Hungary, Bulgaria, and to some extent Greece). When it became obvious that social and economic problems could not be solved by political expedients, the leaders of the Eastern European states faced a choice: they could turn to social and economic reform or they could adopt even more repressive political measures. Unwilling to consider the former solution, which would have undermined their power base, they turned to the latter alternative during the late 1920s and early 1930s. But by this time the fascists had already made their claims to represent the tendencies to which the "old Right" was now willing to turn.

The problem of nationalism and its virulence in multinational Eastern Europe is too well known to demand discussion. Let me only remind you of a few very relevant facts. Most of the states of post-World War I Eastern Europe were only slightly less multinational than was the Austro-Hungarian monarchy. In the interwar period these multinational states were either trying to integrate their newly acquired territories and citizens or were attempting to upset the new political order. Both activities enhanced even further the already virulent nationalistic feelings and tendencies of the people involved. The attempts of those in power to find political solutions for all ills aggravated the situation by raising the question of who was really "reliable," and by manufacturing criteria of "reliability." This search for standards of national dependability led—not unnaturally, given the traditions of Eastern Europe—to equating nation with race. External enemies presented little problem, but the "internal enemy," the group responsible for the failure of the leaders to solve their countries' problems in the 1920s had to be found. When the leadership "discovered" this enemy, the people who were different from them and, therefore, by their definition, not truly part of the nation as they themselves were, it not only turned out that these people belonged to those professions or social strata to which the leaders did not belong, but it also became obvious to those who studied nations with the help of a racist microscope that they were of different ethnic origin. It was at this juncture that the large scale "politization" of anti-Semitism, a long standing prejudice of many Eastern Europeans, occurred. The role of this new political anti-Semitism in Eastern European Fascism is relatively well known. For this reason, although it would deserve detailed discussion, it will not be discussed at length in this chapter. Suffice it to direct the reader's attention to the significance it had in helping the fascists in recruiting followers. By the time the leaders, who might have felt this way for a long time, were ready to make statements of this sort, they found, once again, that they were entering a form of nationalism that the fascists had already defined and claimed as their own.

The people of Eastern Europe had lived for centuries in absolutist empires (Habsburg, Romanov, and Ottoman). Even when these states changed and became constitutional monarchies or when newly formed, independent, constitutional states took their place in the nineteenth century, power remained in the hands of the old ruling elements that operated under the new circumstances only slightly differently from the manner in which they had run affairs previously. On the lower levels of administration the change was even less marked. The little bureaucrat, usually the younger son of a great family or an impoverished member of the elite, was a gentleman dispensing favors in a more or less arbitrary manner and would have resented being considered a public "servant."

The military establishments were even more authoritarian than the civil services and were run by the same social element. The churches also fell neatly into this authoritarian picture. Not only did they preach "the only saving and true dogma," a set of beliefs that could not be questioned, but they were also strictly structured along lines of authority with the pinnacle of power once again in the hands of men who came from the same social milieu that furnished the military officers and bureaucrats. Finally, the church was often "national," if not necessarily in its structure then in its symbolism. It was hardly possible to be a Serb and a Roman Catholic at the same time. Not being a Catholic and trying to be accepted as a Pole was equally difficult. Schools, highly centralized and strictly controlled, reinforced this tendency created by state, army, and church, and preached reliance on the state and the authorities as a public virtue.

While it was difficult, given the newly found self-consciousness of large segments of society, to maintain this demand for unquestioning acceptance of everything handed down to a chain of authority, it was by no means impossible. Centuries of training had drilled a certain discipline and, more importantly, a certain attitude into the majority of the population. Most people were used to being led, felt comfortable with dogmas handed to them, and lacked the habit, practice, and, in most cases, the education to think and act on their own. While the old beliefs and dogmas were dated and had lost their appeal, the habit of relying on them remained and all that had to be done was to present new ones.

Marxism in its various forms tried to do this, but failed. Some of the early manifestations of what later became the "new Right" also understood the need for dogma. But these, like the Szeged idea in Hungary, were voiced too soon before the new lines of power emerged clearly. The reason for the failure of the "old Right," the rulers of interwar Eastern Europe, was that they tried to operate with the help of old ideas and never formulated ideologies that could have been disseminated with the help of the state apparatus which they controlled.

The "new Right" did exactly what the "old" failed to do. It tied the traditional and the revolutionary together, attempting to infuse new meaning into the familiar structures of state, army, school, and, when possible, church. The Ustasa stressed Roman Catholicism, Croat nationalism, and, when they achieved power, returned to such old trappings as the uniforms of the old Austro-Hungarian army to stress continuity while presenting a new program. The apostolic double cross was the symbol of the Slovak Peoples' Party, and in Romania Codreanu went even further by calling his movement the Legion of the Archangel Michael, using religious symbolism as often as possible and making Orthodoxy the first precondition of real Romanianism. The fascists understood the need for leadership and dogma and used old bottles for their new wine.

The remaining pages of this chapter will attempt to spell out in some detail the generalizations presented so far and to show how and why these produced the curious contrast between the very slight political power the fascists enjoyed and the great influence that they exerted. It is my conviction that the picture I will paint has validity for the entire region in spite of the fact that it does not and cannot cover all the variations that occurred and that most samples cited will refer either to Hungary or Romania, the two states that had the largest fascist movements and for which more material is available than for the others.

After the failure of communists and socialists as well as some peasant-based movements to alter the established political patterns of Eastern Europe, the old leadership element was firmly in the saddle again everywhere. No challenge seriously disputed their supremacy after the failure of the communist coup in Bulgaria in 1923. Even those politicians who were not outright conservatives—the major figures in Czechoslovakia or Poland for example—had reached political maturity before 1914 and were set in their ways. All of them were leaders, and, although not the main spokesmen of their parties, they demanded loyalty and obedience from their followers, and looked at politics as a form of war, in that the object is the elimination of the enemy. Their values were usually the same as they had been before the war, and in more ways than one they tried to reestablish the old order under new circumstances.

In their first task, the elimination of the leftist opposition, they were fairly successful. They had the wholehearted cooperation of the future fascists who, in these early years, usually were members of the ruling parties. These parties aimed at gaining a political and power monopoly, to put the organs of the government and state—at least at election time—in the service of the party, to erect barriers against any possible challenge from the left, to equate themselves and their often narrowly selfish interests with those of the state and nation and with true patriotism. They were, naturally, declared enemies of the Soviet Union and everything it represented; they favored economic change to the degree that it was required to get as near to autarky as possible without, however, weakening the mainly agrarian interests of their own followers; they favored the parliamentary form of government, not in its true democratic form, but only as a fashionable mechanism that allowed them to give their rule the veneer of popular approval and legality.

All these parties and leaders were more or less conservative, politically well schooled but ignorant of economic and social problems, highly nationalistic, and firm believers in the state as the embodiment of national sovereignty, power, and as an instrument for ruling.

They certainly had dictatorial tendencies, but these were not totalitarian. They had something paternalistic in them that told them that any method that would keep the ignorant from making mistakes—and the gravest would have been the removal of the truly knowledgeable from power—was not only acceptable but for the public good, and their dictatorial tendencies and methods were in direct correlation to the real or imaginary dangers they saw around them. Unfortunately, as already indicated, their sense was purely political; consequently, political moves, including a gradual but steady move toward dictatorship, were their answers to challenges that were not political in nature. Coupled with the serious crisis produced by the Great Depression, their misreading of the problems of society finally bankrupted their policy and forced them to look, if not for a new approach, then for modifications in this approach and for new allies.

This was the moment when the influence of the fascists began to become serious. Anti-Marxism, nationalism, the belief in political warfare that would end with the victory of the only true approach to the nation's future greatness, an elitist outlook on society, an egotistical self-centered approach to public life, a disdain for all who either were unwilling or unable—because they were congenitally, racially, not of the nation—to see the "truth" were some of the features the "old guard" leaders and fascists had in common. The major difference between the two was one of degree. This difference is well illustrated by the case of the Arrow Cross ideologist, Ödön Malnasi who, in 1937, was indicted on the basis of Law III/1921 originally passed in Hungary to justify the outlawing of the Communist Party. Malnasi published a fascist work, Sincere History of the Hungarian Nation, in which, among other things, he advocated land reform. This, according to the court, represented "an indictment of the system of large estates which sustained the Hungarian state over the centuries." He was condemned because, in the words of the Supreme Court of Hungary, "the crime of insulting the nation can be committed not only by a Bolshevik but also by a well-known anti-Bolshevik and patriotic scholar."[13]

This example brings to light one of the main differences between the "old" and the "new" Right, between outright conservatism and conservative revolutionism. Malnasi and other fascists were just as elitist as the orthodox conservatives were and their interest in the peasants was neither altruistic nor based on a true recognition of economic realities. While some of them were vaguely Populists, their main goal was to take over the leadership of their respective countries from the "old guard." This required something of a social revolution, a certain egalitarian leveling, the raising up of the lower bureaucracy to the level of the upper or, in other terms, the opening of the upper reaches of power to the gentry, the gentry-imitating segment of the middle class, and the lower bourgeoisie. This demand for change also represented the desire of a younger generation to replace its elders on the political stage. Attacks like Malnasi's were well designed to enlist broad support, but their goal was the undermining of the economic bases of the groups that the fascists proposed to replace.

The "old Right" knew which social and political order was to be maintained or, in the case of the Polish National Democrats, to be introduced to its own advantage, while the "new Right" simply wanted power to impose a new order—about which, in Eastern Europe, it was usually very vague—by totalitarian means often modeled on those of Stalin. The fascists were social déclassés, people whose pretensions were not matched by their social or economic positions and who faced the danger of sinking even lower. They could have turned to any form of extreme or totalitarian solutions, but under circumstances in which "the radical left is crushed or otherwise eliminated . . . , where nationalism appears to be a necessary political stance, as in the new nations struggling to free themselves from economic and political bonds that independence has not removed," it was the rightist form of totalitarianism that became almost the natural, logical solution for those who wanted drastic change.[14]

The Eastern European fascist would probably have turned to the right even had his choice been broader than it was. As a true déclassé, he wanted to climb socially, not to lose his identity completely as he would in the full-scale leveling suggested by Marxist theory. He wanted and felt entitled by birth, education, ability, and determination to have what those in power already had. He stood for that for which the ruling group stood, but in an extreme form that included broadening the criteria for those who enjoyed power and privileges just enough to include him. His great advantage over those who ran the various Eastern European states was that he was not in power. This allowed him a somewhat freer hand in analyzing and assessing the situation, permitted him to put his finger on some real problems like the need for land reform, made it possible for him to criticize and to advocate change, and, when the relatively moderate methods used by the "old guard" rulers failed to solve the problems, to attack them for their "softness," demanding drastic, violent, totalitarian change.

I hope it has become clear from what has been said that a close connection existed between the "old" and the "new" Right in Eastern Europe. This connection was based on social origin (nobility in the broadest sense of the word—a relatively small segment of the middle class that was truly "national" and contained the déclassés of the nobility), on occupation (land holding, free professions, civil and military services), on belonging to the "true nation" in the most limited ethnic-racial sense of the word, and on numerous common fears and goals. This group could also be described as the composite of a small upper and a broader lower layer of the socioeconomic "in" group within every state in Eastern Europe. This close connection explains both the strength and weakness of Fascism in Eastern Europe, and, in the final analysis, its influence out of all proportion with its true political strength.

In Western and Central Europe many of the fascist leaders were not déclassés but parvenus, while in Eastern Europe the situation was just the contrary. President Hindenburg's background could not have been more different from Hitler's than it was, and the same holds true of Mussolini and the leaders of Italy. Counts Istvan Bethlen and Fidel Pallfy or Sandor Festetics in Hungary came from the same class. Gajda, Stribrny and Benes among the Czechs, Rydz-Smigly and Piasecki in Poland, and most of the political opponents in the other countries fall into similar pairs. The Nazi Hohenzollern, Prince August Wilhelm, was considered by most of his class an aberrant, but the role of Albrecht von Habsburg in Hungary was regarded as a power play within "proper" circles. The number of military officers going beyond playing roles in veterans' and other "patriotic" organizations into outright fascist leadership was much higher in Eastern than it was in Western and Central Europe. The same was true proportionally of civil servants and professional people.

Consequently, in Western and Central Europe the fascists had to start their movements "out in the cold," had to oppose those in power, and work for a Machtergreifung. They represented an alternative in truly pluralistic societies and reached down into the large masses trying to find support. On the other hand, the Eastern European fascists began their political careers, in almost all cases, within well-established parties or movements whose leaders were not alien to them, and they never thought of reaching too far down the social ladder for support even if in some cases it came from the "lowest" classes. They could hardly have acted in a different manner. They had to work, at least to some extent, with people with whom they identified but who were better situated politically and financially than they were. Otherwise they would not have had any financial or social basis for their activity unless, and this they refused to do, they cooperated with people they regarded as their inferiors.

But the rulers' choice was also limited. The further they moved away from true democracy, the closer they got to dictatorship and, because they needed some additional support, the more they needed the backing of the fascists, those people in their own camp whom they considered too extreme and socially not quite equal or too young. The clearer it became that those in power needed help, the more obvious it became that the policies of the governments were doomed to failure, and the less important it became for the fascists to revolt openly against the existing order. Time was running in their favor, and in the not-too-distant future they saw the moment when those running the show would have to turn to them, accepting the personalities and methods they advocated as the least of many possible evils.

This relatively close relationship between the wielders of power and the fascists had numerous advantages and disadvantages for the latter. Let us begin with the disadvantages. First of all, the connections between the two groups were too close both on the ideological-programmatic and on the personal level. The fascists in Eastern Europe were never able to condemn the policies of the governments they wanted to replace with the vehemence and sharpness of their Central and Western European counterparts. Only those who went beyond mere fascism into outright treasonable activities aiming at the dissolution of the state—the followers of Henlein, Tuka, and Pavelic—could equal their Western fellow fascists in this respect. Furthermore, with the exception of Czechoslovakia, no Eastern European government ever could be accused of "Bolshevist leanings" because socialists were never allowed a share of power even in a coalition. The programs of the governments usually pointed in the right direction from the fascists' point of view, and the most the fascists could do was to accuse the ruling groups of going too slowly, too cautiously, maybe only half-heartedly in the right direction.

Secondly, the personal relationships were often too close. Polish fascist movements could and were systematically absorbed by government-sponsored political movements in 1937-38; men like Ljotic and Szalasi treated the heads of their states with amazing respect, sometimes even deference, making it difficult for them to attack governments supported by an Alexander or a Horthy as unacceptable. Furthermore, these relatively friendly personal relations protected the fascists to a considerable extent from prosecution, making it politic not to break them. As a result only the very extremist fringe of the fascist movements, once again with the exception of those who were also antistate, men like Piasecki, Gajda, Baky, Sima—to mention only a few examples—operated in Eastern Europe exactly as the fascists did in the rest of Europe. These men were relatively minor figures in their respective fascist movements but, together with those who were aiming at the dissolution of the states in which they operated, the Ustasa, the Sudeten parties under various names, and a segment of the Slovak Peoples' Party, had a limited although sometimes very important appeal to certain segments of the population.

The close connection between the "old" and the "new" Rights also worked to the latter's disadvantage when, especially in the

1930s, connections with Italy and Germany became essential for their states. Even the years of World War II began with this tendency unfavorable to the hard-core fascists. It was much more advantageous for Mussolini and Hitler to work with men with fascistic sympathies, with people like Imredy, Gömbös, Stojadinovic, Antonescu, or Tiso who were well-established politicians with well-functioning party machines, than to champion a Böszörmenyi, Szalasi, Pavelic, Sima, or Tuka. Only certain well-known events toward the middle and end of World War II forced Hitler finally to turn to the latter group of men, and, when he finally did, his own satraps became the real masters and not the fascists who were then nominally in power.

Finally, this close relationship also prevented the fascists from gaining power without foreign intervention either in the interwar years or during World War II. While the general trend favored them more and more, and while they were able to capture positions in the governments (Austria, Hungary, Romania), sometimes placing one of their men even in the top position, they never came to power in their own right, with the already-mentioned Romanian exception. Following the deepening crisis at home, following their own personal, if not always political, inclinations, and reacting to changes in Germany, the "old" Right gradually was able to take on more and more features of the "new" without adopting the "new's" most extreme demands or tactics and in this manner keep the fascists from power.

This listing of circumstances that worked against the fascists explains not only why their parties remained politically relatively insignificant, but it also indicates some of the reasons for their steadily growing influence. Operating in countries whose policies they more or less approved—leaving aside for the moment the antistate movements—the fascist parties of Eastern Europe grew within a framework that was favorable to them. It is much easier for authorities to move against people whom they do not need and who attack them than against people who belong to the social stratum whose support they require and whose only "crime" is to demand that the governments go faster and farther on the road that they were already following. In the middle 1920s and especially in the early 1930s even the antistate fascist parties began to influence the policies of governments who attempted to save the integrity of their states. Prague had to make concessions to Tiso to keep Tuka in the background and was, in the last moment, ready even to compromise with the extreme demands of the Sudeten. The Sporazum in Yugoslavia can also be considered in this light. It was a compromise concluded by the central authorities with the moderate Macek faction of the Croatian Peasant Party in an attempt to take away the nationalist plank from the Ustasa-dominated extremist wing of the party.

The circumstantial advantages also include the fact that the fascists were a more determined and active group than were their friends in government circles. Permit me to illustrate this point with a personal experience. When I was 19 years old and worried about the trends around me, I sat with a group of other young people discussing politics. One of them was an impoverished member of the aristocracy. When his turn to speak came he said something like the following: "I neither think nor worry much about politics. I have a fairly well paying governmental job that involves almost no work and gives me lots of free time. If nothing changes, I will get promoted to jobs with even more pay and less work. Should the monarchy be reestablished, I will get a position within the royal household to which I am entitled by birth and will make even more money doing absolutely nothing. If the fascists take over, my cousin, the well-known fascist leader, will take good care of me. In the unlikely case that the reds should come to power, I will go to England and sponge off our English relatives. So why should I worry about political trends."

While this young man's situation was certainly not typical, his attitude was. Those who had jobs often thought as he did, and those for whom the government could not find positions that they considered suitable became déclassés and joined the ranks of the fascists. Educational restrictions placed on Jews and certain social classes, or simply operating through financially erected barriers, produced more and more young men who came from the "correct" circles, who obtained degrees and felt that these, coupled with their social and national-racial background, entitled them to sinecures. But even the most swollen bureaucracies had their limits of absorption, leaving more and more "proper" young men dissatisfied and ready to join the fascists.

The last two disadvantages mentioned, the choice that Hitler and Mussolini could exercise in handling out patronage in Eastern Europe and the ability of some key politicians to move further to the right with ease, are indications of the first of two major reasons why the fascists, usually leaders of relatively small parties never in power, were as influential as they were. They did represent an alternative when the masters of Germany and Italy looked at Eastern Europe. This was important, especially after the Great Depression, when practically every country in the region would have faced total economic collapse without its trade with Germany. Under these conditions Hitler had a choice, but the leading Eastern European politicians really did not. The theoretical choice they had was no choice at all. They could and did turn increasingly toward the extreme represented by the fascists. The alternatives either were displeasing the master of Germany, thus courting economic disaster and, therefore, finally failure and political oblivion, or—provided they had a conscience—abdication, leaving the onus of cooperation with Hitler to the fascists themselves. Giving up power is hard for any politician, even for one with a conscience. Those who had it usually retained power and, consequently, moved closer to fascist policy, either believing or fooling themselves by stating that their action spared their countries the rule of local fascists. Just by being around, by representing an alternative for the foreign masters of Eastern Europe, the fascists of the region were able to influence and in some cases dictate policy.

Many politicians in Eastern Europe did not have a conscience, or if they had one it did not exclude the following of a fascist-type policy. These men always sympathized with and often advocated in one form or another the policies preached by the fascists, but were simply better tacticians then the avowed fascists and waited until it was to their advantage to make a switch. Here the social, educational, and other backgrounds that the "old" and "new" Rights shared created the framework within which each could operate with relative ease. For all these reasons the established politicians were able to and did steal the thunder of the fascists, but it would be a mistake to attribute the need they felt to outroar the fascists simply to economic conditions and German-Italian influence. Home conditions demanded it too.

As has been indicated repeatedly, all the Eastern European countries faced serious problems after World War I, and, once the old guard reestablished its political supremacy in these states by eliminating their opponents, development could move only in one direction. Yet even before the Great Depression and Hitler's Machtergreifung it became fairly obvious that the policies of the numerous governments had failed to solve the ills of the region. Change became more and more unavoidable, and unless those in power changed their approach drastically, introducing the real social and economic reforms that would have undermined their own position, they had to turn further to the right, toward the policies already advocated by fascists of the various countries. The groundwork for this turn had already been laid not so much by the vague and confusing platforms of the Eastern European fascist parties, but by the relatively few individuals placed in crucial positions in society.

These men were army officers, clergymen, and, much more importantly, newspapermen and teachers. They not only represented "authority" for people who were used to being led, but were in fact in posts of authority. Furthermore, among people who were to a large extent either uneducated or undereducated, they were a privileged elite because of their knowledge. Finally, in these scarcely pluralistic societies where their number in the total population was much smaller than in Central and Western Europe, they carried a disproportionate weight.* These people represented a small but crucial element in society whose cooperation was vital for those holding power, notwithstanding the fact that most of them were state employees. It was this group of people also that had the specialized training and the detachment from involvement in day-to-day petty politics to view the national scene "objectively," to see some of its basic problems, and to advocate changes that the governments were unwilling to introduce. Because the really important and influential members of this group came from the same social stratum that furnished the members of both the "old" and "new" Rights, the changes they advocated were seldom democratic, let alone socialistic. The advocates of reforms of a truly popular nature quickly lost positions and influence. It was among these men that the fascists found their most important sympathizers. These, not the party theoreticians, were the individuals who produced the thunder the politicians in power could steal from the fascists.

A well-placed newspaperman could influence thousands of readers; in the army barracks the peasant recruit got not only military training but indoctrination; an anti-Semitic or patriotic sermon in a village church carried much weight; and most of the déclassés were not only the products of the schools, but also carried with them the <u>Weltanschauung</u> that their teachers, mainly the history and philosophy professors, imparted to them. Newspapers were not too numerous and universities even less so. It was easy to mold the readership and even easier to shape the future members of the elite, the university and even the high school graduates, in the image of a few men. Those whom the press and the schools did not reach, the army did. While these armies had no political commissars, everybody familiar with the armies of interwar Eastern Europe knows that the run-of-the-mill officer performed a commissar's duty with great effectiveness. Public opinion, and consequently whatever pressure it could exercise, was shaped by a few men.

It was among this group of crucially placed people that the fascists found—if not party members or even sympathizers—then at least people who shared many of their ideas and were also able to formulate and propagate them with great and far-reaching effectiveness. At least two of the four groups, the newspapermen and the teachers, were also among those who, like the other professionals, had to compete for positions with those, first of all the Jews, whose origins could easily be labeled not quite acceptable from the national

---

*This was true even in the Slovak and Ruthenian parts of Czechoslovakia.

point of view. This made their cooperation with the fascists even easier. They not only were the formulators of ideas that later, in the hands of the politicians moving to the right, became policy, but they also shaped the public climate that, together with the apparent bankruptcy of official policy and later with Italo-German influence, put tremendous pressure on the governments by the late 1920s and early 1930s. This was pressure not only to introduce change but to change in the direction demanded by both a faction of the intellectual elite and of the fascists.

In this identity of views among these two groups we find the second major reason explaining the influence wielded by the Eastern European fascists. While the governments had the power either directly (army and school), or indirectly (church and press) to influence if not to determine the membership of this influential segment of the intelligentsia, it was the fascists who politicized their ideas and turned them into instruments of pressure for the type of change that they favored.

These, then, are the circumstances and reasons that made me write previously that our "states would have produced something that without Mussolini's choice of a label for his party we would possibly not have called fascist, but which, in its essence and numerous manifestations, would have amounted to nearly the same thing."[15] These are also the circumstances and reasons that, while keeping the fascist parties relatively small and away from power, gave them a disproportionate influence in determining the social, economic, and, especially, political policies of most Eastern European governments in the years that both fascists and most other influential politicians considered to be the period of the "long armistice."

NOTES

1. Zbigniew K. Brzezinski, "Totalitarianism and Rationality," The American Political Science Revue, I, 3 (September 1956), 754.

2. Carl J. Friedrich and Zbigniew K. Brzezinski, Totalitarian Dictatorship and Autocracy (Cambridge, Mass.: Harvard University Press, 1965), 2d rev. ed., pp. 9-10. In summary these criteria are: 1. an official ideology; 2. a single mass party led by one man and including in its membership a relatively small percentage of the population; 3. a terroristic police apparatus including a political police; 4. a technologically conditioned monopoly of all means of mass communications; 5. a similar monopoly of all armed forces; 6. a centrally controlled and directed economy.

3. Francis L. Carsten, The Rise of Fascism (Berkeley and Los Angeles: University of California Press, 1967), pp. 230-37.

4. Ernst Nolte, Three Faces of Fascism (New York, Chicago, San Francisco: Holt, Rinehart and Winston, 1965), p. 429.
5. S. J. Woolf, ed., European Fascism (New York: Random House, Vintage Book, 1969), p. 1.
6. Ibid.
7. Hans Rogger and Eugen Weber, eds., The European Right: A Historical Profile (Berkeley and Los Angeles: University of California Press, 1965), pp. 1-28.
8. If one disregards Austria and the publications of emigrés, only Hungarian books deserve mention: Kalman Szakacs, Kaszaskeresztesek [The Scythe-Cross Movement] (Budapest: Kossuth Könyvkiado, 1963); Miklos Lacko, Nyilasok, Nemzetiszocialistak, 1935-1944 [The Arrow Cross, National Socialists, 1935-1944] (Budapest: Kossuth Könyvkiado, 1966); Peter Sipos, Imredy Bela es a Magyar Megujulas Partja [Bela Imredy and the Party of the Hungarian Rebirth] (Budapest: Akademiai Kiado, 1970). Lacko also presented a short comparison of Eastern European Fascisms at the XIII International Congress of the Historical Sciences in Moscow in August 1970, Le Fascisme—Les Fascismes en Europe Centrale-Orientale (Moscow: Editions "Naouka," 1970).
9. Practically all studies dealing with Eastern Europe or individual countries in this region during the interwar period discuss Fascism. Their number is too great to permit listing them. Of the specific works dealing with Fascism already cited, the following sections deal specifically with Eastern Europe: Carsten's fifth chapter; in Woolf's volume, Chapter 5, written by K. R. Stadler, is devoted to Austria, Chapter 6 (J. Erös) to Hungary, Chapter 7 (Z. Barbu) to Romania, and Chapter 8 (S. Andreski) to Poland; the volume by Rogger and Weber has chapters on Austria (Andrew Whiteside), Hungary (Istvan Deak), and Romania (Eugen Weber). These same three countries are also discussed by Eugen Weber, Varieties of Fascism (Princeton-New York-Toronto-London: D. Van Nostrand, Anvil Pocketbook, 1964). A detailed study of Hungarian and Romanian Fascism can be found in Nicholas M. Nagy-Talavera, The Green Shirts and the Others (Standford: The Hoover Institute Press, 1971). Peter F. Sugar ed., Native Fascism in the Successor States, 1918-1945 (Santa Barbara, Calif.: A.B.C.-Clio Press, 1971) contains two essays each on the following countries; Austria (Fritz Fellner and R. John Rath), Czechoslovakia (Jan Havranek and Joseph F. Zacek), Hungary (György Ranki and George Barany), Poland (Henryk Wereszycki and Piotr S. Wandycz), Romania (Emanuel Turczynski and Stephen Fischer-Galati), Yugoslavia (Dimitrije Djordjevic and Ivan Avakumovic).
10. The explanation for this early lack of success given for Hungary by Lacko, Nyilasok, p. 17 is more or less valid for the region as a whole.

11. Lacko, Le Fascisme, p. 9.
12. Ibid., pp. 10-15.
13. George Barany, "The Dragon's Teeth: The Roots of Hungarian Fascism," in Sugar, ed., Native Fascism, p. 76.
14. Rogger and Weber, The European Right, p. 11.
15. Sugar, "Conclusions," in Sugar, ed., Native Fascism, p. 156.

* * * * *

ANALYSES
1. Martin Broszat

I would like to comment about an important aspect of Prof. Sugar's study, namely, social phases and social functions. I do not fully agree with his contention that while Fascism in Eastern Europe was socially closely bound to the ruling elites, in industrial Central and Western Europe its social programs and political activities had to start "out in the cold."

It is evident that in the agrarian societies of Eastern Europe, for reasons that should have been developed, conservative elites took a far stronger stand against the numerically small, but temporarily strong fascist movements than they did in Germany and Italy. But precisely for this reason, and because of the lack of a strong and conscious proletarian class and the absence of elective socialist parties, the conservative establishments of these countries were, in my opinion, less obliged to make concessions to Fascism than the regimes and dominant social groups in Italy or Germany that were facing the masses of the black and brown shirts.

Sugar argues that Fascism in Eastern Europe was more successful than in the more industrialized parts of the continent with more developed democratic political systems because it functioned more or less as an agent of the conservative Right, partly encouraged, partly restricted by the old elite, but basically pursuing the same goals in a more extreme form.

This, however, is only one side of the picture. Historical sources and studies on specific fascist movements in Eastern Europe contain different evaluations of the extreme Right and their social basis and functions. It seems to me that, for instance, Regent Horthy in Hungary or King Carol in Romania were far more aware than

---

Martin Broszat is a staff member of the Institut für Zeitgeschichte, Munich, Federal Republic of Germany.

FASCISM IN INTERWAR EASTERN EUROPE

Hindenburg in Germany that fascist seizure of power would be the definite end of the political and social systems in their countries. Therefore, they did not refrain from severe punishment and even murderous terror to suppress the danger of fascist revolt, although at that time they were strongly dependent on Nazi Germany and knew that their brutal suppression of Fascism was not welcomed there. Of course, if they did not have to fear an actual fascist coup d'état the conservative regimes were indeed ready to show indulgence and tolerance toward Fascism, but only for practical reasons and not because of a basic identity of value systems and social programs as Prof. Sugar would maintain.

Eugen Weber, in his studies of Romanian Fascism has maintained just the opposite point of view. He ascribes the appeal of fascist movements such as the Iron Guard and the Arrow Cross not only to the prevailing anti-Semitism but also to their use of radical social demagoguery and their appeal for land reform that attracted the most backward strata of peasants and laborers, as well as the young intelligentsia and segments of the lower clergy that had risen from these classes. According to him, these Eastern European agrarian fascists, more than middle-class fascists in Central Europe, temporarily constituted the main revolutionary force in their respective countries, claiming to be the only champions of radical change since leftist socialist parties or organizations were either weak or outlawed. Maybe Eugen Weber has exaggerated his point too, but it should be noted that even from a Marxist, although not orthodox Marxist, point of view, (confirmed by the Hungarian historian Lacko in his excellent recent study of the Arrow Cross movement), the fascist movement had its social basis not only in the lower gentry, in the army, local administration, segments of the intelligentsia, and the Christian petite bourgeoisie, but also to a considerable extent in the proletarian groups of landless agricultural laborers and industrial workers. To quote Lacko: "A considerable part of the support for the Arrow Cross came from the class of the workers, semi-proletarians, the backward layer of industrial workers and miners. The Arrow Cross fascist wave had disrupted even the ranks of organized labor in more than one instance."

It is a commonplace, of course, that Fascism, in spite of its temporary successful social demagoguery, nevertheless was led by romantic, conservative or restorative, ideological groups. The historian has to distinguish between the popular proletarian social basis and the real social function of Fascism. Fascist agitation filled not only the middle classes but also parts of the lower classes with antidemocratic, antisocialist, and national sentiment. Offering a pseudoreligious heroism as a kind of moral compensation for poverty, sacrifice, and loyalty, it diverted the hopes and activities of those

classes from their real problems and from a rational evaluation of
their political, economic, and social interests. But it is wrong to
assume that fascist mass movements, by this kind of propaganda and
activity, functioned as a mere stabilizer of conservative or big
business elites. Interpreters often overlook and are sometimes misled
by Marxist views about underlying social content and the effect of
fascist mass agitation and movement. It is true, for example, that
the elite concept of race was a heritage from former upper classes,
but it is also true that the fascists transformed the original social
exclusiveness of this elite conception into an egalitarian conception
for the masses and thereby consciously or unconsciously mobilized
irrational social claims that were misused by the fascists but could
not simply be reversed once stirred up.

It was precisely this social mobilization that was so highly
significant and that was feared most by the conservative authoritarian
regimes of Eastern Europe. Therefore, it is not surprising that the
conservative advisers of Regent Horthy, in 1938, bluntly spoke of
revolution when they talked about the Arrow Cross movement and the
fascist sentiments stirred by it. The example of Eastern European
Fascism also gives evidence of some other social conditions in
backward regions that had potentiality for Fascism. Eugen Weber
found out, for instance, that the Iron Guard movement of Romania
was most attractive in the remote regions of the countryside and to
those social sectors that had been or had felt completely neglected
or inadequately represented in the existing political, cultural, and
economic system. Even in industrialized countries like Germany,
the provinces nourished negative sentiments toward the industrial
centers, big cities, and political capitals, with real or assumed
corruption and superficiality of cultural life. This complex of sentiment in apparently sound small communities has been a common basis
for fascist reaction in nearly all societies.

Closely related to this was the fascist mobilization of students
and those segments of the youth that had been educated by the newly
established schools and universities in the new nation-states of Eastern
Europe but who had not had a chance to realize their claim for higher
positions in economic or public life. The overproduction of young
intelligentsia is a structural problem for all underdeveloped new
nation-states that, for reasons of national integration, give highest
priority to the establishment of a national system of education, but
are unable to make corresponding progress in the economy, thus
making the utilization of this talent possible. In many respects one
might go so far as to say that Eastern European Fascism bears some
particular signs of an unsettled, socially restless, and ideologically
immature young intelligentsia. Organized youth crime, extreme
rigorism, aestheticism, and pseudoreligious traits characterized

the fascist youth movement in Eastern Europe. This was also true, of course, of Fascism in Italy and Germany.

In the final passage of this study, Prof. Sugar has rightly accentuated the strong influence of the small group of intellectuals in Eastern Europe in the process of fascization during the 1930s. Favoring the national intelligentsia was from the very beginning the raison d'être of the conservative regimes of the Eastern European nation-states that used them as a tool in an effort to gain the necessary national support of the masses. But this, in the long run, also meant politicization and social mobilization. It was not only economic crisis in the beginning of the 1930s that disturbed the rather quiet political situation of these countries but also the response of the masses to national propoganda and the disappointing results of the national revolutions that had been nourished by the regimes themselves for about 15 years. The regimes faced the fascist results of this political mobilization that they had favored for national reasons but had to fear for social reasons. Fascism in Eastern Europe was used as a tool by the ruling conservative elite for blackmailing the masses, but at the same time it contributed to the destruction of these elites, for, to the extent that these fascist movements succeeded in implanting their ideologies, methods, and mass appeal into the existing authoritarian regimes, they undermined the basis of the ruling classes. The ruling classes, for domestic as well as foreign reasons, as Prof. Sugar states, competed with Fascism in their anti-Semitism, extreme nationalism, militarism, and police state methods in domestic affairs and thereby increasingly lost credit as rational foreign-policy leaders, as guarantors of independence, and as guardians of the legal and cultural heritage of their nations.

The process of fascization that took place in the Hungarian, Romanian, Slovakian, and Croatian regimes during World War II also unwittingly prepared these countries for the coming of Marxism, not only due to the unhappy alliance with Hitler, but also as a result of the deep loss of political credit that the conservative national elites had suffered in the meantime, and also due to the fact that the fascists themselves proved unable to lead their social dynamism to operational objectives. Fascism did not produce any constructive social reforms, but by its political influence contributed to the undermining of old stagnating social structures and weakened the forces of resistance against the use of social reform and revolution. The fascist episode in the recent history of the European peoples is significant at least for this reason.

2. Istvan Deak

Prof. Sugar points effectively to the "politics of despair" that provoked the rise of Fascism and demonstrates that East Central Europe was an ideal ground for fascist agitation. He explains the momentous differences between the conservative "old Right" and the radical "new Right," and shows us how the dominating "old Right" was able to profit from the dynamism of the "new." He also makes clear how the conservatives were hampered by the radicals and how they were finally driven to adopt much of the radicals' program.

Having said this, there are a few brief statements I would like to make. First, I would like to warn of the temptation to be sidetracked into a lengthy discussion of the question that has already been brought up several times. Namely, who were the fascists? What social strata did they come from, and what social classes did they represent? Prof. Sugar tells us that they were mainly déclassés. I would be inclined to disagree on the basis of my admittedly very limited knowledge of Hungarian fascists and warn that, in order to be able to say anything about the social background of the fascists, we have to do much more digging in the archives for data that are probably nonexistent. The only person who attempted a sociological analysis of the East Central European fascists, and Prof. Sugar in his study refers to him, was the Hungarian historian Miklos Lacko. Lacko concludes, in his Arrow-Cross Men, National Socialists,[1] that a majority of Hungarian fascists came either from "the lower strata of the ruling classes," i.e., they were army officers, landowners, or Christian bourgeois, or they came from "the most backward elements of the proletariat." But even this does not seem to be quite satisfactory because the fascist movement in Hungary included such disparate people as a Habsburg archduke, titled aristocrats, large and small landowners, generals, junior officers, NCO's, civil servants, journalists, artists, clergymen, and many lower class elements. If we take the civil servants as an example, certainly some were déclassés who had lost their jobs in the Depression, but others had their jobs and still were fascist party members. Interestingly, a very large portion of streetcar conductors in Budapest were fascists but the movement was far less successful with the railroad workers. The coal miners tended to be Arrow-Cross followers; other miners stuck to Social Democracy. Many of the young and unorganized workers were fascists, too, but several of the well-organized labor

---

Istvan Deak is Professor of History and Director of the Institute on East Central Europe, at Columbia University, New York.

unions were able to defend themselves against fascist infiltration. Szalasi's Arrow Cross was able to entice an enormous number of small artisans, as well as a lot of hoodlums and gangsters, but very few peasants. What can we conclude from this? That social background and occupation have little to do with membership in right-wing radical parties. If we consider that in East Central Europe, Fascism was the only radical alternative in the 1920s and the 1930s, then it is safe to say that people who were dynamic, fanatic, dissatisfied, and anxious for change were more likely to join the fascist movement than others. This is my first statement.

For my other, I will have to go back in history. I would like to discuss the role that World War I played in the rise of interwar Fascism. It is my contention, first, that the great problems of the interwar period did not stem from the Great War itself but from the period immediately preceding the war. I am in agreement here with many writers on the subject. My second contention is that World War I was not as historically negative a phenomenon as Prof. Sugar perhaps believes. It did solve more problems than it left open. Of course it is hard to measure this with any degree of accuracy. My third contention is that the rise of Fascism was due less to the chaos and misery caused by the Great War and more to the very high expectations and hopes raised by the events of the war. Fascism, in my opinion, was a consequence of these exaggerated hopes and subsequent disappointment.

Many writers, including Prof. Fritz Stern,[2] have commented on the malaise that gripped European public opinion before World War I. It was felt, especially in intellectual circles, that the prevailing order was doomed, and that a general cataclysm was inevitable. Bourgeois materialism had to be rejected and new life forms created. The literati and the artists proceeded to do that in inventing revolutionary art forms such as expressionism and dadaism, which cruelly lambasted the bourgeoisie and its System.

There was a desire for, and premonition of, tremendous change well before World War I. Conversely, although it is hard to establish the evidence, the ruling circles, especially in Germany, were convinced of the revolutionary aspirations of some lower class groups and of the intellectuals. We know today that Imperial Germany's leaders tremendously overestimated the revolutionary potentials of the trade unions and of the socialist movement. They were exasperated by radical agitation and by the rebellious mood of the artists and writers. It is quite likely that the German ruling circles welcomed the war in 1914 as a solution to these problems. We also know from many sources that there were many precursors to Fascism before 1914, in the form of right-wing philosophers, anti-Semitic parties and antiliberal youth movements.

The outbreak of the war came as a release to many. The masses in the streets celebrated not only future victories, but also the end of an era that many found intolerable and many more found boring. The war itself witnessed a series of euphoric celebrations. After each successful battle, people had a renewed sense of a new era dawning. And when, finally, the war was found wanting, new outlets were found for optimism. I am saying all this to show that we are not dealing with a pessimistic period but, on the contrary, with a time when people were filled with undue optimism. When they finally realized, by 1916-17, that the war was not a heady panacea, they looked to peace or revolution as the alternatives to war that could bring about a new era of universal fraternity and general wisdom. Millions found this utopia in the Russian Revolution; others in the Wilsonian program. The revolution of 1918 and 1919 again led to new celebrations in the streets with much of the feelings that existed in 1914. How dull is World War II in comparison! There were no street celebrations in 1939 either on the Allied side or in the German cities. People expected little from the new war. The French, the English, the Poles, the Italians, the Russians, and even the Germans felt they had been driven by their opponents into an unnecessary conflict. The goal now was survival, not utopia. At best, we witness in World War II a grim determination, certainly on the British side, but also on the side of the Russians and the Germans. And because World War II had been marked by pessimism, there was, after the war, less disappointment.

World War I solved many problems and I think it is a good idea to remind ourselves of that. It did away with two anachronistic empires and it ended the rule of two other anachronistic imperial dynasties. Although it did not liberate all the peoples, it did liberate a lot of them and it promulgated the principle of national self-determination. The war did a great deal toward the introduction of universal suffrage and toward the emancipation of women. World War I is now judged negatively, due mainly to the views of Anglo-Saxon historians and writers, but it was not judged so negatively at that time. Many people came out of it convinced that a new happier era was dawning. They were, of course, disappointed.

What then, went wrong after World War I?

There was the economic problem. The economies were not collapsing but they were in terrible shape. Recovery was slow, much slower than after World War II, and people were unwilling to pay for the expenses of the war.

Secondly, there was a psychological problem. A problem of lost illusions and of unrealized expectations. Fascism was a tantalizing escape since it took the form of a new promise.

But if Fascism held out the hope of a new utopia, so did Bolshevism. Why then did the East Central European peoples generally prefer Fascism to Bolshevism? Because Russia was a poor, defeated, and isolated power and because Russia lay to the East. It is very seldom that the East Central Europeans look at the East for new ideas and inspirations. They did in 1917, but this was a short span of time compared with the period preceding and following it when they looked to the West and particularly to Germany. Again, they preferred Fascism because the Central European Bolshevik revolutions in 1918-19 had been a terrible disappointment. Fascism was still untested. Finally, Fascism was tolerated by the East Central European governments whereas Communism was not tolerated. The Bolsheviks were killed or imprisoned and it required great heroism to be a communist in East Central Europe. Fascists, as Prof. Broszat wrote, were also occasionally murdered or put in prison, but mostly they were at liberty to carry on their agitation. Therefore Fascism was generally the only radical activity one could engage in.

If Fascism was such a great promise, why then did it fail to come to power by itself in Eastern Europe? After all, as we all would admit, East Central Europe with its racial and social problems was an ideal ground for fascist agitation. At this point I can do no better than to suggest that we examine Prof. John Weiss' very fine book on The Fascist Tradition[3]. His contention is that "the radical right thrives only in societies where older but still powerful conservative classes are threatened by rapid and modernizing social change; change which creates or gives strength to liberal or radical classes and groups antagonistic to 'the old ways.'" Or as he puts it in another place: "Fascism was not 'the last gasp of monopoly capitalism.' If anything, it was the last gasp of conservatism."[4] In other words, in Western Europe Fascism could not triumph because the conservative forces had already been fatally weakened by industrialization and modernization. In East Central Europe, on the other hand, Fascism could not come to power spontaneously because the conservatives were still strong and they did not feel truly threatened by liberalism and radicalism. The conservatives did not feel the need to entrust power to far-right agitators. Fascism could triumph only in those countries where there was both liberal big business and big socialist trade unions, and where the conservative middle class and lower middle class felt squeezed between the capitalists and the workers. That is, Fascism could triumph only in Italy and Germany.

3. Gyorgy Ránki

Prof. Sugar has given evidence not only of his familiarity with the best available literature on his topic but also of his expertise on the modern history of Eastern Europe and his understanding of the phenomenon of Fascism as it manifested itself in Eastern Europe during the interwar period.

His arguments are well founded when he says that in most of these countries a native Fascism existed, helped but not artificially created by foreign developments. He is right in saying that its influence should not be judged only by whether or not fascists achieved power, for they did have an important function as a pressure group and their influence was extremely great in shaping the policies of government that were based on more traditional forces. They infiltrated the government heavily and they came not only from the lower classes but from the rank and file of the old right as well.

Various theses have been advanced in explaining the phenomenon of Fascism. One of these holds that Fascism is to be studied in a broad sense as a manifestation of vast sentiment in the 1930s in support of totalitarianism. Hans Kohn reflects this view in Political Ideologies of the Twentieth Century,[1] with the difference that Kohn views totalitarianism as being only partially helpful in explaining Fascism which Kohn interprets to be a moral sickness.

Another thesis is that totalitarianism is a natural phenomenon of modern mass society. It has been advanced mainly by sociologists but also by Brzezinski and Friedrich[2] who have provided a rich groundwork for distinguishing between different types of Fascism and for seeing the discontinuity between Fascism and authoritative power.

I will not go into any other aspect of the theory of totalitarianism, the problems of social and historical function, the differences of social structure, historical background, and political and social aims. However, I would like to call attention to the fact that according to this theory, especially as formulated by Arendt, the majority of the parties, movements, and regimes in Europe, especially in East Central Europe, between the two world wars, were not really fascist but only more or less conservative and autocratic, except in Germany and Italy.

Prof. Sugar uses totalitarianism only as a starting point for his general treatment of Fascism, which he places within the general

---

Gyorgi Ránki is Professor of History at Debrecen University, Debrecen, Hungary, and Deputy Director of the Institute of History of the Hungarian Academy of Sciences in Budapest.

context of the interwar social and economic situation, thus limiting the problem in space and time. Therefore Fascism is to him a function of the crisis in the relationship between the old and the new. However, Prof. Sugar has overemphasized this viewpoint and neglected to take sufficient account of the significant changes that took place between the two world wars and the influence of these changes on the "new right."

As to whether or not Eastern European fascists were mostly déclassés, the evidence would suggest that a large part of them were indeed déclassés, but that some of the potential leaders who had aspirations for political activity were in fact acting as revolutionaries and were not as bound to their old regime as Prof. Sugar would believe. Prof. Sugar has generalized too broadly in this sense without sometimes making the necessary distinctions. For example, he speaks of three characteristic trends of the Hungarian fascist movement and the different strands of Hungarian Fascism. He mentions three influences on Hungarian political life during this period, namely that of Gömbös, Szalasi and Imredy. Gömbös was really much closer to the old Hungarian concept of agrarianism than the other two, and Prof. Sugar depicts Szalasi as a revolutionary. I am inclined to challenge the revolutionary character of Szalasi, based on a study of his political conversations with members of his party elite during the war and because of the vagueness of his social program. This is corroborated by Prof. Deak in his chapter in The European Right.[3] This is not to say that a part of his staff or of his political party did not want radical social and economic change. However, by birth, social status, and prestige, Szalasi was tied to the old ruling group, and his party was not only a proletarian but a middle-class party.

There existed a very important distinction between Imredy and Gömbös. This is important because the Hungarian non-Jewish middle class both before and after World War I consisted first of the landed gentry, but in the '30s a new stratum, composed of non-Jewish bourgeois elements and intellectuals, was added to the middle class, strongly supporting Imredy. They were less traditionally agrarian than any conservative or fascist group in Hungary before then. Neither conservative nor agrarian, unlike Gömbös, they were less traditionalist than Szalasi. Therefore it is clear that they were not trying to fit an old reactionary regime with new trappings, and in this respect Prof. Sugar should stand corrected.

Finally, one of the very interesting and critical questions in Eastern European Fascism is the connection between militarism and Fascism. Recently some very interesting studies have been done on this question that make a real distinction between the German-Italian version of Fascism and the less "classical" version. It is important to stress that traditional military Fascism is an outgrowth of conservative reactionary forms into modern forms of government. A study of Italian and German Fascism involves not only the fascist movement but also Fascism in power, whereas a study of Eastern European Fascism only involves Fascism as a movement.

4. Piotr S. Wandycz

I find Prof. Sugar's analysis and presentation most interesting and stimulating, even if, or perhaps precisely because, I disagree with several of his points.

We know that the lack of an adequate and all-embracing definition of Fascism complicates our inquiry. While we can use the term to discuss East European phenomena, we ought to be doubly aware of its arbitrariness given the vastly different conditions within this region. The diversity of the East European scene not only makes generalizations about Fascism difficult, but it almost inevitably leads one to concentrate on one or two countries. Hence Prof. Sugar really concentrates on Hungary and tends to apply his findings per analogiam to the rest of East Central Europe. I do not think that he is fully successful in his approach. I have serious doubts whether the contrast between the "old Right" and "new Right" evident for Hungary existed in a comparable form in Poland, Greece, or Yugoslavia. I do not think that the contrast is valid for Czechoslovakia. There are other instances in his study where the diversity is not sufficiently emphasized. Prof. Sugar is right when he says that all East European countries were in a sense "new," but I think that one must distinguish between those that had preserved most of their traditional institutions—say Hungary, Romania, or Bulgaria—and Czechoslovakia and Poland which were "new" in a different way. I believe that the "old Right" versus "new Right" phenomenon is particularly noticable in the former group—is it not suggestive that the only mass fascist parties were produced in Romania and Hungary?

Prof. Sugar contrasts West and East European Fascism by using an essentially class criterion of "parvenus" versus "déclassés." I am not quite sure that this distinction is either valid or helpful. Surely Sir Oswald Moseley, José Primo de Rivera or Léon Degrelle were not parvenus, while Codreanu was. True, there was a relatively greater "compatibility" between fascists and the ruling group in Eastern Europe than in the West, but I would suggest that the explanation of it be sought elsewhere. To me, the key word is

---

Piotr S. Wandycz is Professor of History at Yale University, New Haven, Conn.

"intelligentsia"—an East European term without real counterpart in the West. Intelligentsia occupied key positions in the Eastern European countries. Both the leaders in power and the rightist extremists were members of it, and thus a special affinity existed between them. It seems to me that the "intelligentsia phenomenon" deserves a more profound scrutiny than it has received in this study.

Prof. Sugar does not fully explore another important issue of the period in Eastern Europe—the generation problem. It is surely important that some of the most prominent fascists were very young. At the time of Mussolini's march on Rome, Piasecki was 10 years old, Codreanu 23, Szalasi 25. Much of their following came from the youth that saw its avenues of advancement blocked. In a sense I would favor the terms "old" and "young" Right rather than "old" and "new" to emphasize this youth element. The "young" and dynamic diplomacy of a Ciano or a Ribbentrop appealed to these youthful fascists and they contrasted it with the "old," hesitant, and ineffective foreign policies of the Western democracies.

Prof. Sugar rightly perceives a pattern of the Eastern European evolution to the extreme right, but I would question some of his explanations. Was the impact of "many centuries" of absolutism all that important? In the case of Czechoslovakia it proved not to be. In the case of Poland the "many centuries" can really be reduced to 123 years. Should we not be a little less sweeping in our statements about the absence of democratic traditions in Eastern Europe? Prof. Sugar mentions a traditional identification of race with nation in Eastern Europe. I would not consider this a long tradition. Surely the concept of "natio Hungarica" and of an ethnically heterogeneous Polish "nation" were not based on race.

Another point that bothers me is the connection between domestic trends and international affairs as presented. The connection was fairly obvious but it lay rather in the sphere of security than economic dependence. Czechoslovak trade with Germany was intensive but it did not produce an evolution toward the extreme right. Polish economic dependence on Germany was decreasing but the country moved politically to the right. In the case of the Danubian and Balkan countries the problem is complex and defies easy generalizations. When Prof. Sugar mentions Prague's concessions to Tiso or to the German Sudeten party, or when he speaks about Belgrade's concessions to the Croats, he seems to view them as examples of a certain compatibility between the ruling circles and Fascism. I would have thought that here we are dealing with a fairly classical case of the outside threat to the country's security. The royal dictatorship in Yugoslavia was introduced to prevent a decomposition of the state endangered from outside. In Poland, parliamentary democracy was attacked by its opponents on the grounds that it was a luxury that a state exposed to German and Soviet enmity could not afford.

I believe Prof. Sugar's analysis would have gained depth if he had emphasized more strongly the diversity of the Eastern European scene, investigated a little more the intelligentsia and the generation problems, and put more stress on foreign policy factors.

NOTES TO ANALYSES

Analysis 2

1. Miklos Lacko, Arrow-Cross Men, National Socialists (Budapest: Akademiai Kiado, 1969), pp. 5-9, et passim.
2. Fritz Stern, The Politics of Cultural Despair: A Study in the Rise of German Ideology (Berkeley and Los Angeles: University of California Press, 1961).
3. John Weiss, The Fascist Tradition (New York: Harper & Row, 1967).
4. Ibid., pp. 4, 5.

Analysis 3

1. Hans Kohn, Political Ideologies of the Twentieth Century (New York: Harper & Row, 1966), 3d rev. ed.
2. Carl J. Friedrich and Zbigniew K. Brzezinski, Totalitarian Dictatorship and Autocracy (Cambridge, Mass.: Harvard University Press, 1965), 2d rev. ed.
3. Istvan Deák, "Hungary," in Hans Rogger and Eugen Weber, eds., The European Right (Berkeley and Los Angeles: University of California Press, 1965), pp. 364-407.

CHAPTER 3

**LEGITIMACY OF POWER
IN EAST CENTRAL EUROPE**
Alfred Meyer

INTRODUCTORY NOTE

After I undertook to write the present study, I sought to gather material for it by reading extensively. My reading material included survey data gathered by sociologists from Eastern Europe and other countries; travel accounts; as well as descriptions of various aspects of social change and social attitudes based on a wide range of impressions and observations. While the totality of this material has doubtless contributed to my own image of the legitimacy of power in Eastern Europe, I have, in the end, refrained from making systematic use of it. Instead, I am offering what Americans sometimes call a think-piece, i.e., an essay dealing, perhaps too abstractly, with the problems faced by the scholar who wishes to deal with the question of legitimacy. I offer my thoughts in the hope that they will stimulate opposition and dissent from among my colleagues as well as constructive advice on how to overcome some of the obstacles to knowledge that I see.

Under the term legitimacy we customarily understand a quality inherent in certain relationships of power, namely, that quality that justifies the power relationship and thus renders it acceptable. If we define power as a relationship in which one actor has the ability to determine the actions of another, then legitimacy is that quality of power relationships that turns them into relationships of authority. Hence one current and useful definition of authority is "legitimate power."[1]

Alfred Meyer is Professor of Political Science at the University of Michigan, Ann Arbor.

Power can take many forms and manifest itself in a wide range of human endeavors. In politics it manifests itself as the ability to control, command, and regulate; to settle disputes; to establish, change, and abolish institutions; to make laws and supervise their execution. When we use the term within the context of national and global affairs, it usually denotes the political leadership exercised over an entire national system. In analyzing power one can focus either on the nature of the relationship itself or on those who "hold" or "wield" it—the locus of power. Concerning the locus of national power in Eastern Europe, there is universal agreement: power in Eastern Europe is in the hands of an elite dominated by the top leadership of the Communist parties. This statement must be hedged in by two reservations: first, the elite is not very easily identifiable, because the dominant top leadership of the party shares power, to an extent not well known, with other groups in the population; and it does so in a manner that changes from one period to another and varies greatly in the different countries. Second, the power of the East European top elite is limited, also in changing fashion, by the power of the Soviet Union. Power in Eastern Europe, by and large, is the power of client states.

In light of these definitions, the problem of the legitimacy of power in Communist Eastern Europe focuses on a concern with the questions, how successful the top leadership groups of the East European Communist parties have been in establishing themselves and their parties as those who are entitled to rule; or, how acceptable they have managed to render their political systems? In this study I shall explore a variety of ways in which one might attempt to answer such questions.

THE ETHICS OF LEGITIMACY

Since legitimacy concerns the measuring of certain realities against a hypothetical standard, it is, in the final analysis, a moral concept. One determines the legitimacy of power by applying principles of ethics to political systems. Given certain assumptions about human nature and the purpose of human activities, what kinds of power relations are legitimate, and what kind of people ought to exercise power over their fellow men, in what circumstances, and in what areas of life? To answer these and similar questions we require principles of ethics. If it has not been clear before, it ought to be apparent now that theories of legitimacy are, in effect, theories of political obligation or duty. By defining certain powers as legitimate, they command us to submit to them and indeed to do so cheerfully. Of course, theories of obligation easily turn into justifications of rebellion; for, by setting moral standards of legitimacy, they provide methods for demonstrating that incumbent systems fall short of these standards.

There are as many different moral justifications of power as there are schools of philosophy but it would not be useful here to survey them, for two reasons. First, there exist a bewildering variety of theories of legitimacy. In order to do justice to it, one would have to survey the entire history of moral philosophy. Second, even if we refrain from a historical survey, a survey of moral arguments current today would be almost as bewildering in its variety. Ours is a world as pluralistic in ethical philosophies as in every other respect. If there was ever unity of philosophic views, that unity is gone. If there was ever a possibility to engage in moral discourse, even that possibility seems gone. We seem no longer to agree sufficiently on terms or first assumptions to be able to sustain moral discourse. For that reason, some people argue that ethics is dead.

If ethics indeed is dead—and I shall not argue for or against that proposition—then it has been done in not only by the prevalent philosophic pluralism, but also by the scientistic, positivist, and empirical biases of contemporary intellectual life. Aware of the shakiness of all moral arguments, many of us have developed a strong and open aversion to the very use of moralistic arguments. In the case of political ethics, to which all arguments concerning legitimacy of power belong, the aversion against any moral defenses of power is intensified by the great strength of democratic convictions throughout the contemporary world. For one of the most persistent assumptions underlying democratic political thought is a suspicion of all power and all rule.

All this might be restated in highly abstract form by pointing out that contemporary political philosophy throughout the world lays great stress on the development and cultivation of human freedom and human reason. Long before the age of democracy and science, however, great philosophers pointed out that power tends to be a threat to both freedom and reason. The Augustinian argument that no existing system, or no system fashioned by mortals, can ever be legitimate, has had a lasting influence on all subsequent political philosophy, so much so that even the most emphatic philosophic apologists for powerful rule have remained aware of the strain they imposed on the moral credulity of their readers. The most forthright of such apologists have boldly expressed this strain by legitimizing power through deliberately paradoxical formulations, beginning with Augustine, who argued that dominatio est contra naturam and yet urged submission to the magnum latrocinium of the state; through Hobbes, who urges the criminal to consent voluntarily to his own execution; or Rousseau who thinks we might be forced to be free.

Terms such as "popular sovereignty," "the consent of the governed," "legitimate usurpation," the "dictatorship of the proletariat," "democratic centralism," and others, neatly express the remarkable brittleness of all attempts to provide moral theories of legitimacy. It could easily be shown that all such theories are based on meta-rational assumptions, and that, therefore, power can be legitimized only by faith and myth, or, to express this more cynically, by lies and fraud, which are accepted only because ultimately they are backed up by power. So that, in the final analysis, the only thing that legitimizes power is power itself.

Once such a point of view, which is based on the assumption of universally valid moral commands, is accepted, all legitimacy is indeed deception or self-deception; and the argument suggests itself that a system with a certain amount of legitimacy is morally more reprehensible than one which is felt to be illegitimate. For the system which has managed to gain legitimacy in the eyes of its subjects or citizens has managed to institutionalize itself; and power accepted is worse than power recognized for what it is.

I do not wish to maintain such Augustinian views here. For it seems that there are indeed moral standards by which the legitimacy of one system of power can be compared with that of another. Each of us, however reluctant to moralize, can be assumed to have some such standards of legitimacy, which, if nothing else, might enable him to determine under what system of power it might be preferable to exist, if a choice were necessary or possible. Given the philosophical pluralism of the contemporary world, these standards may turn out to be highly personal, hence comparatively meaningless or unacceptable to many others. And yet, it might be possible to work out some relatively vague and abstract maxims on which all participants in a scholarly conference such as this could agree; one might even elaborate a vaguer set of principles on which he would obtain broad agreement throughout the so-called Western world. We are likely to find, however, that were we to bring our colleagues from Eastern Europe into the discourse, we would have great difficulties agreeing even on such vague and abstract maxims. And yet, there may be some standards of decency that could be accepted by people throughout the contemporary world, and if not standards of decency some other measure by which to assess the legitimacy of political systems. The trouble is, first, that such standards are likely to be exceedingly vague. We all believe in the value of freedom, justice, material security, stability, and the like. But we give quite varying meanings to all of these terms. And even if there were universally accepted definitions, people still differ in the manner in which they arrange these standards and the different weights they give them. In other words, the values we hold high may not have changed much since

LEGITIMACY OF POWER

Socrates; but the hierarchies of values we work out for ourselves remain matters of controversy; and so, finally, do our different views concerning the implementation of these values. Hence we might all agree on the importance of freedom, justice, and the like, but we will still fight over the most effective method of creating the proper conditions for their development and flourishing. In short, as political moralists we are accustomed to think in terms of complex systems, in which all real manifestations of power are assigned places of greater or lesser importance depending on their salience to the total system. This makes it impossible to make universally acceptable moral judgments between different systems of power. By what standard can we measure the inefficiency of Western parliaments against the inefficiency of Communist bureaucracies? Which is morally more reprehensible, massive unemployment or the exploitation of collectivized peasants, Katyn or Hiroshima, correctional labor camps or Attica prison? Or which is more praiseworthy, the absence of large-scale unemployment or the freedom of the affluent to lead lives of pleasure?

If we despair of applying a universal moral standard to the measurement of the legitimacy of various systems, we can still inquire into the extent to which the population in Eastern European states has accepted the political formula of Marxism-Leninism, which provides the official moral standard. It will be very difficult to do this in practice; and even if we could gather concrete information about degrees of acceptance, and numbers of people who accept or reject the official ideology in different ways, we should not yet be able to assess the legitimacy of the regimes. For one thing, rejection of the official myths does not necessarily mean lack of legitimacy. Many citizens in a variety of political systems accept their system even though they are skeptical about the legitimation myths employed. The reasons for accepting them may range from the realization that there is no alternative to calculations of group or class interest, in which case the legitimating factor would be the regime's performance. The legitimacy of power, in other words, can be derived from prudential arguments that neglect questions of political or moral philosophy altogether. At the same time, it is equally possible, and indeed likely, that we will find plenty of people who accept the tenets of Marxism-Leninism used by the East European regimes to legitimize themselves, but nonetheless sharply criticize these regimes, and do so in the name of the official ideology. The problem of assessing the legitimacy of power is complicated, in other words, by the fact that legitimacy can be attributed either to the system (as an abstraction) or to the way it actually functions and to the people actually wielding power. The two kinds of legitimacy can be mutually exclusive, although they can also reinforce each other.*

Altogether, therefore, the attempt to measure the legitimacy of any power system on purely moral grounds will remain highly challengeable. Moral standards, however, are not the only possible foundation for a theory of legitimacy. Political philosophy provides us with several alternatives to it. One of these, suggested by Aristotle's distinction between "good" and perverted forms of rule, identifies the culture of the community as one of the chief criteria of legitimacy. For, according to Aristotle, that kind of power relationship is best for a community that most closely matches the views, customs, and traditions of that community. This view has a conservative flavor because it places so much weight on well-established traditions; but it could be made compatible also with theories of change, if it acknowledges the changeability of culture itself. (In writing this, I am aware that the notion of changeable culture may be self-contradictory.) Whether culture is sufficiently capable of being defined for the purposes of determining degrees of legitimacy is, perhaps, open to question. The fact that some scholars derive their definition of political culture from the attempts made to legitimize indicates a certain circularity in argument.2 Moreover, in complex societies there usually are several cultures, one for each major class of the population; and in Eastern Europe matters are complicated even more by the ethnic variety of the populations; Yugoslavia, Romania, and Albania have more than one distinct national culture.

---

*In real life, the two kinds of legitimacy are intertwined inextricably, so that very often it is difficult to tell one from the other, or to assert with confidence whether a given political sentiment indicates legitimacy or illegitimacy, precisely because people for whom the system has lost its legitimacy often find it convenient to justify their actions or intentions, which aim to destroy the system, by reference to the commonly accepted values and ideologies. Those totally alienated from a given political order express their alienation by a fierce loyalty to an idealized image of that order, which they claim the incumbent wielders of power have betrayed. This is the stance taken by Trotskyite critics of Stalinism, by fascist superpatriots, indeed by most reformers and revolutionaries. Revolutionaries claim they seek to fulfill the professed ideals that do have legitimacy in their eyes; radicals on the far right speak in the name of established laws and a hallowed order; yet they show all intentions to abolish the laws and the order they claim to defend. In both cases, symbols of legitimacy are manipulated for a political purpose springing ultimately from the conviction that the system is not legitimate at all.

National culture becomes a tricky criterion for legitimacy also in political systems that proclaim themselves to be revolutionary systems. For revolutions often declare the destruction and replacement of the prevailing culture to be one of their chief aims. Hence to measure their legitimacy against the very criteria that they reject would be a futile exercise in denunciation, all the more so when it can be argued, as it might be possible for Eastern Europe, that the political culture that had prevailed before World War II had already been destroyed and discredited, if not totally, then to a large extent. In the course of the German occupation, a large portion of the old ruling classes had been destroyed; those that survived often did so only at the cost of collaboration with the occupier, so that after liberation they were tainted. Capitalist property had largely been confiscated by the occupying forces and could, after liberation, easily be taken over by the new governments, so that the coming of socialism, in some form or another, appeared as a relatively easy step. To this one must add the fact that Communist parties emerged, throughout Eastern Europe, with a kind of prestige and power they had never had before, an image that they had gained by their leadership in underground struggles and by martyrdom. Indeed, throughout Europe (and not only in Europe) Communist parties after the war could successfully claim to be patriotic parties. In that sense, communism had become respectable. One might generalize about this by suggesting that there are periods in which traditional political culture disintegrates or weakens. These are periods of crisis or revolution. In the course of very deep crises the traditional political culture tends to be replaced by a mixture of despair, cynicism, and strong hopes for delivery through drastic, or even catastrophic, deeds. In a genuine revolution, that group of people that most clearly expresses such hopes (which are sometimes labeled "millennial") is likely to come to power; and because its power corresponds to the prevailing millennial mood of broad masses of the population, the power is legitimate, at least as long as the revolutionary mood has not evaporated. Max Weber has called this temporary legitimacy of power created in genuine revolutions "charisma." The revolutions of Eastern Europe were not, on the whole, genuine, because the eventual distribution of power was profoundly affected by the presence of the Soviet armed forces. And yet, because of the discredit in which the prewar political culture had fallen among broad strata of the population, a certain amount of charismatic legitimacy must nonetheless be conceded to the Communist regimes at the time they acquired power.

As I pointed out above, that kind of legitimacy by its own nature cannot survive the revolutionary period. Charisma is an ephemeral phenomenon linked to periods of sharp crisis.

I shall discuss below the inevitable threat to legitimacy that is posed by the disappearance of the revolutionary crisis. At this point, however, an additional observation must be made about the national political culture. Revolutionary systems typically regard it as one of their tasks to eradicate the traditional political culture. Yet they do not seem ever to succeed entirely. There are certain cultural elements that seem to persist through and beyond revolutions. Perhaps these could be called elements of a national political style, in want of a more precise term. Whether political science has found a method for analyzing and describing such styles adequately is questionable. We are therefore discussing an extremely elusive phenomenon. And yet it seems without doubt that there are certain kinds of behavior or relationship in political life which a Prussian, a Pole, a Magyar, will somehow recognize as consonant or not consonant with the way he and his compatriots expect political actors to behave or to relate to each other—a Prussian, Polish, or Magyar style of politics. If that is correct, then the legitimacy of power in Eastern Europe would, in the long run, be determined in part by the sensitivity of the power-wielders to such national styles; in other words, by their ability to create distinctly Polish, Magyar, or Prussian styles of communism, or by the success of these several peoples to compel the wielders to make such adjustments to the national political culture. Once in a while the observer gets vague impressions that in at least some of the East European countries such a process is taking place already.

If moral theories of legitimacy are vitiated by the lack of universal agreement on underlying maxims or on specific hierarchies of values, and cultural theories by the vagueness of our understanding of what constitutes a culture, it might be feasible to agree on a theory of legitimacy based on purely formal criteria. According to formal criteria, legitimacy would be conceded to any power system that has been established in conformity to existing constitutional and legal rules concerning the acquisition, transfer, and use of political power. In order to assess the legitimacy of power in Eastern Europe, one would then have to examine whether power was acquired in violation of then existing laws, constitutions, treaties, and other established formal rules, and whether today it is being wielded in violation of rules now in force.

A cursory examination of the evidence will yield a very inconclusive picture. First, most of the East European Communist leaders showed awareness of the problem and therefore tried to come to power with as much formal legitimacy as possible. At the same time, they also showed their contempt for formal legitimacy by allowing coercion to remain visible just behind the formalities. Communists have always voiced such contempt. They have always maintained that

LEGITIMACY OF POWER 53

all politics consists of struggle, and that superior power not only ensures victory, but also legitimizes; at least as long as it is their power, the power wielded in the name of the proletariat. One need not agree with them to recognize that in certain historic situations formal criteria of legitimacy become fairly meaningless, and reference to them becomes futile if not ridiculous. These situations are war and revolution. The distribution of power in Eastern Europe is, to a large extent, the result of the fortunes of war; and conquest has always been an argument to which there is no effective response. But in the case of Eastern Europe, conquest was in fact recognized as legitimate in the treaties and other arrangements made by the wartime allies at the Teheran, Yalta, and Potsdam conferences. To be sure, both sides have accused each other of having broken these agreements in creating their respective systems of client states in Eastern and Western Europe. The fact is, however, that the agreements were deliberately worded so vaguely that each side could claim justification for its sovereign arrangements. The deliberate vagueness of the agreements, in other words, was a tacit legitimation of the law of conquest, but a legitimation that, by the same token, could be repudiated at will.

The law of revolution, at first sight, does not seem to have any legitimizing force, even though most political systems, including those that are commonly considered to be among the most legitimate, have been born in revolution. Yet one might argue, as all spokesmen for tyrannicide, regicide, and revolution have argued, that revolutions are legitimized by the lack of legitimacy of the systems they replace. Certainly most of the wartime regimes in Eastern Europe, being occupation regimes or under the domination of an occupation force, had little or no legitimacy; and many of the prewar regimes had little more. The postwar order therefore was legitimized in part by the illegitimacy of the wartime and prewar usurpers of power. But the resulting legitimacy must be assigned not to the Communist systems but rather to the immediate postwar regimes that were more broadly based coalitions. If revolutions confer legitimacy, then we must recognize that the revolutions in Eastern Europe were, to some extent, contrived. While it is undeniable that the prewar systems had forfeited their legitimacy, the communist parties acquired full power only because the Soviet Union was able to channel the revolution in this direction. All that one might point out in addition would be that this kind of interference was then practiced by both of the superpowers. Contrived revolutions in Eastern Europe were matched by contrived counterrevolutions in the West, including American interference in a crucial Italian election campaign; British-American interference in the Greek civil war; the establishment of the Federal Republic of Germany; and numerous other acts of intervention and usurpation. In a way, one might argue that American and Soviet practices of usurpation legitimized each other, albeit totally unintentionally. The entire argument simply shows that there are periods in history where one cannot apply formal criteria of legitimacy, certainly not with any conviction. For systems of power that originate in war or revolution, the only question one can ask is whether they can render themselves legitimate afterwards.

If formal criteria are an inadequate basis for assessing the legitimacy of power in Eastern Europe, and if the real question is whether this power can render itself legitimate, or whether it has succeeded in doing so, there is one standard that may be more reliable. The criterion of legitimacy I have in mind is that of performance.

Again, this is suggested by Aristotle, who approved of those power systems that served the public interest, in contrast with regimes that serve only the wielders of power. Thus, according to Aristotle, the legitimacy of power depends on a standard that gives positive weight to the furtherance of the public welfare, and negative weight to the well-being of the power elite. Although, in the abstract, this notion might be universally acceptable, it is a difficult measure to elaborate concretely. To be sure, all of us could come up with a shopping list of human wants or human needs that we wish the wielders of power to satisfy. We want them to provide stability and internal peace; international prestige and adequate defense forces for our community; avenues for participation in public affairs and an open road for upward mobility, if not a well-elaborated merit system. There seems some general consensus also that power is rendered legitimate if it is used for the purpose of securing and improving the material well-being of all citizens, i.e., if it succeeds in promoting economic growth. But, lest there be any illusion that the performance criterion is a measure easily applied to different systems of power, it should be pointed out that, in this case, too, there will be interminable argument over the proper mix of the different areas of performance. Further, the current philosophic controversy over the definition of human needs (where "genuine" needs are contrasted with "false" ones) indicates we cannot even expect significant agreement on any individual criterion of political performance. All contemporary politics, indeed, can be explained by the fact that within any one community differences exist over the definition of the public interest.

ACQUIRING LEGITIMACY

I have tried to demonstrate the impossibility of determining the legitimacy of power on the basis of any universally accepted criterion. There are no such criteria. The concept of legitimacy is thus revealed to have no objective meaning. It makes sense only within highly subjective value schemes.

This does not, however, mean that legitimacy is meaningless as a descriptive category or, to use the jargon of contemporary social science, as a behavioral phenomenon. On the contrary, legitimacy is something that can be stated to exist or not to exist in specific systems; the legitimacy or nonlegitimacy of power is something that, perhaps, can even be measured. Measurable or not, legitimacy or its absence is a matter of vital importance to both the wielders of and the sufferers of power.

It is a trite and ancient observation that power by itself is insecure. If it is to become stable, it must be supported by belief, by faith, by myth, or by a political formula—by some subjective state or some symbolic communication that transforms mere power into law, and mere compliance into duty. And, to make power truly secure, the beliefs, the myths, the lies and truths that make up the political formula must appear plausible and convincing to both actors in the power relationship—the wielders no less than the sufferers. Legitimacy is synonymous with this subjective acceptance, by both, of the political formula.

The task of a study investigating the legitimacy of power in Eastern Europe would therefore consist in inquiring how the wielders of power in Eastern Europe have sought to create this legitimacy, how successful they have been, and what obstacles they have faced or are facing in maintaining it. I shall begin with a brief and sketchy historical treatment, in which I shall summarize some observations made in a previous article,[3] and then go on to the problems of measuring the legitimacy of power at any one moment.

I maintain that power in Communist Eastern Europe was of dubious or shaky legitimacy in the immediate postwar period; that the attempt to make it legitimate was seen as a most urgent task by the communist leadership; that they have succeeded remarkably well, on the whole, to acquire legitimacy; but that nonetheless there have been recurrent legitimacy crises, and that therefore there are great strains in their power systems still.

Reference has already been made to factors that have legitimacy to communist power in Eastern Europe in the first postwar years—the disappearance of the old elites or their loss of legitimacy because they were tainted by collaboration; the destruction of capitalism by the occupation regimes, which made a transition to some sort of socialism easy; the emergence of some Communist parties as parties of national liberation and as acceptable coalition partners. Perhaps one should add to this the fact that in some circles the Western powers had discredited themselves by the weakness of their stand against German policies of aggression. At the same time, while the Communits parties of Czechoslovakia and Yugoslavia derived legitimacy from being associated with liberation, in Hungary and Romania they were associated more with national defeat; and their legitimacy was lowered even more by the predominance in their leadership of people alien to the dominant culture.

Even where the Communist parties had a certain measure of legitimacy, they forfeited much of it in the period where they consolidated their power, in general, because of the ruthlessness with which they pursued this aim and the thoroughness with which their regimes were made into virtual carbon copies of the Soviet system. Hence the need that the leadership felt for acquiring legitimacy appears to have been very great. The hostility of large segments of the population must have given the leaders themselves a feeling that their power was illegitimate. Indeed one can go so far as to ascribe to the Communist systems of the 1940s and 1950s an aim that I am tempted to call the primitive accumulation of legitimacy, i.e., a desperate attempt to transform power into authority as quickly as possible, and against great obstacles. For this concerted effort to acquire legitimacy, the wielders of power employed all the traditional means at the disposal of usurpers—coercion, socialization, organization, and rewards. Coercion means the use or threat of punishment through all the familiar devices of the police state. Socialization denotes the education of the population in the spirit of Marxism-Leninism. Organization symbolizes not only the attempt to subject all societal activities and all human relations to central bureaucratic management, but also the institutionalization of this relationship of rule. Rewards, finally, include not only the promotion of economic growth and the manipulation of material incentives, but also other manifestations of benevolence toward the population.

The four modes of legitimacy-building blend into each other. At the same time, they may also get into each other's way. In any event, all power elites have a choice concerning the relative weight they wish to give to each of the four. As for the Communist regimes of Eastern Europe, they have always been willing to use coercion, even though they are alert to the need for building a more durable legitimacy on the basis of ideological conviction. At the same time they have been relatively skillful in the use of both organization and the manipulation of rewards to win over the masses of the indifferent. In the early years of postwar economic austerity, the last of these was doubtless the least significant method.

The term I have suggested, primitive accumulation of legitimacy, is coined in analogy to terms used by Marx and Preobrazhenski. As anyone familiar with these usages knows, it implies a bloody process to which its perpetrators are impelled by a desperate urge. Hence the ruthlessness of the terror, the relentlessness of indoctrination efforts and the related attempts to seal the societies off from any alternative ideas; the thoroughness of the attempt to coordinate all organizational and associational life under the guidance of the party; and the readiness to abandon egalitarian ideals for the sake of a system of differentiated rewards.

The task must have seemed all the more difficult, and the situation the more desperate, to the Communist leadership because what was involved was not merely the accumulation of legitimacy, but a thorough restructuring of the traditional cultures, involving not only the dethroning of old authorities, such as the church and the family, but also the transformation of premodern peoples or classes into modern ones, of peasants into proletarians, or rural folks into city dwellers. Again, the Communist orders that established themselves in Eastern Europe in the wake of World War II were quite impatient in their desire to compress this process of cultural modernization—a process that in some western countries has gone on for many generations and even then is painful enough—into as short a time span as possible.

It must be terribly difficult, however, to accumulate or acquire legitimacy in a period of rapid, planned, and induced social and cultural change. The very act of inducing change threatens the legitimacy of an incumbent power, because the power seeks to maintain itself while changing the society. This in itself is a difficult political balancing act; and to strike a balance between attitudes of accepting some continuities and accepting some changes is equally difficult. It is almost inevitable that the attempt will produce some credibility gaps. Crises involving a rapid turnover of cadres will threaten the legitimacy of the entire power elite. The imposition of an ideology which is simultaneously rigid and flexible, dogmatic but subject to new interpretations, strains its credibility, especially because the ideology must be transformed from a legitimizer of revolution to one of obedience. A credibility gap can result also from the fact that actual power is in the hands of a dictator whose very existence at the top of the power pyramid is at odds with socialist tradition and Communist ideology—a discrepancy that the ideology seeks to overcome by a deliberate cult of personality.

The reference to the cult of personality brings to mind the dictatorial nature of power in Eastern Europe. What is significant here, in a discussion of legitimacy, is the fact that this is openly acknowledged. Power in Eastern Europe, by being in some sense more honest and in many ways more open, more direct, more immediate than power in western systems, seems to be going out of its way to make its own legitimation difficult. This, too, explains the desperate urge of the indoctrination effort.

In general, the kind of legitimacy that is generated through ideological indoctrination appears to be quite unstable. It threatens to disintegrate or even turn into its opposite, not only because of changes in circumstances, which cause the ideologist's dilemma of steering a course between flexibility and rigidity; it also can collapse when it is challenged by facts that the ideology has hitherto ignored or declared impossible. Examples from Communist political history would be Stalin's crimes, the German-Soviet pact of 1939, the great purges, or the reports about the Slansky trial that were published in Czechoslovakia in recent years.* The legitimacy-shattering impact of such facts is proportionate to the degree of uncritical commitment that the population had to the legitimating ideology; the stronger the commitment and the more uncritical the adherent, the greater the resulting credibility gap and the ensuing cynicism and loss of legitimacy. One might conclude from this that there is danger in excessive legitimacy, or at least in overindoctrination, because it can turn into deep disappointment with, and alienation from, the system. The implication would be that ruling elites would do well not to rely very much on indoctrination lest the message backfire. But such restraint would be unnatural to ruling elites, who seem to be under a compulsion to overindoctrinate—especially themselves. The tendency therefore is to allay the danger of credibility gaps by maintaining control over potentially dangerous information, i.e., over information that might threaten the rulers' legitimacy. Hence the effort of people in power to brand as criminal or subversive those who reveal compromising facts.

If overindoctrination is a general cause of credibility gaps in contemporary politics, by far the most important special cause in Eastern Europe probably is the fact that the entire crash program of economic development initiated in the late 1940s was dysfunctional to the real needs of the Eastern European states: whereas socialism in some form was something that seemed likely, normal, and acceptable after the liberation from occupation forces and puppet regimes, its imposition in the Stalinist form was not only unnecessary but, indeed, could be explained only on the basis of the needs and aims of the Soviet Union. Socialism therefore came to Eastern Europe as a system

---

*In the West, the Pentagon Papers, the Spiegel and Globke affairs, or the facts of the Indochina war have served similar functions. In the Third Reich, the best example of a fact clashing with myth and leading to the collapse of legitimacy is the battle of Stalingrad.

of domination and exploitation by a foreign power; and the East European politicians who acquired and wielded power in its name were identified with these aims. Moreover, power in Eastern Europe not only is dependent on a superior superpower; but it appears at times as if that superpower had a certain measure of interest in the weakness, and indeed in the illegitimacy, of the client regimes, because a client power that becomes too popular may also, by the same token, become too independent. Thus the lack of legitimacy may be a source of worry for the East European political leaders; but it may be a source of reassurance for their comrades in the Moscow Kremlin.

Despite these great handicaps, one could argue that the power of these regimes has succeeded in gaining a substantial amount of legitimacy, even though this legitimacy still appears to be quite brittle, subject to easy challenge, and at times ready to collapse altogether.

Several factors account for this growth of legitimacy. One of them is the sheer longevity of the regime, which might be restated by saying that power has, to some extent, been institutionalized. A survey of the criteria established by Samuel Huntington for the institutionalization of a political system would indicate that the communist regimes of Eastern Europe will score high on any test of their degree of institutionalization; indeed, Huntington, despite his obvious antagonism to these regimes, seems to agree with this judgment. The institutionalization of Communist power in this area of the world has been aided, among other things, by the effective elimination of all alternatives. This has been made clear not only by the Berlin Wall, but also by the failure of the United States to interfere in Hungary in 1956 and by the intervention of the Warsaw Pact powers in Czechoslovakia in 1968.

Longevity turns into institutionalization because both the exercise of power and compliance with its commands will, in the end, turn into routines. With this, the organizational forms and functional procedures through which power is exercised and obeyed become routines as well, so that the system itself gets taken for granted. Once this takes place, the holders of power are able to mobilize broader masses of the population into participation within the system. Links with the people are thus established. The distance that at first separated the powerful from the powerless is bridged, at least in the minds of the people. And this is what counts; for when we examine legitimacy we are concerned with what goes on in people's minds.

Once this process of institutionalization has begun, the indoctrination effort too pays off—again, if only because it has gone on for a sufficient time, and because there are no meaningful alternatives to official political formulas. Here, too, isolation from the Western world may have been a significant factor. But in the most recent 15 years that isolation has not been complete. Indeed, it seems more and more impossible for the holders of power in Eastern Europe to keep out news from the outside. At the same time, however, as contacts with the Western world were resumed and intensified, that world began to be looked at, from Eastern Europe, with growing ambivalence. The impression one gets from conversations with a wide range of Eastern Europeans is that their image of the West has been tarnished in recent years. The news they receive from the outside is sufficiently unattractive so that the danger of its serving as a de-legitimizer has decreased. In particular, America seems to have been the dream goal for Eastern Europeans only a decade or two ago. But the younger generation focuses its attention on the urban ghetto, on the fate of Angela Davis, or on My Lai. For many of them the West is morally bankrupt.

The picture is quite complicated. It is without doubt, for instance, that the consumer societies across the Western borders of the region exert great fascination and attraction, which challenges the legitimacy of the incumbent powers with their stress on consumer austerity. Yet the contrast between the two worlds has also engendered, in some Eastern Europeans, a certain pride in their own more frugal life, indeed an attitude of moral righteousness about it, so that the luxurious life of the affluent in the West becomes a count of indictment against the West. One could describe similarly complex and ambivalent attitudes toward the new forms of radicalism in the west and toward various aspects of avantguardist culture and life styles. In the final analysis, it is probably true that increased contact with the outside world will not greatly threaten the legitimacy of power because of people's tendency to practice self-censorship by perceiving only those things that confirm views that they already have, avoiding cognitive dissonance. For anyone who has, in some fashion, accepted the system as given and inevitable, there is always plenty of evidence not only for the inferiority of Western systems, but also for the view that the East European regimes have, individually or collectively, managed to establish themselves as factors in world affairs the importance of which can no longer be disregarded, and indeed, as morally or politically superior systems.

Communist power in Eastern Europe thus has come to be identified with the nation. It has done this not only by tapping latent anti-Western sentiments and the ever-present need that many people have to feel themselves as participants in a successful national enterprise. It does this also by feeding upon some of the remarkably strong antagonisms within the Communist camp. For the American observer the fierceness of the hatred expressed, even in some official circles, of the most immediate neighbor nation is a recurrent source of amazement. Magyars and Romanians, Germans and Poles—a long list of nationalities could be made that continue to feel extreme bitterness toward each other. And, to a considerable extent, the incumbent powers have made themselves (or give themselves the appearance of being) mouthpieces of such hostile sentiments. This applies not only to hatreds felt toward the nation across the border, but also, at times, to the antagonisms within a given nation; an example would be Polish anti-Semitism. With the toleration or encouragment of this kind of national and ethnic antagonism, a portion of national traditions is resurrected that in the early postwar years seemed buried forever. When irredentism, anti-Semitism, and similar sentiments are utilized by the power wielders, when figures prominent in prewar fascist movements survive in contemporary political life, or when their memory is cherished officially, then one gets the impression that power in Eastern Europe bolsters its legitimacy by tapping some of the same feelings that a generation ago provided some of the mass following of Fascism.

To this one must add general achievements made by the Communist regimes in such disparate areas as economic growth, living standards, science, the arts, and even international sports. In a wide range of endeavors, and to a variety of publics among their citizens, the regimes have managed to give plausibility to the claim that they wield power for the benefit of the nation. Partial successes in any field thus make the promises of the ideology more believable. If at the same time the image of the West as a desirable alternative disappears or becomes tarnished, the wielders of power can afford to become less compulsively dogmatic; they can describe the world somewhat more realistically. Indoctrination, once a desperate effort at the re-socialization of entire nations, can itself become more of a routine; it can be institutionalized, and the doctrine internalized. In that way the established power becomes legitimate. Again, my impression is that much of this complex process has taken place and that there is, as a consequence, considerable general legitimacy, of the kind that David Easton calls "diffuse support," of the incumbent powers in Eastern Europe. No one has expressed this more sharply than Samuel Huntington, who asserts that the Communist regimes of Eastern Europe are based on widespread mass participation, that the masses identify with them, that the Communist parties have managed to secure deep roots in the population, and indeed that it is the specific genius of communist elites to succeed very quickly in establishing viable, legitimate new orders on the ruins of discredited ones.[4]

This is nevertheless a one-sided and inadequate account because, while it is obvious that a substantial degree of legitimacy has accrued to the East European powers, it is equally obvious that there have been repeated legitimacy crises; and these recurrent crises attest to a lingering shakiness of the legitimacy of power in Eastern Europe. Evidence of this is so plentiful that it need not even be summarized here: various kinds of unrest in the population and within the Communist parties; illegal emigration; obvious discontent among the intelligentsia; the persistence or revival of widespread devotion to views and life styles considered alien to the system. The evidence comes to us in many forms, and from many sources—ranging from official party publications to the research reports of Radio Free Europe. The scholar is left with the problem of weighing this evidence against the information that indicates the growth of legitimacy; to assess trends of development; and to offer systematic explanations for the trends he perceives.

There are some obvious causes of the recurrent legitimacy crises in Eastern Europe, chief among them probably the failure of the regimes to maintain sufficiently high rates of economic growth, or, more precisely, perhaps, the various factors contributing to this failure: the disadvantages of the economic dependence on the Soviet Union; the inefficiencies of the command economy; perhaps also the resultant distortion of national economic goals. As the regimes begin to make adjustments in the economic system, the legitimacy of power is strained by the growing discrepancy between the new economic model and the old political model. Hence by reforming the economy, the system invites trouble as much as by not reforming it. And a similar dilemma must be confronted in the purely political arena as well, as illustrated by the question concerning the amount of reliance that the party should place on that kind of enforcement mechanism that in Eastern Europe is called "administrative measures," and in the West is usually designated as "terror." Here, too, the regimes endanger themselves both by employing and by not employing this method.

These dilemmas, in turn, result from the successes won by the Communist regimes of Eastern Europe in establishing themselves as viable orders. They have managed to establish their parties in a politically monopolistic position by eliminating all rivals, by establishing links with all segments of the population through a complex system of organization, and thus to integrate their nations into new political entities. But in doing this they have also promoted important social changes, resulting in the emergence, among other things, of new social groups, including groups important enough to challenge the legitimacy of the party that created or strengthened them in the first place. Vigorous modernization programs always endanger the power of those who initiate these programs.

One can restate this, perhaps somewhat less dramatically, by arguing simply that Communist rule, even while it has integrated the societies of Eastern Europe in significant ways, has simultaneously strengthened pluralistic tendencies in them, so that more clearly than ever before we can or must divide them into distinct groups. Now, perhaps, we can take it for granted that different methods must be used to create subjective legitimacy in different groups, because different goals may have priority for each of these groups. To oversimplify grossly, it might be assumed that the legitimacy of power is dependent, for industrial workers, on the regime's success in providing tolerable work conditions and a reasonable material living standard; peasants may measure the legitimacy of a regime by how much it leaves them alone; the technocratic elite, by the degree of autonomy it is given in its professional work or by the readiness of the political elite to allow it to participate; the creative intelligentsia, finally, may consider democratization as the overriding goal that alone can render power legitimate. Meanwhile, all groups may be interested in the growth of national prestige and a variety of other identifiable goals, on which they may or may not agree with each other.

These groups are neither of equal size nor of equal importance; and for assessing the legitimacy of power in Eastern Europe it is important to single out that group or those groups whose attitudes are most essential to maintain the system. Contemporary political science seems in broad agreement that opinions, attitudes, expectations, and other subjective traits of those people matter most who are closest to the top of the pyramids of power, status, and prestige. Speaking most broadly, then, the alienation of the masses is more tolerable to a power system than alienation among the elites. Yet this too must be qualified: some elites seem expendable, and some groups among the masses count more than others. Thus, in the eyes of the power wielders in Eastern Europe, the industrial workers are the most important social class, whose allegiance is so crucial that its loss would imperil the entire system.* At the same time, the observer at times gets the impression that those in power often disregard or discount the attitudes and opinions of the most literate and best educated group in the entire population, i.e., the intellectual elite.

---

*In the American political system, certain segments of votes play a similar role—the South, gerrymandered rural areas, and certain "swing" states.

Let me discuss the attitudes customarily ascribed to this elite in relation to that of other elites in Eastern Europe. Any survey of Eastern European politics in recent years enables us to identify three clearly distinguishable goal orientations. One of these can be labeled conservatism. Its aim appears to be the maintenance of the present system, its institutions, its procedures, its power distribution, and opposition to all endeavors for change. A second, usually labeled reformism, can be identified as a belief in the need for bureaucratization, in the Weberian sense of the word. It is, in other words, a form of technocratic elitism, expressing the need for the functional optimization (Hegedüs) of society or in what Soviet sociologists and planners call the scientific organization of work. Reformism may be a challenge to the legitimacy of incumbent power when it expresses its opposition to conservatism or when it seeks to extend the technocratic transformation to the party itself. Indeed, the party seems to be a frequent and convenient target of their criticism. It provokes criticism from the technocratic elite because its leaders are not as highly educated as the professionals; because they often are overaged; because they are subservient to the comrades in Moscow; because they have blood on their hands; or simply because they can be held responsible for the failures of the past.

While reformists challenge conservatives, they may be equally or even more opposed to the third major trend in East European politics, which we may label democratization, although some of its protagonists prefer to call it humanization. Against those who argue that technocracy is the image of the best possible social system we can attain in the most highly developed countries of our time, democratic or humanist dissenters repudiate technocracy as much as they reject the conservative formula, criticizing both as a betrayal of democratic, socialist, humanist, and/or Marxist principles.

In any three-cornered conflict, combinations are possible; and any assessment of political trends in Eastern Europe will have to keep such possible combinations in mind. Unmitigated conservatism (the Stalinist formula), technocracy pure and simple (a solution that many members of the professional elites seem to favor), and radical democratization are not the only possibilities. There are various possible compromises between conservatism and technocracy as well as combinations of one or the other with democratizing trends. The Khrushchevian formula, and possibly the Gomulkan one as well, might be described as democratic conservatism, in which conservatism enlists mass participation and mass sentiments. It turned out to be one of the causes of Khrushchev's, as well as Gomulka's, downfall. One can speak also of a trend toward democratizing technocracy or elitist democratization, a tendency promoted by many East European social scientists (such as Hegedüs, Wiatr, Ostrowski). The Soviet writer Y. Davydov defines this ultimate goal as one in which the technical culture has become the property of all citizens: "every member of society will be a scientist."[5] For him and for many of his East European colleagues, this merger of technocracy with democracy is attainable only in the very long run. "So long as advances in science and technology are not rationally controlled in all their social and human implications, we shall be faced with a cleavage between the professional and democratic aspects."[6]

Meanwhile, the cautious reformers must fight a tricky two-front war against conservative resistance and "vulgar egalitarianism." Whatever arrangement is made between the various contending tendencies, each solution creates its own problems. Indeed, one might assert that all the legitimacy crises of Eastern Europe in the past 15 years can be explained as the results of experimentation with these various solutions. Moreover, whatever the eventual outcome of these trends and countertrends, some people in Eastern Europe will be dissatisfied and disaffected and will tend to consider the trend illegitimate. The most likely candidate for chronic disaffection, at the present time, seems to be the creative intelligentsia and the educated youth: in other words, the same groups that seem permanently alienated from their systems in the Western world, especially the United States. They are the people whose humanitarian and democratic ideology makes them unready to accept either a conservative or a technocratic solution. If this prognosis is correct, then the most important gulf is not that between the Communist parties and the remainder of the population, as Western scholars usually assume. Instead, the deepest gulf will divide the party, the technocrats, and their mass supporters, on the one hand, from the dissenting intelligentsia, on the other, with the proviso that the different elites who consider the system legitimate are divided among each other and that their antagonism will be affected by occasional outbreaks of dissatisfaction among the masses of workers or peasants.

THE MEASUREMENT OF LEGITIMACY

A group of scholars such as the one for whom this study is written might agree or disagree with my observations. But neither my statements nor any counterstatements that might be offered are subject to convincing verification or falsification. For the fact is that it is impossible to measure the legitimacy of power anywhere at any moment. This is not only because we have only limited access to the people of Eastern Europe, whose attitudes we would wish to explore. Even in totally accessible political systems there are no reliable indicators of the many factors that make for legitimacy, from the strength of ideological convictions to a vague yet meaningful phenomenon such as diffuse support. All the indicators that readily come to mind turn out to be unreliable. Is a power system legitimate when there is universal compliance with its commands? Such compliance can be the result of terror as much as of genuine legitimacy. Do we measure legitimacy by the absence of expressions of dissent and criticism? The same answer must be given. Indeed, there is more open complaining in Yugoslavia than in the German Democratic Republic; there certainly was more under the rule of Dubcek than under Husak. Would anyone argue that power in the DDR is more legitimate than that in Yugoslavia, or the Husak regime more than that of Dubcek? A similar aura of unreliability adheres, it seems to me, to all other alleged behavioral and attitudinal indicators of legitimacy, even where they can be observed. The conclusion suggests itself that legitimacy is something that cannot be measured at all. At best, we can, perhaps, sense the lack of legitimacy. That means, we can observe legitimacy <u>crises</u>, periods when it becomes apparent that legitimacy has broken down. The indicators of such crises are riots, rebellions, and waves of disobedience of the law, but also more subtle indications of alienation such as mass delinquency, alcoholism, or suicide. But even here one must be cautious. Does the presence of corruption in the system indicate a lack of legitimacy? Or all forms of criminality? What is the function of political jokes in strengthening or undermining the legitimacy of power? By asking these questions I am trying to hint at the elusiveness of the concept of legitimacy.

And behind this is the nagging question whether it matters at all, i.e., whether there are not some highly successful systems of power of the past and present that have maintained themselves quite nicely without much legitimacy except among a relatively small group of those who benefited from it. The present regime in Taiwan seems to have only minimal legitimacy; indeed, the United Nations vote of October 25, 1971, has robbed it of whatever legitimacy it had in world opinion. Yet it appears to be quite viable for a number of reasons and might maintain itself for a long time to come.

The difficulty or impossibility of ascertaining the legitimacy of power in countries that are not readily accessible is attested by the poor record of Western scholarship on Eastern Europe. Political observers specializing in the study of this area during the last 25 years have been wrong far more often than they have been right in their assessment of the degree of legitimacy of power in these countries. Most developments and events there since 1945 have come as surprises—the Polish workers revolt in 1970, the growing stabilization of the German Democratic Republic and of the Kadar regime, the Romanian developments as much as the ups and downs of policy in Czechoslovakia. And reference to any of these events or developments must remind us that any generalization, even though it may be true for one East European country, may be false for all the others; or, if it is true today it may become false tomorrow. If anyone of us had dared, say, in 1955, to rank the East European states according to the degree of legitimacy they possessed, that rank order would have been overthrown by events in the subsequent five years; and a similar statement could be made about almost any five-year span since then.

I am told that scholastic disputations about the number of angels who might dance on the tip of a pin did in fact take place and that, far from being idle exercises of befogged minds, they were meaningful debates about the nature of space and other aspects of reality. If in these pages I have reduced the concept of legitimacy to scholastic nonsense, I feel duty-bound to call attention to the fact that meaningful questions may be concealed underneath the nonsense. One question inquires about a defensible moral attitude toward the power systems now established in Eastern Europe. This is a question that every person must answer for himself, in the light of the moral standards he is ready to apply to all other systems of power. The second question inquires into the amount or intensity of support that the incumbent powers have among their own citizens. That question cannot be answered reliably. The semiinformed guesswork we must use is insufficient. It can be answered definitively only in retrospect; once a regime has fallen, we must assume that it was not very legitimate. Whether a regime that has maintained itself for a long time can therefore be assumed to have rendered itself legitimate is a question we must answer with great caution.

As I look over what I have written, I am struck by its negativism. I believe the reason for the negativism is yet another implication that hides behind the problem of assessing the legitimacy of power in Eastern Europe. Implicit behind our problem is a comparison of Eastern Europe with other systems of power and, in the light of past Western scholarship, the assumption behind such comparisons seems to be that power in Eastern Europe is not legitimate, while power in Western regimes is, regardless of the standards we apply to gauge legitimacy—morality, national culture, performance, or attitudes and behavior. What I have tried to show in this study is that comparisons of this kind cannot be made because we cannot assess legitimacy with sufficient precision anywhere. And even if this were too pessimistic a statement, even if it could be shown that some solid knowledge is attainable, comparisons with other systems would run into new problems. I shall not dwell on the nature of these problems, but, instead, point out one additional reason for hesitation in the face of such comparisons. At a time when the legitimacy of power in the leading nation of the Western world appears to be shaken to its very foundation, when in the space of the last eight years one President has been murdered, another forced to abdicate; when the armed forces are totally demoralized and the country troubled by deepening cleavages—at such a time it somehow does not seem quite appropriate for an American or a West German scholar to inquire into the legitimacy of power in Eastern Europe.

NOTES

1. See my article on "Autorität," Sowjetsystem und demokratische Gesellschaft; eine vergleichende Enzyklopadie, Vol. I (Freisburg, Germany: Herder Verlag, 1966), pp. 546-64.
2. According to Dolf Sternberger, ". . . attempts to clothe a usurping power with legitimacy, whether successful or not, have often revealed what the standards of legitimacy are for a given society or civilization." "Legitimacy," in International Encyclopedia of Social Science, Vol. 9, p. 244.
3. Alfred G. Meyer, "Authority in Communist Political Systems," in Lewis J. Edinger, ed., Political Leadership in Industralized Societies (New York: John Wiley, 1967), pp. 84-107.
4. Samuel Huntington, Political Order in Changing Societies (New Haven: Yale University Press, 1968), pp. 310, 315, 335.
5. Y. Davydov, Trud i svoboda (Moscow: Izd. vysshaia shkola, 1962), p. 113.
6. Ota Klein and Jindrich Zeleny, "Dynamics of Change: Leadership, the Economy, Organizational Structure, and Society," in R. Barry Farrell, ed., Political Leadership in Eastern Europe and the Soviet Union (Chicago: Aldine, 1970), p. 215.

* * * * *

ANALYSES
1. Oskar Anweiler

Professor Meyer's very provocative study innovatively illustrates the problem of the legitimacy of power in Central and Eastern Europe. However, as I am not a political scientist, this analysis will of necessity be limited to my observations as an historian and educator.

Prof. Meyer, after his survey of ethically founded theories of legitimacy, comes to the conclusion that it is impossible "to apply a universal moral standard to the measurement of the legitimacy of

―――――――――

Oskar Anweiler is a Professor at the Institut für Pädagogik at the University of Bochum, Federal Republic of Germany.

various systems." The criteria of political philosophy, legality as distinct from legitimacy, political culture, and the performance of all these criteria are questionable. "The concept of legitimacy is thus revealed to have no objective meaning," and seems useful "as a descriptive category or as a behavioral phenomenon." I do not wish to decide here if it might be possible to give a sociological characteristic to a historical concept such as legitimacy, which has its roots in constitutional law, in order to render it useful in a functional sense, for this would abolish its relation to a moral value system and would bypass the question of the real source of political power. The concept of legitimacy appears to be in a state of tension between normative value judgments and an empirical and analytical usage with all the epistemological problems of sociological concepts.

Be that as it may, there are two basic problems concerning the legitimacy of the Communist systems in Eastern Europe. First, the self-legitimization of the ruling political system. Second, the legitimacy of the regime in the eyes of the population. With respect to both of these the study contains remarkable observations and explanations.

First, the problem of a distinct national political culture, manifested in certain attitudes or styles in political life, proves ambiguous when applied to the basis of the legitimacy of the Communist regimes. On the other hand, compromises must be made, given the strength of national traditions in the interest of the stability of the regime. An example is the Polish Catholic Church as a thousand-year-old legitimate representative of the Polish nation. But a national brand of communism is, in the opinion of the Soviet Union, a danger to Soviet supremacy. Thus the supranational principle of legitimacy of the worldwide movement of communism (class revolution) is called into question by another principle, that of the sovereign national state. The Communist leaderships in all Eastern European countries and in East Germany based their legitimacy at first entirely on the historical law of the socialist revolution, and subsequently tried to identify with the country's national historical heritage, thus shifting the basis of legitimacy. This identification can easily lead to a strengthening of the claim for legitimacy in the population, as happened in Romania, but in the long run it will result in the loss of the former legitimacy based on Marxist-Leninist ideology. We can validly speak of a gradual change in the factors affecting legitimacy; besides the factors of time and institutionalization, there is the important process of incorporation into national traditions.

Second, in the process of legitimizing their rule, the communist regimes in Eastern Europe attached much value to political education and political socialization of the youth as well as the adult population. Prof. Meyer calls this procedure ideological indoctrination and thereby reveals his own conceptions of education that are in contrast to

indoctrination. His observation that overindoctrination turns to apathy and alienation, however, seems valid, though sufficient empirical proof is yet to come. It can be asked whether these effects would be compensated by indirect educational influences, which would probably be more effective in bringing about the internalization of the communist rules of behavior than formal schooling and direct indoctrination.
The effectiveness of direct political and ideological influence varies from country to country and with time. In the GDR it has always been the highest; in Czechoslovakia intensified ideological indoctrination has gained increased momentum since 1969, after the Dubcek era; in Hungary it has remained relatively low; and in Poland indoctrination is strongly patriotic.

A third, most important, point is the problem of periodic crises of legitimacy—it might be more accurate to speak of authority crises— due to lack of or to uncertain legitimacy. The rise of such crises invalidates Samuel Huntington's thesis, mentioned by Prof. Meyer, of a widespread mass participation in politics in the Eastern European countries, if by mass participation one understands effective political influence and something more than mass parades. One could argue almost in the opposite direction. Effective political mass participation in the Eastern European countries has so far taken place in periods of crisis in the lives of the communist regimes, affecting their basis of legitimacy. This was most dramatic under Dubcek, and in Poland in December of 1970. The reasons for these crises were specified in Prof. Meyer's study. I agree with him that the economic reasons were on the whole probably preeminent. To restore authority, the Communist governments in the GDR, Hungary, and Czechoslovakia had to have recourse to the military forces of the Soviet Union. In Poland the crisis was settled twice, in 1956 and in 1970, and the balance of power within the party shifted. It is interesting to note that the new Polish leadership, when analyzing the motives for the December crisis of 1970, explicitly referred to certain mechanisms of authority relations. I quote now from the materials of the Eighth Plenum of the Central Committee of the Polish Communist Party in February 1971: "By the events of December, 1970 the party must be taught that in order to avoid future conflicts with the community, safe alarm systems have to be installed signalling the danger of commencing conflicts. Furthermore, provisions must be made for settling the conflict within the organizations and the institutions of our state."

A fourth point. Prof. Meyer has developed, in a most interesting fashion, theories of groups in the society as the most important factor for the legitimacy of power. His analysis in this area concentrates primarily on the Soviet Union. The differences in national political cultures should be brought into a sharper focus here. For instance, the Czech and Polish elites are oriented toward the Western

European liberal democratic political traditions. Generally, I agree with the statement that "the most important gulf is not that between the Communist parties and the remainder of the population . . . instead, the deepest gulf will divide the party, the technocrats and their mass supporters, from the dissenting intelligentsia, with the proviso that the different elites who consider the system legitimate are divided among themselves and their antagonism will be affected by occasional outbreaks of dissatisfaction among the mass of workers or peasants."

Lastly, some remarks on the skeptical attitude the author has toward cross-cultural comparative studies in this field. I fear that Prof. Meyer has come to false conclusions here due to what he regards as a regrettable moral deficiency of Western societies and due to his choice of analytical categories for understanding the legitimacy problem of which I spoke in the beginning. At first, he has tried to eliminate the value orientation inherent in the older concept of legitimacy, and then applied the same values to the criticism of the system and to the research of those who study these systems and the problems of legitimacy of other political systems. This approach, on supposedly political-ethical grounds, would lead to a voluntary dismissal of scientific research in a field that is most appropriate for study by comparative analysis, namely questions of political behavior and political order, and the question of the legitimacy of power. This, of course, would result in the loss of concepts that would be useful in the search for a better reordering of this society. In other words, a rigorous scientific Gesinnungsethik could well destroy the Verantwortungsethik that alone can activate practical policy.

2. W. Harriet Critchley

Professor Meyer's study is a brilliant tour de force of a multitude of theoretical approaches to the idea of legitimacy. He discusses moral or ethical theories, cultural, formal, and performance theories of legitimacy. He is to be congratulated and admired for his capacity to deal with such a multitude of theories in a very clear and lucid fashion, especially as the words involved—power, authority and legitimacy—are some of the most fundamental philosophical ideas used in political science, sociology, and history.

There are many points of departure for comment. I will confine my analysis to that part of the study that deals with legitimacy as a descriptive category, or tool of analysis, since it is the most bothersome

---

W. Harriet Critchley is a Ph.D. candidate in the Department of Political Science, Columbia University, New York.

for political scientists. The pessimism that Prof. Meyer expresses, or, to use his own word, his negativism, is a reflection of the difficulties we experience whenever we start to think deeply about such fundamental ideas. Our experience often suggests the analogy of proceeding down a dark tunnel only to find it ending in a proliferation of equally dark tunnels. The general tenor of my comments will imply that we can proceed down the tunnel with a serious expectation of finding at least a faint light at the end. In accomplishing the latter, the crucial factor is how we proceed.

Prof. Meyer's definition of legitimacy is as follows: "Under the term legitimacy, we customarily understand a quality inherent in certain relationships of power, namely that quality that justifies the power relationship and renders it acceptable. If we define power as the relationship in which one actor has the ability to determine the actions of another, then legitimacy is that quality of power relationships that turns them into relationships of authority." In telescoping this into a few words, I think Prof. Meyer is saying in effect, "authority equals legitimate power." There is a clear connection here with the Weberian conception of the three legitimations of domination, or authority types—charismatic, traditional, and rational-legal.

I would like to suggest a rearrangement of the relationship between the three words—power, authority, and legitimacy—as follows: authority equals power relationships; legitimacy is a quality attaching to some authority relationships. This suggested rearrangement stems from David Easton's concept of authority that is broad enough to encompass all command-obedience relationships, including coercion. According to Easton's concept, we would regard coercion in an authority relationship as a form of illegitimate authority. On the other hand, with Prof. Meyer's definition that authority equals legitimate power, nonlegitimate power would be called something else: overlordship or tyranny, if you will. For example, using the latter definition of authority, a British Prime Minister has authority, whereas the leadership of some of the East European regimes in the late 1940s and early 1950s did not have authority but exercised tyranny. If, on the other hand, one broadens the definition of authority to encompass all power relationships and uses the idea of legitimacy to describe some of the possible varieties of authority, then one can say that both the British Prime Minister and the Eastern European leaders have or had authority: the British Prime Minister having a form of legitimate authority and the Eastern European leaders having a form of illegitimate authority.

By rearranging these three terms, I am not proposing simply an exercise in semantics although, as scholars of Communist political systems, our professional analysis would benefit by the elimination from common and unrestricted usage of such emotion-laden terms as "tyranny." I am suggesting something much more fundamental. Power carries with it the notion of force—in other words, compliance—and power can be defined as the capacity to demand compliance successfully. Authority incorporates two notions, compliance and support. Support means some form of voluntary obedience. Using these concepts of power and authority, legitimacy can then be described in terms of the support aspect of authority. Legitimacy refers to a capacity to engender enduring support; that capacity, as Prof. Meyer and others have pointed out, being anchored in the beliefs of the population.

If we adopt this relationship between the three ideas of power, authority, and legitimacy, where some authority is legitimate and some is not, then we can begin to distinguish various types of authority in terms of their relative combinations of compliance and support. Perhaps my argument can be clarified by referring to that part of the study where Prof. Meyer introduces the idea of a "primitive accumulation of legitimacy" defined as "a desperate attempt to transform power into authority as quickly as possible using such traditional means as coercion, socialization, organization, and rewards." I would submit that this definition contains a contradiction that stems from his original definition of authority. First, authority equals legitimate power. Second, coercion is defined as one of the means of acquiring authority. Thus we find that coercion is a mode of acquiring legitimacy. But legitimacy, as Prof. Meyer has pointed out, is "a subjective acceptance of a political formula." If coercion is used to engender legitimacy, one is using _force_ to generate _voluntary_ obedience. This is more than a semantic and logical contradiction, that probably cannot be demonstrated empirically. By contrast, if one defines authority more broadly, acknowledging a variety of degrees of legitimate and illegitimate authority, coercion remains a means of acquiring authority, but that authority would be categorized as one of the illegitimate forms, since coercion cannot engender subjective acceptance of a political formula, or, in other words, voluntary support.

A typology of authority patterns using the compliance and support variables has been constructed by Richard Rose in an article in World Politics in 1969. An expanded version is contained in his book Governing Without Consensus.[1] I am following his typology as an example of the analytical utility to be gained by broadening the definition of authority. Rose writes: "The type of authority that a regime exercises can be distinguished by the degree to which its population acts in accord with regulations concerning the maintenance of the regime, and has diffuse cultural orientations approving the regime." The typology therefore has two components: compliance, which "emphasizes the power of the regime and gets its nominal subjects to act as de facto subjects"; and support, "the enduring and diffuse basis of voluntary obedience to a regime's regulations." Actually, Rose has constructed a six-fold typology. The point is that in such a typology one has a range of authority patterns at one's disposal. Some of these patterns, depending on where they fall on the compliance-support axis, are fully legitimate, some are partially legitimate, some are intermittently legitimate, and there are various types that are illegitimate: for example, coercive and semicoercive patterns. This particular typology is one illustration of the utility of such approaches to the relationship between power, authority, and legitimacy. Another equally interesting approach can be found in the Bachrach and Baratz essay "The Two Faces of Power" in their book Power and Poverty.[2] Using these typologies we would be able to trace the movement of the Eastern European regimes along the dual axes and discuss their movement in terms of variations of legitimacy and illegitimacy.

Again, with respect to the relationship of coercion, authority, and legitimacy, if authority is defined more broadly, so that some authority can be legitimate and some illegitimate, then one can deal more effectively with the idea of political leaders designing a ruling strategy. A relative weight can be assigned among the four modes outlined by Prof. Meyer: coercion, socialization, rewards, and persuasion. But one can also discuss the various moves that the leadership makes within the compliance-support typology in the same way. Taking the two polar opposites of Prof. Meyer's four modes, coercion is then a strategy for gaining compliance; reward-giving, for example the development of a consumer industry in an Eastern European state, is a strategy for gaining support. Whether the support is generated from a belief in the system or person, or from an acceptance of the inevitability of the regime is not germane at this point in the discussion. The central fact is that one can engender support with rewards. I doubt that anything other than compliance can be engendered with coercion.

Within this compliance-support typology of authority, our chances of qualitatively or quantitatively measuring the presence, absence or degrees of legitimacy are increased. We can break down both the concept of compliance and the concept of support into their various types. Indicators can be assigned. A small example: along with the Weberian types of authority—the charismatic, traditional, and rational-legal—we could consider the idea of congruence of leadership styles. First, we can analyze the degree of congruence of leadership styles of Eastern European regimes today in terms of past leadership styles in those states. Then we can consider the relative mix of compliance and support components in that leadership style for a comparison both across time and among states. What I have in mind here is the well-known idea of the authoritarian leadership style and the congruence of that style between Czarist Russia and the Soviet Union. Or, to take Yugoslavia as an example, the congruence of an individualistic leadership style based on the individualistic ethnic political cultures in the prewar period, which is apparent again at present as the regime implements a greater degree of federalism, in opposition to the centralism advocated by Leninist doctrine. Choosing a congruent or an incongruent pattern can be a matter of leadership strategy and an element of legitimacy. Also, congruence of leadership styles inherently includes one of the other factors that Prof. Meyer has emphasized, that factor being national political styles, in that one can discuss national political styles in terms of congruence and incongruence. Rose has suggested other strategies that are available to the leadership. I will refer to them briefly as they illustrate the utility of this approach to power, authority, and legitimacy where analysis of trends in Eastern Europe is concerned: a "popular strategy" that places a high value on both support and compliance; an "authoritarian strategy" that seeks to maximize compliance without regard for maintaining support; or a "confederal strategy" that values support so highly that compliance demands are limited.

If one defines authority more broadly as proposed, one can also deal more effectively with such marginal situations as the Polish government-in-exile or the Benes group. Deutsch, in The Nerves of Government[3] notes that shortly after the war both groups found themselves in a position of having much less actual power (that is, authority) than their symbolic legitimacy would have implied. These two groups had the voluntary support of at least a substantial portion of their respective populations—but this is only one component of authority. For a variety of reasons, they lacked the ability to be successfull in demanding compliance. Prof. Meyer has concentrated on leaders or regimes that have authority and are endeavoring to acquire legitimacy. Deutsch notes two examples of the reverse situation. A comparative analysis of the type that juxtaposes the authority and legitimacy of the prewar or wartime regimes in Eastern European states with that of regimes in those same states at various points in the postwar period would help us to refine the rough distinctions of support and compliance, their relative weight in various authority patterns, and, finally, trends of change in authority and legitimacy patterns.

By viewing legitimacy as an attribute of certain patterns of authority on the compliance-support axis, the possibility that Prof. Meyer raises near the end of his study of the "shakiness" of legitimacy would be couched in terms that are independent of any labels that might be attached to the type of regime, Communist or democratic. That is, we can see "shakiness" as a possibility in Eastern Europe, in the Western democracies, in nations of Africa, Asia, and Latin America. This kind of perspective on legitimacy, and therefore the "shakiness" of it, might avoid the moral problem alluded to in the paper, when a scholar makes a professional analysis of legitimacy and the "shakiness" thereof in one region of the world, while experiencing the same phenomenon at home. The moral problem is germane and relevant, but on a philosophical, rather than a descriptive, level.

3. George L. Kline

The first part of Prof. Meyer's study is sweepingly skeptical about the possibility of specifying criteria for political legitimacy. Prof. Meyer insists that we cannot formulate "universally acceptable judgments [which would permit us to distinguish] between different systems of Power"; he denies the validity of all four of the proposed criteria of legitimacy, namely, (1) moral acceptability, (2) furtherance of, or harmony with, national culture, (3) the performance of the rulers, and (4) the attitudes of the ruled. He goes so far as to claim that the "concept of legitimacy" has "no objective meaning" since "even in totally accessible political systems there are no reliable indicators of the many factors that make for legitimacy."

But just as even the most skeptical epistemologist, after having called into question every item of his sense experience, nevertheless goes on to distinguish decisively between a rotten apple and a sound one, trusting his eyes, nose, and tongue, so Prof. Meyer, especially in the last half of his study, expresses a number of categorical judgments about the legitimacy of given regimes, both Eastern and Western. He suggests that the "illegitimacy of the client regimes" of Eastern Europe may be welcomed by the Soviet Union and asks rhetorically, "Would anyone argue that power in the GDR is more legitimate than that in Yugoslavia, or the Husak regime more (legitimate) than that of Dubcek." Finally, he asserts that the "legitimacy of power" in the United States "appears [today] to be shaken to its very foundation."

I agree entirely with Prof. Meyer's ranking of Yugoslavia and the GDR, and of the Dubcek and Husak regimes in Czechoslovakia, in terms of legitimacy, although I disagree with his assertion about legitimacy in America. But at the moment I wish to stress that the formulation of such categorical judgments of legitimacy cannot be squared with Prof. Meyer's systematic skepticism about the possibility of establishing criteria of legitimacy.

In the last half of his paper Prof. Meyer exhibits a robust readiness to distinguish between good and bad political apples. But the tendentiousness of his classifications is shocking. He seems to

---

*George L. Kline is Professor of Philosophy at Bryn Mawr College, Bryn Mawr, Penna.

me to: (1) overestimate the legitimacy of the Eastern European regimes, (2) misequate Soviet and Western, especially American, policy in Europe, and (3) underestimate the legitimacy of Western regimes, in particular that of the United States.

1. Power in Eastern Europe, Prof. Meyer says, is "more honest and in many ways more open . . . than power in Western systems," and "plenty of evidence" is available to Eastern European citizens "not only for the inferiority of Western systems, but also for the view that Eastern European regimes have . . . managed to establish themselves . . . as morally or politically superior systems." I dissent vigorously from these judgments, agreeing rather with Prof. Leszek Kotakowski, who describes the current regimes in Czechoslovakia, Poland, etc., as forms of "despotic socialism" that are dying a slow political death,

> sinking down into an inert boredom and numbness, relieved only by everyone's fear of everyone else. . . . The loss of its ideas means a loss of its raison d'être for the system. Let us note some small changes in phraseology. The word "freedom" was always on Stalin's lips when torture and massacres were the order of the day in his empire; today, when the massacres have stopped, the faint cry of "freedom" puts the entire police force on the alert.[1]

2. "Contrived revolutions in Eastern Europe," Prof. Meyer asserts, echoing the revisionist historians of the Cold War, "were matched by contrived counterrevolutions in the West" and by numerous other acts of Soviet and American intervention and usurpation including, on the American side, the "establishment of the Federal Republic of Germany." Comment, it seems to me, would be superfluous!

3. Prof. Meyer declares:

> at a time when the legitimacy of power in the leading nation of the Western world appears to be shaken to its very foundation, when in the space of the last eight years one President has been murdered, another forced to abdicate; when the armed forces are totally demoralized and the country troubled by deepening cleavages—at such a time it somehow does not seem quite appropriate for an American or a West German scholar to inquire into the legitimacy of power in Eastern Europe.

This astonishing assertion raises at least three questions. (a) Is American society as tattered and riven as Prof. Meyer claims?

(b) Even if it were, would that fact disqualify American scholars as students of the legitimacy of power in Eastern Europe? (c) Do the alleged facts bear on the question of the legitimacy of power in the United States? My answer to question (b) is an unqualified negative, my answer to question (c) a qualified negative. My answer to question (a) requires a bit of elaboration.

Prof. Meyer's claim that the American armed forces are "totally demoralized" and the country as a whole beset by "deepening cleavages" is highly controversial. In another context I would be glad to controvert it.

The claim that an American President has been "forced to abdicate" strikes me as not only controversial but also irrelevant. In the first place, "abdication" is hardly the term a responsible historian would use to describe Lyndon Johnson's decision not to run for the presidency in 1968. But even if Johnson had retired to his Texas ranch in midterm, in 1966, such an "abdication" would not have called the legitimacy of power in the United States into serious question.

As for the assassination of John Kennedy, the fact that it was an American President who was killed in 1963 rather than the ruler of an Eastern European country seems to me to have nothing whatever to do with political legitimacy. It was partly a matter of historical contingency and partly a result of the greater size, experience, and efficiency of Communist (as compared to non-Communist) security forces. The relevant and interesting question concerns not the act of political assassination but the institution of succession, the machinery for an orderly transfer of power. How, in 1963, would the successor to a hypothetically assassinated Gheorghiu-Dej, Gomulka, Kadar, Novotny, Tito, or Zhivkov have been chosen? We do not know, but it seems highly probable that the new leader or leaders would have emerged from a labyrinth of Byzantine intrigue and infighting rather than from any stable procedure for the orderly transfer of power, such as that which made Johnson President upon the death of Kennedy.

It strikes me as odd that in an extended discussion of legitimacy in Eastern Europe—in the course of which he found space for such peripheral topics as affluence, Attica, and Angela Davis—Prof. Meyer had nothing whatever to say about the succession problem.* Any institutionalization of legitimacy must provide for an orderly process of political succession. The lack of any such process in contemporary Eastern European regimes casts the most serious doubt upon the

---

*There is a tangential reference to it in Prof. Meyer's comment that crises involving a rapid turnover of cadres will threaten the legitimacy of the entire power elite.

legitimacy claims of those regimes, quite apart from the nature of their power systems at any given moment.

Two brief final comments:

1. Prof. Meyer writes: "Once a regime has fallen, we must assume that it was not very legitimate." Presumably he meant to include some such qualification as "in the absence of external intervention" or what Kotakowski has called the "fraternal cannon muzzles from the East"; otherwise this claim would contradict Meyer's assertion that the fallen Dubcek regime was more legitimate than the Husak regime that succeeded it. To be sure, there is still the delicate question of what constitutes "external intervention," since it is notorious that there are subtler forms of interference in the "internal affairs" of a country than the movement of armored divisions across national borders.

2. Prof. Meyer declares that America, which was the "dream goal" for Eastern Europeans only a decade or two ago is now viewed by the younger generation in Eastern Europe as "morally bankrupt." I doubt this very much. The young Eastern Europeans of my (direct and indirect) acquaintance still view Western regimes, including that of the United States, as offering broader personal freedoms, greater privacy, and a better chance to pursue one's work—especially intellectual or creative work—than the Eastern European regimes. I detect a possible ambiguity in Prof. Meyer's disparaging remarks about Western "consumerism." A young Czech, Hungarian, Polish, or Romanian intellectual or professional person who aspires to have a room of his own might be said to have been corrupted by the "reified values of a consumer society." But he might also be viewed—more sympathetically and, to my mind, more accurately—as seeking not just things or gadgets but a certain quality of life, a quality that includes and requires privacy. And privacy, although it presupposes a minimum level of "affluence," is not a "consumer value."

4. Rudolf Tökes

I shall comment about five different points that I feel have been insufficiently analyzed in this study.

The first relates to the concept of continuity and change in Eastern European politics; the second to the problem of Marxism, communist nation-building and political legitimacy; the third to legitimacy and Soviet-Eastern European relations; the fourth to strategies

---

Rudolf Tökes is Professor of Political Science at the University of Connecticut, Storrs.

and crises of legitimacy-building in Eastern Europe; and the fifth to legitimacy and comparative implications of the so-called Eastern European pattern.

1. First, with respect to the broad concept of continuity and change, Prof. Meyer argues that the defeat of the old order in Eastern Europe created a vacuum of legitimacy that the Communist Party could fill easily under the flag of patriotic, democratic, or charismatic modes of legitimacy and create the foundations of a new order. In arguing his case, I think Prof. Meyer understates aspects of continuity and vastly overstates aspects of change. I have four points in mind in supporting my case for continuity. First of all I would like to know how we interpret the term "normalcy" in Eastern Europe. After all if we talk about continuity and change, we have to have a point of departure by which to measure subsequent changes. Would it be authoritarianism? Would it be democracy? Turning to traditional concepts, and in particular to the area of party politics, it is evident that there is complete continuity in that respect. The postwar traditional classical four-party mix in Eastern Europe—socialists, communists, bourgeois middle class, and the peasant party—differs from the prewar pattern only in the substitution of an extreme leftist party for an extreme rightist party.

Second, with respect to continuity in ideology, Prof. Meyer understates the importance of surviving non-Communist leftist ideologies as alternative modes of legitimacy-building in Eastern Europe. Quite surely, Fascists and Nazis were eliminated; their ideas did not matter at this juncture. However, there were a good many socialists, peasant radicals, and liberal bourgeois thinkers, parties and other formations that did put forth alternative methods of nation-building that did challenge the presumed monopoly of Communist ideology.

Third, in terms of economic institutions and government economic policy, there was remarkable continuity between pre- and postwar Eastern Europe. One must remember that the state has traditionally played a role in Eastern Europe in terms of owning and operating transportation networks, commodity monopolies, regulating industries, and directly promoting economic modernization. These functions were easy to assume by anyone who took over power in Eastern Europe. Foreign ownership and control of key industries played the role of legalizing and legitimitizing Soviet ownership of appropriate sectors of the national economy. Therefore postwar nationalization of the so-called private sector was little more than a coup de grâce of a small part of the national economy and was far from creating a radical legitimacy as Prof. Meyer has implied.

Fourth, as far as continuity in political style is concerned, surely it would be wrong to assume that the traditional Eastern European elites, again with the exception of the extreme right, were completely shattered. This would be overstating the case; Eastern Europeans were yearning for strong leadership of any kind that seemed to promise peace and stability. Generally, the kind of revolutionary legitimacy-creating acts of the Communist Party that Prof. Meyer speaks of should be put in this kind of perspective, for the communists took advantage of existing demands and yearnings and, at least initially, drifted along with the popular ground swell rather than proposing drastic reforms. Eastern Europe ought to be viewed in a nonapocalyptic way. Moreover, the notion of primitive accumulation of legitimacy as Preobrazhenski conceptualized it in Russia in the 1920s was by and large irrelevant for Eastern Europe 20 years later.

2. My second point refers to the question of Marxism, Communist nation-building, and political legitimacy. I feel that Prof. Meyer offers an important insight in proposing a distinction between the legitimacy of the system as an abstraction and the legitimacy of the manner of its operation. He argues that the two are intertwined and cannot be viewed apart. I would maintain that the two are in fact analytically distinct. Actually, one can argue that they are in a dialectical relationship. From this I would formulate the proposition that in a communist system, political legitimacy is founded on an unstable equilibrium between the ideology or system as an abstraction, on the one hand, and the extent of official ideology supporting popular orientations toward the way the system actually functions, or the policy outputs of that particular system, on the other. Obviously tensions are inherent and Prof. Meyer refers to a certain degree of illegitimacy. The real ethical question here is whether it is only the Communist Party or all developing systems and all one-party systems in developing countries that are compelled to use coercion to implement their goals. In either case we do know that Communist systems have been partial to coercion and illegitimate ways of doing things. But this is a session on philosophy and ideology. Perhaps we can pursue later the point whether this is a characteristic unique to communist systems or whether it is a problem common to all developing systems.

3. My third point refers to the problem of legitimacy and Soviet-Eastern European relations. I would maintain that the legitimacy of the political power of a communist party-state in Eastern Europe is directly related to the degree of esteem in which the Soviet Union is held by the citizens of that particular country. From this I would hypothesize that under such circumstances the legitimacy of political power is a composite of the regime's <u>indigenous legitimacy</u> and its <u>derivative legitimacy</u>, that is, the kind of legitimacy the Communist Party has accumulated by virtue of its association with the CPSU (Communist Party of the Soviet Union) and the Soviet Union in ideological, political, economic, and military fields as well as in

international affairs. I would argue that there is a very delicate balance between these two components of legitimacy and that they fluctuate over time. I would also argue that the growth of indigenous legitimacy, that is the party's own indigenous support, tends to lessen the importance of derivative legitimacy. Paradoxically, I would maintain that the growth of the regime's derivative legitimacy need not weaken the regime's indigenous legitimacy. That is to say that the association of a national Communist Party leader with the leadership in Moscow actually tends to strengthen the former's own legitimacy as a leader as far as the population is concerned. Kadar's relationship to Khruschchev comes to mind in this connection. This kind of association, of course, did precious little to help Novotny and Gomulka, to be sure, but on the other hand, one might argue that Ulbricht's regime was strengthened by building the Berlin Wall, however paradoxical this may sound.

I would conclude from this that, contrary to Prof. Meyer's arguments, the Soviet Union for various practical, military, political, and economic reasons, has no interest in weakening the political legitimacy of its Eastern European clients. Rather, the Soviet Union is interested in maintaining a viable balance between the two indigenous and derivative components of any given Eastern European client state's legitimacy. The balance should allow the Soviet Union to continue to exercise a great deal of control without having to resort to intervention that is invariably a costly proposition. Also, I would argue that this study did not give due weight to some of the intrinsic advantages that the Soviet Union enjoys in regulating the behavior of its Eastern European clients. Some of these include the still explosive heritage of postwar territorial arrangements, nationality and language disputes, and equally potent age-old tensions along Eastern European borders. The Soviet Union may reactivate its control at any time without moving a single soldier from one place to another.

4. In connection with the fourth issue, strategies and crises of communist legitimacy-building in Eastern Europe, I would like to talk about two problems. One is the role of the Communist Party in the Eastern European countries. As we all know, at the beginning most communist parties had a native and a Muscovite wing. The Russians, of course, supported the Muscovite wing and liquidated the natives. The Stalinist purges in Eastern Europe left two unresolved questions as far as legitimacy was concerned. First, we still do not know exactly why some national leaders and some of their Muscovite counterparts acted the way they did. In other words, we do not know why they opted for certain forms of legitimacy. I would suggest that in each case, their personal experiences in the Soviet Union and their understanding of the Soviet pattern had a lot to do with these choices. The other problem, again within the sphere of Communist parties, is

the ideological legacy of the liquidated natives, which of course is a long-term problem. It is very hard to sort out the issues here, but I think we can argue that this legacy has always interfered with the legitimacy of the incumbents. This interference can be conceptualized as providing ideological ammunition for the incumbents' native opponents and also giving the Soviet masters, the leaders, a choice in selecting between them and the natives as well as between their respective policy alternatives at any given point in time.

With respect to the various crises of legitimacy in Eastern Europe, we know that such crises have ranged from isolated opposition to national uprisings, from bread riots to pitched battles between insurgents and heavy Soviet armor. In each case something went wrong with the given system's legitimacy. I think that legitimacy should not be a mythical term. It might be, for purposes of analysis, sorted out and divided into various aspects. I would at this time tentatively identify five aspects of legitimacy, one or more of which went wrong when a crisis occurred. These five aspects are, very briefly, political legitimacy, i.e., elite and public orientations concerning the Communist Party's ability to provide effective leadership to the country and the community; economic legitimacy, i.e., elite and public orientations concerning the economy's actual performance in terms of continued modernization, growing productivity, and ability to satisfy expectations generated by the regime's political socialization programs; ideological legitimacy, i.e., mainly elite but also popular orientations concerning the Party's ability to reconcile inherent dichotomies between the system's stated and feasible goals via doctrinal flexibility and readiness for ideological innovation through the adoption of nonparty elite intellectual values and specific ideological perferences; cultural legitimacy, i.e., elite and public judgments concerning the efficacy of the regime's cultural policies in terms of achieving a viable synthesis between a socialist form and a national content in literature, the arts, and sciences; finally, psychological legitimacy, the most complex of all, for it relates to the regime's ability to evoke supportive or nonhostile responses to its ruling style, political symbols, and key policy outputs. I would argue that each aspect of legitimacy is maintained by a set of "aspect-specific" legitimacy-building techniques that may indeed be called coercion, political socialization, and rewards, or simply legal, rational, traditional, and charismatic means.

5. Finally, I would like to join Prof. Kline and Prof. Anweiler in commenting on Prof. Meyer's views on the comparative implications of the Eastern European pattern. There are three issues I would like to discuss. First is the legitimacy of political power in Eastern and Western Europe after the war. Prof. Meyer has maintained that contrived revolutions in Eastern Europe were neatly balanced by analogous developments in the West. Specifically he refers to direct

Soviet interference with virtually every aspect of Eastern European postwar politics, as well as to United States meddling with Italian elections and strengthening noncommunist forces in France, among other things. I could entertain this proposition if Prof. Meyer could prove that, first, thousands of French, Italian, and other communists were deported to American prisons or to northern Norway at least, and that opposition politicians, professed atheists, and others were arrested, tortured, and executed, and further that the United States Army actively cooperated in putting down popular uprisings against bourgeois democracy. He would then obviously have a case. Otherwise this kind of comparison is gratuitous and must be dismissed as nonsence.

Second, the ambiguity of postwar arrangements in Europe, as a general proposition. I think that Prof. Meyer follows in this respect the revisionist school of modern United States history, implying that both superpowers were guilty of deliberate deceit in their respective spheres of influence. While I am inclined to doubt the existence of a Soviet blueprint of conquest, whatever that might be, there is still sufficient evidence to argue that the Soviet Union had a much better idea about its postwar plans for Eastern Europe than the United States had for Western Europe. In short, idle comparisons between the moral objectionability of Soviet occupation of Czechoslovakia and the United States involvement in Viet Nam, between the Soviet suppression of the Hungarian revolution and the Suez affair, and the presumed complacency of the superpowers in the face of these events offer no valid explanations about the legitimacy of power in Eastern Europe, or anywhere for that matter.

The third matter is popular orientations toward the legitimacy of political power in Eastern Europe. I think that Prof. Meyer is quite correct in suggesting that there exists a great deal of diffuse support of the Eastern European regimes by their respective populations. However, instead of saying that this support is highly correlated with the regimes' economic performance, satisfaction of popular expectations associated with the welfare state aspects of the systems, he maintains first, that Eastern European elites take pride in their austerity of life, and consider it superior to the culturally shallow, materialistic, and vulgar life styles of the West. He also implies that Eastern Europeans, while conceding that things could be better under socialism, temper their hostile feelings by thinking about Angela Davis, My Lai and the Chicago Seven, racial inequality in the United States, and so on. Unless Prof. Meyer's findings are based on conversations with some extremely peculiar and severely disoriented Eastern Europeans, it seems more plausible to argue that Eastern Europeans are not at all austerity-loving but are decidedly a hedonistic lot, who perhaps put too much emphasis on good living and not enough on the moral quality of their environment. They, of course, may be guilty of hypocrisy, now and then, but they are certainly not fools as Prof. Meyer implies. The peoples of Eastern Europe, unlike most Americans, have been living in the last 40 years with memories of brutalities, genocide, of man's inhumanity to man as a matter of daily existence. Katyn, Buchenwald, Duchau, Treblinka, the Warsaw ghetto, purges, deportation, and bloody Communist counterrevolutions have done much to develop a sense of callousness toward the sufferings of the Vietnamese and the American Blacks, not to mention the private agonies of Western intellectuals of the non-Communist left. In the absence of such Eastern European empathies, Prof. Meyer should have thought of more plausible and certainly more immediate objects of Eastern European compassion, such as Solzhenitzyn, Daniel, Sinyavsky, Ginzburg, and many others, not to mention the still-hounded intellectuals of Prague, Warsaw, and Bucharest. I think it is objectionable scholarship to project one's politics or intellectual guilt into elites of a distant land who have no opportunity to take exception to examples of academic escapism that one can observe when contemplating arguments of this kind.

In summing up, I think that Prof. Meyer's study is a delightful and stimulating example and perhaps the first of its kind of what one might call the "Greening of Eastern European Scholarship." In a more serious vein, I wish to reiterate that legitimacy is knowable without resorting to mystification of the kind to which he has treated us. As I tried to show, the concept of legitimacy is amenable to quantification, especially when we are talking about "the way the system works." After all, there are objective ways of measuring decisional outputs, living standards, indices of cultural development, services, and many other aspects of a political system.

It is gratifying to know that Eastern Europe has again become an academically recognized field of political-science inquiry rather than a neglected appendage of Soviet studies. I hope that both the historically oriented old, and the methodologically sophisticated, but factually uninformed new students of the area will soon join forces and develop together a body of new evidence with which to put some methodological backbone into discussions about Eastern European politics and the legitimacy of political power in that part of the world.

NOTES TO ANALYSES

Analysis 2

1. Rose, <u>Governing Without Consensus</u> (Boston: Beacon Press, 1971).

2. Bachrach and Baratz, <u>Power and Poverty</u> (New York: Oxford University Press, 1970).

3. Deutsch, <u>The Nerves of Government</u> (New York: Free Press, 1966).

Analysis 3

1. Leszek Kotakowski, "Hope and Hopelessness," <u>Survey</u>, XVII, 3(80) (1971), 50.

CHAPTER 4

SPHERES OF INFLUENCE AND SOVIET WAR AIMS IN 1943
Vojtech Mastny

Soviet striving for a division of Europe into spheres of influence has been almost a truism for Western authors, whether of the "traditional" or the "revisionist" variety. The former have tended to agree with Arthur M. Schlesinger that "the Kremlin... thought only of spheres of interest"[1] and have blamed the narrow-minded intolerance of the Soviet leaders for the subsequent breakdown of East-West collaboration. The latter have taken a somewhat more benevolent view of Stalin's desire to control areas to which he was supposedly entitled for both historical and military reasons, and have merely resented his putting this goal above that of social revolution. But is it really true that the Soviet Union wanted spheres of influence or is this hypothesis rather a retrospective projection of the subsequent reality?

During the first year and a half of their belligerence, the Russians indeed extended to the West several secret proposals in favor of spheres of influence. In December 1941, Stalin outlined to Foreign Secretary Anthony Eden a grandiose scheme that implied that Britain would have a free hand in Western, the Soviet Union in Eastern Europe.[2] After London had proved unreceptive, Moscow submitted a somewhat more modest plan in May 1942. It asked for recognition of its predominance in Finland and Romania, which would be confirmed by special treaties, and offered in return to support a corresponding British arrangement with the Low Countries.[3] At a time when the Soviet Union was still fighting desperately for its very survival, these projects were premature to say the least; dependent as they

---

Vojtech Mastny is Assistant Professor of History, Columbia University, New York.

were upon a foreign fiat, they also suggested a deficiency of might though not of ambition.

After Stalingrad had turned the military fortune, the Russians showed conspicuously less interest in an agreement about spheres of influence, at least with their coalition partners. The high cost of victory seems to have led them to explore briefly the possibility of making such a deal with Germany but without success.[4] In August 1943, they expressed their preferences to the Western powers in different terms. Ambassador Ivan M. Maiskii told Eden that the West and the East could each have a sphere of influence but that the Soviet government preferred to "admit each other's right to an interest in all parts of the continent."[5]

Thus, by August 1943, the Russians regarded the partition of the continent as but the second best choice; but what really did they consider their top preference? Stalin of course never disclosed his true vision of the ideal European order to his capitalist allies or, for that matter, to his disciples among the foreign Communists. But since he always tried to make all his followers act in accordance with his design, that design can be deduced from the guidance they were receiving from Moscow. In this respect, the relations between the Communists from central Europe and their Soviet mentors are of particular import for it was in this part of the continent that the lines between the two power blocs were eventually drawn.

An interesting clue to the Russian calculations in 1943 may be found in the little known programmatic writings of Alfred Lampe, who as the chief ideologist of the Polish Communist exiles may be regarded as an authentic voice of Moscow. Discussing the future of Poland, Lampe emphasized that the party must fend for itself and not count upon the presence of the Red Army in the country.[6] His reasoning seems to corroborate the view, not uncommon among contemporaries, that the Russians might stop upon reaching their own frontier of 1941.[7] And indeed, Stalin had good reasons to take this alternative into account while planning for the future.

From Stalin's point of view, the path of military conquest entailed the incalculable risk of exposing his troops to the allurements of different ways of life, from which he had tried so hard to shelter all his subjects. By the same token, the impression that the Red Army would give abroad was likely to deprive the Soviet Union, as it later did, of much of the sympathy gained during the war. Moreover, the administration of occupied countries involved many unpleasant obligations besides prerogatives. But the greatest uncertainty in Stalin's mind concerned the readiness of the West to stand by until complete victory.

Although none of these considerations ruled out the use of military force in order to achieve Soviet aims abroad, they all

SPHERES OF INFLUENCE 89

supported the wisdom of relying upon political means as well. And at no time in the war was this axiom more topical than during the critical period between Stalingrad and the great Allied conferences at the end of 1943. On the one hand, the Red Army's ascendancy gave the Russians a foretaste of victory, though no certainty about its extent. On the other hand, the absence of any agreement with the West about the future European settlement gave them freedom to maneuver for the greatest possible rewards. It was during this period that they elaborated the concept of the National Front as the central feature of their political strategy.

Devised originally in 1941 in order to facilitate the collaboration of the Communists with other enemies of Fascism in the resistance movements, the National Front formula assumed by 1943 definite long-term implications. At the beginning of that year, the top officials of various European Communist parties held secret sessions in Moscow to discuss their postwar tasks; the Czechoslovak party leaders, for example, met on January 5, the German ones on January 28 and February 10-11.[8]

The ultimate purpose of the National Front strategy, which envisaged coalition regimes with an important but not necessarily predominant Communist participation, has been the subject of much speculation ever since the sorry fate of such regimes in Soviet-dominated Eastern Europe after the war.[9] In 1966, historians from Yugoslavia, Poland, and Czechoslovakia devoted to that intriguing topic an entire conference in Belgrade.[10] But having studied thoroughly the pertinent records in their party archives, they unearthed no evidence that Moscow had anticipated or encouraged postwar Communist seizures of power. Indeed, an important internal policy directive now available in print—the Czechoslovak party resolution of January 5, 1943—shows that the confidential instructions did not contradict what Moscow's spokesmen were saying in public.

The document, published in Prague in 1965, advocated cooperation across class and party lines and directed the Czechoslovak comrades to respect the authority of the "bourgeois" government of President Benes.[11] The passage that "the international status and relations of the liberated republic will be determined after the liberation"[12] suggested that the Soviet Union was not yet commited to any particular course in these matters. At the same time, however, the Communists were encouraged to create a counterpart of governmental power by controlling local committees of national resistance. Established without regard to constitutional formalities and uncomfortably reminiscent of the 1917 Russian Soviets, the committees were part of the Communist program in all countries of Hitler's Europe.

Thus the Soviet advocacy of the National Fronts by no means implied abstention from interference in the politics of other nations.

On the contrary, here was a strategy ideally suited to maximize Moscow's influence abroad no matter how far its military power would reach. Governments merely infiltrated rather than controlled by Communists were likely to be weak, thus enabling the Soviet Union to act as arbiter in a prostrate Europe. In contrast, any Communist bid for total power might prompt intervention by the Americans or British, whom the Russians preferred to keep away from the scene. Barring such revolutionary attempts, there was a good chance that neither Western power would fill the vacuum of power left after the defeat of Germany—the former for lack of interest, the latter for lack of resources.

From the Russian point of view, therefore, Communists in every country ought to be so strong that they be influential, yet not too strong that they develop ambitions of their own. Ideally they should hold the key to the political balance. Aside from that, the main prerequisites of their effectiveness as potential Soviet fifth columns were both tight organization and prompt responsiveness to orders from Moscow. Yet in this very respect, their condition in 1943 left much to be desired. In Central Europe, the pro-Russian underground had suffered especially severe blows. In the fall of 1942, the Gestapo destroyed the "Red Orchestra," the impressive Soviet espionage network in Germany. The few surviving Communist resistance groups in Germany, Austria, Czechoslovakia, and Hungary remained largely isolated from one another and from the outside world.[13] Viewed from Moscow, central Europe was indeed the most remote part of the continent.

The Soviet Union sent agents in order to remedy this unsatisfactory situation. During 1941 and 1942, their principal task was to organize sabotage and guerrilla warfare. Later, however, the emissaries went on political missions as well. Besides restoring the interrupted contacts, they tried to enforce the program adopted by the leadership in Moscow. Thus, for example, some of them brought the text of the Czechoslovak party resolution of January 5, 1943, to the home country; they reached the Czech lands in March of that year, Slovakia four months later.[14] Confidants carrying political directives came to Austria by way of Belgium and France at the end of 1942 and in early 1943.[15]

The results, however, fell far short of the target. Not only did Moscow fail to establish regular contacts in central Europe—with the exception of Poland—but its efforts to do so led to a major disaster in at least one part of the area. In the spring of 1943, the Gestapo tracked down the main Soviet emissary to Czechoslovakia within a few weeks of his arrival and kept him under surveillance for almost a year. Undercover agents meanwhile infiltrated the Communist organizations in that country so thoroughly that even one of the three

SPHERES OF INFLUENCE   91

top party officials there was in fact a police informer. The Nazis went so far as to organize "clandestine" conferences in order to identify the remaining members of the resistance movement.16

Besides the extensive infiltration of the underground by enemy agents, the less than enthusiastic reception of the Moscow line was for the Russians a reason for concern. The Czech and Slovak clandestine central committees, for example, endorsed the January 5 resolution only reluctantly.17 In Germany, Communists were not altogether happy about Soviet support of the "class enemies" on the Free Germany Committee and in the League of German Officers.18 Even among the comrades in Poland, doubts persisted about both the wisdom and the feasibility of the directives urging them to come to terms with at least some of the pro-London resistance groups.19

Close coordination between Moscow and the Communist resistance movements was therefore rather an ideal than a reality. The extreme sensitivity of pro-Soviet historians to this topic only underlines the magnitude of the problem that the Russians were facing during the war. It matters little that the disagreements did not in fact impair the overwhelming devotion of most Communists to the "Fatherland of Socialism." For the very shortage of reliable information about the actual situation in the occupied countries tended to generate suspicions in Moscow. And Stalin was not a person to take chances in matters of discipline; having punished severely much smaller manifestations of nonconformism before, he was hardly inclined to be more tolerant in wartime.

This was the setting for what was, perhaps, Stalin's most important, as well as most controversial, decision during the critical year of 1943: the dissolution of the Comintern. With little justification, anti-Communist authors have usually disparaged the importance of that move. Most of the interpretations offered have been not only unconvincing but also contradictory. They have ranged from the theory that the organization was obsolete anyway to the assumption that its machinery continued to exist, so that nothing really changed in any case.20 Yet the Comintern's former employees have testified that its apparatus was in fact dismantled. And the contemporary confidential explanations by authoritative Soviet spokesmen stressed that the dissolution was to be taken literally, not as a mere tactical move to reassure Russia's "capitalist" allies.21

A close reading of the carefully worded official declaration that announced the decision to the world on May 21 shows quite clearly that the intended audience was the Comintern's followers rather than its adversaries. The text included the conspicuous, but altogether unconvincing, compliment to the "growth and political maturity of the communist parties," which had supposedly rendered superfluous their direction from one center.22 Another passage asserted that the war had

> sharpened the differences in the situation of the separate countries, and has placed a dividing line between those countries which fell under the Hitlerite tyranny and those freedom-loving peoples who have united in a powerful anti-Hitler coalition.23

National animosities of course existed, but the struggle against the common foe had also generated strong feelings of solidarity and a desire for European unity—among Communists and non-Communists alike. For its part, Moscow left no doubt that its sympathies were on the side of nationalism against any form of internationalism. Averse to social revolution, the Soviet program was less radical than many Communists wished and their adversaries feared; it was radical all the same. As Jesús Hernández, a disillusioned former member of the Comintern's executive committee observed,

> Stalin's vision extended far. He realized that his imperialist ambitions might create misgivings among the national parties. He did not want to be forced to justify his policy to the foreign Communists. He eliminated in advance any possibility of an uncontrolled reaction by an international body no matter how tame.24

The dissolution of the Comintern, therefore, served above all to establish a new institutional framework for the expanding Soviet war aims. Consistent with the principle "divide and rule," Moscow dealt from now on with each of the "fraternal" parties directly and separately. Its policies differed from country to country, since its stakes were greater in, say, Poland than in the more remote parts of the continent. But, significantly, no line was drawn to indicate where Soviet aspirations began and where they ended.

To sum up, Stalin's ideal was to achieve continental hegemony— neither by military conquest nor by social revolution, but by promoting internal weakness in the European nations and their disunity with the active help of Communist fifth columns. As a prudent politician, however, he did not seek this goal at any cost but rather adjusted his ambition to opportunities. In this sense, its extent depended very much upon the behavior of others, particularly of Russia's coalition partners.

In the first year of Soviet belligerence, British and American leaders were disturbed about Stalin's insistence upon the restoration

of the lands he had acquired during his collusion with Hitler. They
also resented the imperialistic connotations of his proposals for
spheres of influence in 1941 and 1942.[25] Anticipating with certainty
a tremendous increase of Russian power by the end of the war, they
probably overestimated the actual goals that Stalin had set for himself
at that time. But in the long run they assessed correctly the Soviet
potential for future expansion.

Although by different means, Western statesmen initially tried
to check what they regarded as excessive Russian aspirations. The
United States government, convinced that all decisions concerning
territorial sovereignty should be postponed until after the war, refused
to sanction Moscow's title to the territories seized in 1939 and 1940,
let alone its claim for control of any countries farther west. The
British, for their part, were quite prepared to recognize the pre-1941
Soviet frontier, except that with Poland, hoping that by satisfying
these relatively minor demands, they would prevent the Russians from
seeking more.[26] There is something to be said for both policies—
the one more principled, the other more pragmatic—provided they
would have been applied consistently.

The official American attitude gave signs of mellowing during
Molotov's visit to Washington in May 1942. At that occasion, President Roosevelt hinted at his idea of four "world policemen" who would
be responsible for peace and order in their respective precincts.[27]
Although he did not get down to specifics with his Soviet guest, particularly about the extent of the Russian precinct, he gave the impression
that he regarded strong Soviet presence in Europe favorably. The
President's exaggerated notions about a great power concert as the
main safeguard of peace and order were matched by his doubts about
Europeans' competence in handling their own affairs.

Churchill's opinion about the beneficial impact of Soviet power
was less optimistic and his faith in the Europeans greater. In October
1942, he confided to Eden that "it would be a measureless disaster
if Russian barbarism overlaid the culture and independence of the
ancient States of Europe."[28] In order to avert this melancholy prospect, he hoped that "the European family may act unitedly," regain
its self-respect and uphold its heritage of freedom. The British
government therefore encouraged strongly efforts at regional integration, particularly in Eastern Europe. The ideal was, besides the
resurrection of a strong France, the establishment of several confederations of the small nations farther east: one in the Balkans;
another made of Hungary, Austria, and portions of dismembered
Germany; a third uniting Czechoslovakia and Poland.[29] On March
21, 1943, the Prime Minister delivered a major speech in which he
appealed to the great powers to support the movement for European
unity.[30]

The speech was Churchill's response to an editorial published 11 days earlier in the London Times and widely suspected to be expressive of the views held by the government. The article envisaged joint British-Russian guardianship of Europe, suggesting that Britain's frontier was on the Rhine, Russia's on the Oder.[31] Although particularly explicit, this was not an exceptional opinion; and in the cabinet itself, Lord Beaverbrook represented an influential minority that favored the acceptance of the Soviet insinuations for spheres of influence. He wrote in a confidential memorandum in January 1942 that

> Stalin has expressed himself willing to underwrite any claims we may make for bases in western Europe and particularly on the French Channel coast. We should take advantage of this willingness.[32]

The Americans were initially far less sympathetic to the Russian aspirations than the British were, but after Stalingrad the situation began to change. True, much of the local press continued to express reservations about the Communist ally. But the more prestigious journals, regarded abroad—rightly or wrongly—as representative of the overwhelming public opinion, tended to adopt the view that Moscow's "cooperation could be obtained only by acquiescing in the leadership asserted by the Russians in Eastern Europe."[33] Most liberals, and not a few conservatives, agreed with Walter Lippmann that "it is not only unavoidable but eminently proper to recognize that each great power does have a sphere in which its influence and responsibility are primary."[34] Such an ostensibly realistic belief was curiously enough often blended with the doctrinaire notion that the Soviet Union deserved what it wanted not so much because of its ability to take it as because of its alledgedly growing resemblance to a true democracy.[35]

What was written in the press did not, of course, necessarily coincide with the policies of the government. However, responsible leaders could not remain too much out of step with the disposition of a great many of their constituents. The Russians were no doubt alert to this phenomenon in democratic politics although, in conformity with the Marxist theory, they probably exaggerated the extent to which both the press and the government responded to impulses by the same "capitalist wire-pullers." In Soviet terminology, "progressive capitalists," convinced about the necessity of making concessions to the Land of Socialism, now appeared to be in the ascendancy.

The Russians welcomed the Western trend in favor of spheres of influence not so much because they were inclined to accept the restraints inherent in that formula as because of the support it lent to their opposition against regional integration. They expressed their opposition ever more forcefully, having as early as July 1942 applied diplomatic pressure in order to hamper preparations for the confederation between Czechoslovakia and Poland.36 Shortly after Churchill's call for European unification, Maiskii told Eden explicitly that the Soviet government might tolerate a Balkan grouping without Romania and a Scandinavian one without Finland—for such associations would be "vegetarian"—but that it was opposed strongly to any combinations in Central Europe.37

Moscow's campaign against confederations coincided with its diplomatic offensive against Poland. Yet for several months after Stalingrad, the Russians hesitated to press their hegemonial aspirations elsewhere. Characteristically, they remained cool to the idea of concluding an alliance with Czechoslovakia desired ardently by its President, Eduard Benes.38 Similarly, they refrained from backing his plan for the expulsion of the German minority from that country—another project that promised to enhance Moscow's status in Central Europe after the war.39

The Soviet reserve was no doubt related to the June 1942 "gentlemen's agreement" between Molotov and Eden that the great powers should not seek bilateral treaties with the minor Allies.40 One may also speculate to what extent Stalin's remaining illusions about possible accommodation with Germany accounted for his reluctance to make commitments to its victims. But the most likely explanation is that the fulfillment of the Czechoslovak project depended upon priorities, and that the Polish question commanded for the time being the top priority.

When the discovery of the murdered Polish officers at Katyn strained the Soviet-Polish relations, Moscow skillfully used the Czechs in order to isolate the Poles. At the height of the crisis, on April 23, Ambassador Aleksandr M. Bogomolov notified Benes that his government would conclude the treaty with Czechoslovakia well before the end of the war and that it also favored a similar arrangement with Poland "in principle."41 This sufficed to assure Czechoslovak quiescence when Moscow broke off diplomatic relations with Poland on the next day.

The rationale of the Czechoslovak President has ever since evoked contradictory evaluations.42 Whereas sympathizers have defended his efforts as a desperate attempt to mitigate the rigors of inevitable Soviet supremacy in Central Europe, critics have blamed him for actually helping to usher it in—unwittingly, or not so unwittingly. Not surprisingly, the Poles have always been among his most bitter critics. But already in 1943, a minority of Western conservatives voiced concern when the President assumed the role of something of a mediator between the East and the West.43

In early May 1943, Benes traveled to the United States. He arrived there at a very important juncture of the war, when the policies of all the major Allies were in a state of flux. Stalin had just started to improve his relations with the West after a period of ostentatious coolness during which he seems to have tried and failed in a bid for a separate peace with Germany.44 Churchill was in Washington at the same time as Benes, discussing among other topics two items closely related to the future of Soviet power in Europe: the confederations and a possible Allied landing in the Balkans before the Red Army might get there first.45 Roosevelt, for his part, harbored misgivings about both projects although he, too, was worried about the uncertainty surrounding the Russian aims. But he hoped to dispel it in a rather different fashion by proposing to Stalin a tête-à-tête without Churchill's presence. He was about to convey the proposal to Moscow through a special emissary, Joseph Davies, who was known for his uncritical admiration of the Soviet system.46 But before dispatching him to the Russian capital, the President talked with Benes.

Roosevelt held the Czechoslovak leader in high esteem not only for his reputed expertise in affairs Russian but also for his excellent connections in both the West and the East. The President held two long meetings and although, rather surprisingly, no minutes of their conversations have been preserved, indirect evidence suggests that Roosevelt sought above all his guest's advice about Soviet intentions.47 And the nature of the advice given can be deduced from other statements on that subject which Benes made during his numerous public appearances in the United States and Canada.48

In his speeches and articles, the Czechoslovak President ridiculed the Soviet bogey as but an invention of Nazi propaganda and pleaded for a sympathetic understanding of the tenets of the Bolshevik revolution. He blamed the lack of Western sympathy for it as the main cause of mistrust on the part of the Russians and saw the principal remedy in the recognition of their legitimate aspirations, including "influence in Central and Western Europe which [is] rightly due to them as a great world power."49 At the same time, Benes criticized the confederation projects, expressing his preference for sovereign national states. But he pleaded for their independence and integrity with much less vehemence than he did for a benevolent Soviet protectorship over them.

Benes elaborated his ideas before large and attentive audiences ranging from business executives to university students, government officials to Americans of Czech ancestry. Although most of his arguments did not differ in substance from current left-wing and liberal theses, they carried particular weight as the opinion of a prominent representative of a small nation who might be expected to be apprehensive about Russian supremacy and yet was not. Comtemplating that prospect with serenity, he did not hesitate to deliver a coup de grâce to the confederations.

The performance of the Czechoslovak President in the United States evoked favorable response in Moscow.[50] Stalin and Benes, after all, had shared in common a mistrust of any internationalist schemes; the former considered them dangerous, the latter ineffective. But most pleasing to Moscow was the sympathetic portrayal of its power by Benes and the evident approval his estimates received from the rank and file in the greatest capitalist country. On June 5, the Soviet government expressed its gratitude by finally sanctioning the expulsion of the Sudeten Germans from Czechoslovakia.[51]

Thus, by mid-1943, the time had ripened for Stalin to seek for his country a greater role in the postwar world than he had thought possible earlier. Not only had the opposition, so adamant in 1942 to his outright territorial claims, all but disappeared; also that against his indirect domination of foreign countries was diminishing. Indeed, proposals for granting Russia a large though unspecified domain in part of Europe were now emanating from the West itself. From mid-1943 onwards, the Soviet Union acted more decisively to create the most favorable conditions for its supremacy.

On June 7, Moscow sent to London a memorandum about the treatment of the countries currently allied with Germany.[52] It suggested four fundamental conditions that were to be imposed upon them: military surrender, retrocession of all annexed territories, reparations for the damages caused to the Allies, and the punishment of war criminals. In return, the victors would guarantee the territorial integrity and national independence of the nations ready to abandon the Axis cause. These were ostensibly unobjectionable demands. Yet they were, in fact, an expression of the same desire to keep Europe divided and weak that had also motivated the dissolution of the Comintern three weeks earlier.

Unlike the Western Allies, who had committed themselves to the principle of unconditional surrender, Moscow was prepared to offer terms of varying harshness to the defeated countries, thus inviting them to compete for its favors. A similar calculation inspired the demand for the restitution of annexed territories as indicated, for example, in the Soviet support for the return of Transylvania to Romania by Hungary. From the Russian point of view, this particular transaction had the triple advantage of obligating the former, weakening the latter, and keeping both countries hostile to each other. The compulsory reparations, too, were intended to cripple the defeated countries economically for a long period of time. And as far as the punishment of the war criminals is concerned, that offered a way to weed out inconvenient political figures.

Finally, the promised guarantees of independence and integrity, far from imposing restrictions upon the Russians, served above all to erect barriers to supranational integration. In order to avoid any misunderstanding, Molotov notified the British ambassador specifically that Austria and Hungary ought not to be included in any regional associations.53 And shortly afterwards, the Soviet press started an intensive campaign against the confederations.54

The campaign also advertised Russian dissatisfaction with the British attempt to block the Czechoslovak-Soviet treaty. London perceived the significance of the project as a possible precedent that might sanction in advance a client relationship of the small nations of East Central Europe to Moscow—a prospect made particularly topical during Benes' recent American journey. Eden further feared that such an ostentatious display of Soviet-Czechoslovak intimacy would only accentuate the deplorable state of the Soviet-Polish relations, thus making their satisfactory settlement even more difficult.55 For the Czechs, indeed, there seemed to be no need to cement Moscow's friendship by a special treaty that, on the contrary, would "give everyone the impression that [they] are completely under the Soviet hat."56 Through diplomatic channels, London drew Moscow's attention to the 1942 understanding that either government abstain from concluding bilateral treaties with the small nations.57

In reply to the British intervention, Maiskii argued that no such general "self-denying ordinance" in fact existed—an assertion facilitated by the ambiguous record of what had exactly transpired between Eden and Molotov in June 1942.58 Furthermore, the Russians reversed themselves and put pressure upon Benes, urging him to come as quickly as possible to Moscow in order to finalize the agreement. On July 5, Czechoslovak Ambassador Zdenek Fierlinger reported ominously from the Soviet capital that they "do not say that they would not sign the treaty later, but they do not know when and under what circumstances it could be signed if not now."59

In early July, two important developments on the battlefields added urgency to the competition for power in Europe. On July 12, the Soviet Union won the great victory at Kursk—a dramatic demonstration of its growing military might. But the Western Allies, having landed in Sicily two days earlier, actually preceded the Russians in beginning to take physical possession of foreign territories in Europe. Italy became the first liberated country in which the East and the West confronted each other.

The importance of the Italian case for the evolution toward spheres of influence has often been noted.60 Having excluded the Soviet Union from an effective share in the administration of Italy, the Western powers supplied Moscow with a strong argument for their own exclusion from the countries later to be conquered by the

SPHERES OF INFLUENCE 99

Red Army. But, in 1943, neither side seems to have regarded this outcome as inevitable. In any case, their respective attempts at defining the role of the victors in the liberated countries show that both the Western and the Soviet governments were still trying to avoid a partition, although for different reasons.

London submitted on July 1 a memorandum to Moscow and Washington that envisaged the establishment of joint American-British-Soviet commissions to supervise the execution of any armistice agreements.[61] In the occupied areas, the Allied military commanders would have complete responsibility but a "United Nations Commission for Europe" would "direct and coordinate the activities of the several Armistice Commissions, the Allied Commanders-in-Chief and any United Nations civilian authorities that may be established."[62] Although both the major and the minor Allies would sit on the commission, the dominant position of the great powers would be safeguarded by means of a tripartite steering committee whose actions would require unanimity. On the whole, the arrangement would enable each Allied power to run the territory it had liberated, but the potentially divisive effects of their different policies would be mitigated by the influence of the international bodies.

Stalin, for his part, proposed on August 22 to his Western colleagues "to create a military-political commission of representatives of the three countries... for the consideration of questions regarding negotiations with different Governments falling out with Germany."[63] According to a subsequent Soviet addition, this single commission should exercise authority "not only in relation to Italy, but also correspondingly in relation to other countries."[64] The Russians would have liked to assign it the executive powers that the British wanted to reserve to the military commanders. The Soviet-sponsored commission would have also differed from the European one envisaged by London in being exclusively a great-power agency, in which the minor Allies would have had no voice. Moreover, its authority would extend not only over former enemy countries but also over liberated friendly countries.[65]

The differences between the two respective viewpoints were subtle but significant. In the last analysis, the West wished to regulate the relations among the great powers, whereas the Russians sought ways and means of influencing the situation in the occupied territories in their own favor. They tried to deprive the military administrations of any significant role in internal politics, especially regarding the restoration of local self-government. Instead, decisions on all such important matters would be in the hands of a commission in which Soviet representatives would have a strong voice. Admittedly, the system might work the other way around in case of the occupation, as yet hypothetical, of foreign countries by the Red Army. But then, regardless of whether the Soviet Union would be ready to reciprocate, it could still benefit from the additional assistance available from the local Communist parties and their front organizations. Thus the Soviet leaders demonstrated again their inclination to think in terms of political rather than of military penetration.

If the proposals about the Military-Political Commission hinted at Moscow's short-term tactics, its long-term strategy is evident from its little-known desiderata toward Czechoslovakia. The Russian amendments to the treaty drafted by Benes in August 1943 aimed at changing its meaning from a fairly straightforward anti-German defense pact into a mainly political agreement, at once broader and tighter.66 They defined very flexibly the conditions under which the pact was to be operative by referring to putative danger from "states allied with Germany directly or in any other form."67 This interpretation was reminiscent of the formula of "indirect aggression" developed in 1939 to support the Soviet claim to intervene at discretion in the neighboring countries. The revised draft also circumscribed Czechoslovakia's freedom to seek other friends by inserting the prohibition to take part in any "directly or indirectly" hostile combination. Incredibly enough, the Russians even deleted the adjectives "full international" when referring to the sovereignty of their junior partner that they pledged to respect.68 Finally, they demanded that the treaty become effective upon signature by government plenipotentiaries prior to ratification by any representative bodies, and that it remain valid for 20 years. To sum up, the pact was to make the most of the natural inequality of the 2 signatories, giving the stronger party prerogatives without commitments, the weaker one obligations without protection against abuse.

It is characteristic of the prevailing contemporary misapprehension of the Soviet power that these fairly transparent allusions did not create grave concern among their recipients. Admittedly, Benes hesitated for a while, estimating correctly that "Moscow is playing a game with us. . . , wishes to weaken our republic and make it into a pliable tool."69 But having himself originated the alliance project, he became convinced that the prospective advantage to his country's security outweighed the threat to its sovereignty.

Moreover, the President was under strong pressure from his many Anglophobe collaborators to whom "Moscow appeared as the only reliable partner."70 In an important sense, the unequal treaty was to codify the considerable gains that the Soviet Union had made already in Czechoslovakia without really trying very hard. They were symbolized by the remark of Benes' Foreign Minister, Jan Masaryk, who was aware of having "in his office people who report everything to the Communists and to the Soviet Embassy."71 Indiscretion and outright disloyalty were frequent among the officials of the

SPHERES OF INFLUENCE

government-in-exile, whereas in the home country its Russophile policies met with considerable popular approval.[72]

By late 1943, the leading Western statesmen, though averse to spheres of influence in principle, had in practice become all but reconciled with the prospect of at least the Russian one. On September 3, 1943, Roosevelt confided to Francis Cardinal Spellman, the Archbishop of New York, the opinion that "the European people will simply have to endure the Russian domination in the hope that. . .in ten or twenty years the European influence would bring the Russians to become less barbarian."[73] He anticipated that Germany and Austria would become Communist, perhaps even without Soviet military intervention, and that Austria, Hungary, and Croatia would "fall under a sort of Russian protectorate." The President hoped to obtain from Stalin a pledge not to expand beyond a certain line but did not expect that his wish would be granted. As far as Churchill is concerned, he did not take such a resigned view, although he had by then given up his confederation projects. And a year later, he actually authored the famous "percentages agreement" with Stalin regarding the Balkans— the only clear wartime arrangement about spheres of influence in Europe.[74]

Indeed the failure of the Allied leaders to face the issue squarely earlier was the crux of the problem. True, at the Moscow meeting of foreign ministers, the subject came up for discussion—having been introduced by the British rather than by the Russians—but it was not settled.[75] The Soviet delegates objected to a public statement against spheres of influence on the plausible grounds that such a gesture would encourage rather than discourage speculation about the intent to create them.[76] At United States behest, the conferees finally issued a vague "Declaration on General Security" in which they dissociated themselves from that disreputable device of imperialist diplomacy implicitly rather than explicitly.[77]

But in the course of the Moscow conference, several important compromises were reached that in effect strengthened the trend toward partition of Europe. Rather unexpectedly, Eden gave up without discussion his opposition against the Czechoslovak-Soviet treaty— possibly because of the Russian-inspired last-minute addendum inviting the participation of Poland.[78] His attitude suggests that a solution of the Polish problem along the Czechoslovak model—the voluntary subordination to Soviet leadership in foreign policy—would have been agreeable to London, no less than to Moscow, if only a Polish Benes could have been found.

Another compromise concerned Italy and the related question of the European commission. By consenting to the creation of a special Allied Commission for Italy instead of the general Military-Political Commission they had hoped for, the Russians weakened their bid for influence in other countries that were to be liberated by the Western Allies. At the same time, however, they took the teeth out of the British proposal for an international body that would handle the problems of the continent as a whole. The resulting European Advisory Commission therefore confined its agenda mainly to technical questions concerning armistice and the administration of the former enemy countries.

At the Teheran conference, the military representatives of the Big Three agreed upon zones of operational responsibility, described retrospectively as "precursors of the postwar spheres of influence.[79] No attempt was made, however, to define precisely the extent of either the zones or of the responsibility. This was bound to create difficulties once, in the next year, the Russians followed the Western example in expanding their military presence abroad. In the end they had to settle for control over only parts of Eastern Europe while for the West even that was all too much to tolerate. The lines were eventually drawn via facti amidst mutual accusations of bad faith, providing the atmosphere in which the Cold War mushroomed.

Whether or not this outcome could have been avoided is a topic beyond the scope of the present study. There was no doubt a strong element of predetermination in the trend toward partition. Yet the policies of the main actors were not without fault in precipitating it. The Western behavior very likely misled Moscow to believe that, regardless of the official protestations to the contrary, the West in fact approved of spheres of influence. As far as the Russians themselves are concerned, they considered such an arrangement perhaps second best but still eminently acceptable. In their version, exclusive Soviet control over most of Eastern Europe was to be taken for granted, while the rest of the continent would serve as an arena for political competition—a concept which even 30 years later commands intense topical interest.

NOTES

1. Arthur M. Schlesinger, Jr., "Origins of the Cold War," Foreign Affairs, XLVI (1967-68), p. 29.
2. Llewellyn Woodward, British Foreign Policy in the Second World War, Vol. II (London, 1971), pp. 222-23.
3. Eden's report on conversation with Maiskii, May 5, 1942, Memorandum No. 190, CAB 66/24, Public Record Office (London) [PRO].
4. Vojtech Mastny, "Stalin and the Prospect of a Separate Peace in World War II," American Historical Review, LXXVII (1972).

5. Anthony Eden, The Reckoning (Boston, 1965), pp. 469-70. Cf. Winant to Roosevelt, January 28, 1945, Foreign Relations of the United States [FRUS], The Conferences at Malta and Yalta, p. 130.

6. Antoni Przygonski, "Z rozwazan Alfreda Lampe o nowej Polsce" [Alfred Lampe's Thoughts on New Poland], Z pola walki, VII, 2 (1964), 98-115.

7. Cf. Maurice Matloff, Strategic Planning for Coalition Warfare, 1943-1944 (Washington, 1959), pp. 286, 411.

8. Lothar Berthold, "Der Kampf gegen das Hitlerregime— der Kampf für einneues, demokratisches Deutschland," Beiträge zur Geschichte der deutschen Arbeiterbewegung [BGDA], VI (1964), p. 1016.

9. Cf. Ruth A. Rosa, "The Soviet Theory of 'People's Democracy,'" World Politics, I (1948-49), pp. 489-510, or Zbigniew Brzezinski, The Soviet Bloc: Unity and Conflict (Cambridge, Mass., 1960), p. 47.

10. Narodni fronta a komuniste: Ceskoslovensko, Jugoslavie, Polsko, 1938-1945 [The National Front and the Communists: Czechoslovakia, Yugoslavia, Poland] (Prague, 1968). Parallel editions in Serbo-Croatian and Polish.

11. In Vilem Precan, ed., Slovenske narodne povstanie: Dokumenty [The Slovak National Uprising: Documents] (Bratislava, 1965), pp. 37-43.

12. Ibid., p. 42. For an interpretation of the resolution by a moderate party historian, see Oldrich Janecek, "Na ceste k narodni fronte: K vyvoji politicke linie moskevskeho vedeni KSC v letech 1939, 1941-1943" [Toward the National Front: The Development of the Political Line of the Moscow Leadership of the Communist Party of Czechoslovakia], Odboj a revoluce, VII, 4 (1969), 208-20.

13. About the situation in individual countries: Gertrud Glondajewski and Heinz Schumann, Die Neubauer-Poser-Gruppe (Berlin, 1957), pp. 67-70; Die Kommunisten in Kampf für die Unabhängigkeit Österreichs (Vienna, 1955), pp. 139-41; Stanislav Kotrsal, "O cinnosti III. ilegalniho vedeni KSC" [The Activities of the Third Underground Leadership of the Communist Party of Czechoslovakia], Odboj a revoluce, V, 4 (1967), 7-46; Legyözhetetlen Erö: A Magyar Kommunista Mozgalom Szervezeti Fejlödësenek 50 Eve [Invincible Might: 50 Years of the Organizational Development of the Hungarian Communist Movement] (Budapest 1968), pp. 137-44.

14. Kotrsal, "O cinnosti...," pp. 33-34. Wolfgang Venohr, Aufstand für die Tschechoslowakei (Hamburg 1969), p. 65.

15. Hermann Mitterācker, Kampf und Opfer für Osterreich (Vienna, 1963), pp. 98-99. M. A. Poltavskii, "Ob osobennostiakh dvizheniia soprotivleniia v Avstrii" [Characteristics of the Resistance Movement in Austria], Novaia i noveishaia istoriia, No. 2 (1965), p. 112.

16. Kotrsal, "O cinnosti . . .," p. 34. Josef Klecka, "O zrade" [On Treason], Odboj a revoluce, V, 4 (1967), 47-52. Vilem Kahan, "O nekterych nedostatcich v konspirativni cinnosti" [Some Shortcomings in the Conspiratorial Activities], Odboj a revoluce, pp. 94-100.

17. Kotrsal, "O cinnosti . . . ," pp. 34-38. Josef Kral, "Organizace a struktura III. ilegalniho vedeni KSC v letech 1942-1943" [The Organization and Structure of the Underground Leadership of the Communist Party of Czechoslovakia in 1942-1943], Odboj a revoluce, VII, 4 (1969), 82-85.

18. Gerhard Rossmann, Der Kampf der KPD um die Einheit aller Hitlergegner (Berlin, 1963), p. 51. Gertrud Glondajewski and Gerhard Rossmann, "Ein bedeutendes politisches Dokument des illegalen antifaschistischen Kampfes der Kommunistischen Partei Deutschlands," BGDA, VIII (1966), pp. 647, 657.

19. Marian Malinowski, Antoni Przygonski, and Jerzy Pawlowicz, "Boj Polske delnicke strany o vytvoreni narodni fronty v letech druhe svetove valky" [The Struggle of the Polish Workers' Party for the Formation of a National Front in the Years of World War II], Narodni fronta a komuniste, pp. 290-91.

20. For examples of different views, see Franz Borkenau, European Communism (London, 1953), p. 282, and Kermit E. McKenzie, Comintern and World Revolution, 1938-1943 (New York, 1964), p. 190. Cf. also Alexander Dallin, "The Use of International Movements," in Ivo J. Lederer, ed., Russian Foreign Policy: Essays in Historical Perspective (New Haven, 1962), p, 329.

21. Wolfgang Leonhard, Child of the Revolution (London, 1958), p. 242.

22, Jane Degras, ed., The Communist International, 1919-1943: Documents, Vol. III (London, 1965), p. 479.

23. Ibid., p. 477.

24. Jesús Hernández, La grande trahison (Paris, 1953), p. 249. Cf. also Enrique Castro Delgado, Mi fe se perdió en Moscú (Mexico City, 1951), pp. 228-30.

25. Cf. Herbert Feis, Churchill, Roosevelt, Stalin (Princeton, N.J., 1967), pp. 23-24.

26. Ibid., pp. 57-64. Woodward, British Foreign Policy in the Second World War, Vol. II, p. 245.

27. Hopkins' memorandum on Roosevelt-Molotov conversation, May 29, 1942, FRUS, 1942, III, pp. 572-74.

28. Winston S. Churchill, The Hinge of Fate (Cambridge, Mass., 1950), p. 562.

29. Ibid., p. 803. A. Eden, "Post-War Settlement," Memorandum No. 292, July 1, 1943, CAB 66/38, PRO.

30. "A Four Years' Plan," in Winston S. Churchill, Onwards to Victory (London, 1944), pp. 33-45.

SPHERES OF INFLUENCE

31. "Britain, Russia, and Europe: Conditions of Continental Security," London Times, March 10, 1943.
32. Beaverbrook's memorandum, January 31, 1942, Hopkins Papers, Box 123, RG-24, F. D. Roosevelt Library (Hyde Park, N.Y.).
33. "Mr. Hull," Washington Post, November 12, 1943.
34. New York Herald Tribune, December 18, 1943, quoted in Andrzej Wojcik, The War Settlement in Eastern Europe (New York, 1964), p. 75.
35. Cf. Warren B. Walsh, "American Attitudes Toward Russia," Antioch Review, Vol. VII (1947), pp. 183-90, and Paul Willen, "Who 'Collaborated' with Russia?" Antioch Review, Vol. XIV (1954), pp. 259-83.
36. Piotr S. Wandycz, Czechoslovak-Polish Confederation and the Great Powers, 1940-43 (Bloomington, 1956), p. 81.
37. Robert E. Sherwood, Roosevelt and Hopkins (New York, 1948), p. 714. Eden, The Reckoning, p. 371.
38. Benes to Fierlinger, February 1943, Dokumenty z historie ceskoslovenske politiky [Documents on the History of Czechoslovak Politics, DHCSP], I (Prague, 1966), pp. 311-12.
39. Radomir Luza, The Transfer of the Sudeten Germans (New York, 1965), pp. 243-44.
40. Minutes of the Molotov-Eden conversation, June 9, 1942, Memorandum No. 220, CAB 66/24, PRO.
41. Foreign Commissariat to Bogomolov, April 21, 1943, Sovetsko-chekhoslovatskiie otnosheniia vo vremia Velikoi Otechestvennoi Voiny [Soviet-Czechoslovak Relations at the Time of the Great Patriotic War] (Moscow, 1960), p. 72. Smutny's note on conversation with Benes, April 24, 1943, DHCSP, I, pp. 327-28.
42. Cf. Vojtech Mastny, "The Benes-Stalin-Molotov Conversations in December 1943: New Documents," Jahrbücher für Geschichte Osteuropas, 1972.
43. Cf. F. A. Voigt, "Constants in Russian Foreign Policy," The Nineteenth Century and After, CXXXIV (1943), p. 246.
44. Mastny, "Stalin and the Prospect of a Separate Peace..."
45. Minutes of Roosevelt-Churchill conversation, May 12, 1943, FRUS, Conferences at Washington and Quebec, pp. 26-33. (See also note 29.)
46. Roosevelt to Stalin, May 5, 1943, Stalin's Correspondence with Roosevelt and Truman (New York, 1965), pp. 63-64. Standley to Secretary of State, May 25, 1943, FRUS, III, 1943, p. 654.
47. Ibid., p. 529. Cf. OSS report A-9072, August 3, 1943, RG-165, National Archives (Washington).
48. His statements are collected in President Benes on War and Peace (New York, 1943).

49. Speech at the University of Chicago, May 24, 1943, ibid., p. 91. Cf. Eduard Benes, "Russia and the Postwar World," Liberty, August 21, 1943, pp. 13-15, 72.

50. "Vystupleniie Benesha" [Benes's Address], Pravda and Izvestiia, May 22, 1943.

51. Ripka to Benes on conversation with Bogomolov, June 6, 1943, Sovetsko-chekhoslovatskiie otnosheniia, p. 85.

52. V. L. Israelian, Antigitlerovskaia koalitsiia [The Anti-Hitler Coalition] (Moscow, 1964), p. 268.

53. British Embassy to Department of State, August 28, 1943, FRUS, 1943, I, p. 515.

54. "Chto skryvaetsia za proektom Vostochnoevropeiskoi federatsii ili konfederatsii?," [What Is Behind the Project of the East European Federation or Confederation?], Voina in rabochii klass, July 15, 1943, pp. 23-27.

55. Cf. Memorandum No. 423, September 28, 1943, CAB 66/41 PRO.

56. Smutny's note on conversation with Benes, November 1, 1943, DHCSP, I, p. 407.

57. Eden's report to War Cabinet, July 5, 1943, Minutes No. 93, CAB 65, PRO.

58. See note 40.

59. Fierlinger to Benes on conversation with Korneichuk, July 14, 1943, Sovetsko-chekhoslovatskiie otnosheniia, p. 99. Cf. "K voprosu o poezdke g. Benesha v Moskvu" [Concerning Mr. Benes' Trip to Moscow], Voina i rabochii klass, October 1, 1943, pp. 21-23.

60. For example, Martin F. Herz, The Beginnings of the Cold War, reprinted in James V. Compton, ed., America and the Origins of the Cold War (Boston, 1972), p. 134.

61. "Suggested Principles Which Would Govern the Conclusion of Hostilities With the European Members of the Axis," FRUS, I, 1943, pp. 708-10.

62. Ibid., p. 709.

63. Stalin to Roosevelt and Churchill, August 22, 1943, FRUS, I, 1943, p. 782.

64. Stalin to Roosevelt and Churchill, September 12, 1943, ibid., p. 786. Cf. Molotov to Clark Kerr, October 14, 1943, Sovetsko-frantsuzskiie otnosheniia vo vremia Velikoi Otechestvennoi Voiny [Soviet-French Relations at the Time of the Great Patriotic War] (Moscow, 1959), p. 217.

65. Cf. Feis, Churchill, Roosevelt, Stalin, pp. 213-14.

66. Bogomolov to Foreign Commissariat, August 24, 1943, Sovetskochekhoslovatskiie otnosheniia, pp. 103-105. Foreign Commissariat to Bogomolov, October 2, 1943, ibid., pp. 107-09.

67. Ibid., p. 108.

SPHERES OF INFLUENCE   107

68. Ibid., pp. 108-09.
69. Smutny's note on conversation with Benes, September 28, 1943, DHCSP, I, p. 379.
70. Smutny's note, August 22, 1943, ibid., p. 362. Cf. his essay, October 4, 1943, ibid., pp. 383-87.
71. Note on Masaryk-Eden conversation, October 8, 1943, ibid., p. 388.
72. Cf. estimates from August 1943, ibid., II, pp. 721, 723.
73. Robert I. Gannon, The Cardinal Spellman Story (Garden City, 1962), p. 224.
74. Winston S. Churchill, Triumph and Tragedy (Cambridge, Mass., 1953), p. 227.
75. Summary of proceedings, session of October 26, 1943, FRUS, 1943, I, pp. 638-39. "Draft of Declaration on Joint Responsibility for Europe," ibid., pp. 736-37.
76. Summary of proceedings, session of October 30, 1943, ibid., p. 680.
77. "Declaration of Four Nations on General Security," November 1, 1943, ibid., pp. 755-56.
78. Summary of proceedings, session of October 24, 1943, ibid., p. 626.
79. Philip E. Mosely, The Kremlin and World Politics (New York, 1960), p. 200.

* * * * *

ANALYSES
1. John C. Campbell

This analysis covers three points. First, what Prof. Mastny said was the strategy of a broad coalition in relation to the postwar aims of the Soviet Union as conceived by Stalin and his colleagues in 1943; second, the dissolution of the Comintern; and third, some thoughts on the attitudes of the West.

Prof. Mastny's main argument is that the view that the Soviet Union strove for the division of Europe into spheres of influence during the postwar period is only a Western view. He closed his remarks by saying that it was really Western statesmen, representatives, and public opinion that advocated this cause, rather than Soviet leaders. He cites to support his thesis the lack of instructions

―――――――――

John C. Campbell is Senior Research Fellow at the Council on Foreign Relations, New York.

to Communist parties to prepare to take power after the war, and
also the general line given to them ordering cooperation with other
anti-fascists, progressives and other groups fighting against the
Germans. I think perhaps that one should look at this evidence also
in the framework of the fact that the war was in progress and that
much of what was said publicly by the Soviet government and much of
what was said privately to its fraternal Communist parties in occupied
territory had to do with the fighting of the war. Emphasis was placed
on creating trouble for the Germans, and this could be done better by
collaboration among forces, Communist and non-Communist, that
were in the resistance rather than by giving orders to the Communists
to prepare to take over power themselves at some given time.

Much of the Soviet attitude in this period, moreover, had to do
with the fact that they did have to take account of their Western allies
and needed their help. For example, the instructions or the advice
that they gave to the Yugoslavs—to Marshal Tito—not to create too
much trouble for the government of King Peter by setting up a specifically
Communist regime and to continue collaboration with non-
Communist parties seem to confirm the view that the interests of the
Soviet Union were to get the maximum amount of coordinated resistance
and to have the least trouble with Western allies, on whose
help the Soviet Union depended in large degree.

Prof. Mastny's study then presents the idea that the Soviet Union
attempted to attain eventual political hegemony in Europe through
mixed governments in which there would be Communist participation,
that is, a political strategy in lieu of military occupation and one in
which there would not be a grab for power on the part of the Communists
alone. He presents this as a policy of the Soviet Union for
the whole of Europe, from Poland all the way to the Atlantic. One
wonders how much of a distinction this really is. Clearly they were
giving thought to the possible occupation of some countries; they
must have expected to share in the occupation of Germany. This was
certainly in the wind as they were leading up to the international
conferences that took place at the end of 1943. At what point they
may have made some decision not to stop at their own frontiers but
to go forward is not clear. I do not know the whole story of the attempts
at separate negotiations for peace or some kind of truce with the
Germans. Nevertheless it does seem that they must have looked
forward to political action that they would take as their armies crossed
the frontiers established in 1939-41.

Actually, the strategy that Prof. Mastny's paper describes is
what turned out to be their policy in Western Europe after the war.
It is clear that at least in France and Italy they did hope that the
Communist Parties would play a considerable role in the politics
of those countries, stay within coalition governments, and, in effect,

SPHERES OF INFLUENCE

serve Soviet interests. But this seems like a minimum for what they must have expected for Eastern Europe. Was this not perhaps a stage, particularly in their dealings with President Benes of Czechoslovakia, that they expected to turn to at a later time, and in fact did? It may also be argued that this was necessary for a displacement of any real power still remaining in the hands of bourgeois parties and for the introduction of a kind of national front in which the Communist Party would have as its partners only those remnants of the non-Communist parties or constructed pseudoparties with which they would presumably but not actually share power. If they had this in mind for Czechoslovakia, is this also necessarily the case for Poland? Prof. Mastny's study presents a bit of evidence indicating that perhaps the Communists in Poland would have to make it on their own somehow without military occupation by the Soviet Union, although it is questionable how realistic this is. After all, from the time of the break of relations with the Polish government-in-exile in London after the Katyn affair was made public, were they not preparing their own government for Poland through the Union of Polish Patriots, which was the nucleus of the Committee of National Liberation that they eventually set up in Lublin? It is surely open to question, therefore, whether there was any time when they seriously felt that they would not go beyond the line of 1941 in Poland, the line on which Stalin and Hitler had agreed before the war even started.

Another point the paper makes is that Stalin was concerned lest the individual Communist Parties and their leaderships in Europe become too strong and too ambitious for power and therefore escape from his control. Was he thinking of Yugoslavia at this time, in 1943, and is there any other evidence about such thoughts with respect to any other Communist Party in Europe? Central Europe was indeed remote in 1943 at the time that the Russians were just beginning to move westward from Stalingrad toward Kursk, though the tide definitely had turned. They knew they were coming back; their policy was one of keeping open their opportunities, as the study says. Certainly they played on this national front theme both in their public propaganda and in the creation of groups like the Polish group and the German National Committee in Moscow. It seems rather difficult to believe that Stalin ruled out the kind of situation and policy that actually happened when his troops entered Polish territory in 1944.

The dissolution of the Comintern was indeed a more complex matter than has been generally assumed. Comments on it here are limited to those that relate to what has been said above. In getting rid of an organization that perhaps they felt had served its purposes and might be in the way of their direct relationship with and control of Communist Parties in the various countries of Europe, the Soviet leaders had devised a differentiated approach, geared to the different conditions of countries where there could be no commonly proclaimed Comintern doctrine that covered what they wanted to do. There would be certain territories in which the Red Army would be present as an occupying power alone. There would be other territories in which by agreements with the Western allies, as in Germany, there would be different zones of occupation and different policies in each case. Others would be under new national governments, over which Moscow would have varying degrees of influence. So far as Western Europe was concerned, the Soviets would necessarily want to have flexible means and policies in order to deal with each situation, particularly in the use of Communist Parties in France and in Italy. The distinction between friendly and enemy countries was made only for tactical reasons, it would seem.

Finally, a few points about Western policies and attitudes, especially those of the United States. Prof. Mastny says that it was really the West that awakened the Soviets to the idea of spheres of influence and that heretofore the Soviet Union had not been thinking very much in those terms. The question of Roosevelt has always been a puzzle. He, more than anyone else, had the idea that Russia had a place in Europe, west of its own frontiers, but he was never very specific as to what he had in mind. He had some idea, as he expressed it to Harry Hopkins and others, that Russia was like a big St. Bernard dog that maybe somehow would be housebroken if we just let it into Europe, but at the same time we should have a leash as well as a mop in the closet. But he was not specific on the concept of the four policemen and this was never developed into a policy by the Department of State or by any other branch of the government. It is difficult to draw from the concept of the four policemen that he had an awareness of the threat of Soviet domination of Europe or any part of Europe. Prof. Mastny cites remarks as reported by Cardinal Spellman as follows: "A lot of Europe is going to have to live under Soviet domination for awhile and maybe eventually they will get out of it." One wonders just how much weight to put on that, or whether this really represents Roosevelt's thought or not.

Prof. Mastny writes of the idea of granting the Soviet Union a sphere of influence in Europe as one that gained great popularity in the United States. It is true that Walter Lippmann wrote about it in this sense. It is true also that the Washington Post and other newspapers were speaking along those lines at the time. However, it is hard to determine what this meant for the formulation of governmental policy. It seems to me that perhaps something should be said of the poor old Department of State, which has been the target for most of the abuse for all that went wrong at that time and since. Certainly it never had in mind, in any of its postwar planning, the division of Europe into spheres of influence. It had more and not less apprehensions as the war went on and Soviet forces approached Europe. It was not prepared to recognize any sphere when Cordell Hull went to Moscow for the Moscow Conference in 1943. It was not going to oppose the return of the Soviet Union to its 1941 borders, although there was a question of just where the final borders might be. We certainly were not going to take a stand for the frontiers set by the Treaty of Riga. Nevertheless it is quite clear that there was no idea that the Soviet Union would have any right to dominate territories it occupied west of the Curzon Line and the Prut River, although we were aware that it could assert itself in spite of its allies. Certainly we were not going to use military measures to oppose it, but nevertheless the fact that American policy remained on the same principle of no spheres of influence was true in 1943 as well as in 1944, and even when we met Soviet policy with the Declaration of Liberated Europe at Yalta.

2. Herbert S. Dinerstein

Professor Mastny has made a very good case of Soviet war aims on the basis of the positions and actions of Communist Parties in wartime Europe. But he has also given us a sense of the opportunities that they did not take.

Mr. Campbell, while accepting Professor Mastny's evidence, argues that Russian war aims went beyond their statements to others. The question has been posed, but can the differences be composed? I do not think they can, but in our profession we have to try. The approach that I would like to suggest is a very familiar one, that is, to try to reconstruct as best we can Stalin's rationale. We must start with the assumption, and we have lots of evidence on that score, that his rationale was not ours and there is not much point in calling it rational or irrational. What we are really interested in is trying to reconstruct the picture he had of the way that events were shaped. I think the most important thing to say, and this applies as much to other statesmen as to Stalin, is that 95 percent of our clues should be sought in domestic politics, not foreign politics. This is true for any nation; anyone who attempts to understand Franklin Roosevelt's foreign policy would be well advised to try to understand his relations with some of the individuals prominent on the American political scene.

Herbert S. Dinerstein is Andrew W. Mellon Professor of Soviet Studies at the School of Advanced International Studies, The Johns Hopkins University, Washington.

What do we know about Stalin's own life experience? We know that he felt that most friends become traitors and he had most of his closest associates put to death. It he was anything like the rest of us, he had to believe that he did it for a good reason, that they were indeed traitors. He was therefore very suspicious of all his associates, especially those that might be influenced by his opponents. Stalin's very hard course toward other Communist Parties, as we all know, antedated the outbreak of World War II. The Polish and the Korean parties had been abolished and others had come close to the same fate. The course of the war convinced Stalin that these parties were not to be trusted. As Prof. Mastny describes it in his study, agents sent to make contact with the Germans were soon picked up by the latter, who obviously had prior knowledge; this of course meant that the parties were infiltrated, and were creatures of foreign intelligence. Since the Soviet Union itself was very active in this kind of activity, there was a kind of professional appreciation for German competence. This reinforced Stalin's inclination to distrust independent people he could not manage. He was therefore very sensitive to proof of the untrustworthiness of Communist Parties. I might repeat an anecdote that one of his still prominent Soviet admirers told me about these parties. I am not sure that this admirer was totally serious but I think he might have been. A few years ago he asked me a peculiar question: Why was Castro making so much trouble for the Soviet Union? I said that it was all the Russians' fault, that they should not have dissolved the Comintern. His reply gave me reason to think. He said: "We did not dissolve the Comintern; it dissolved itself. They ran away." Whether he was serious or not, I think this does reflect the then prevailing Soviet attitude about these parties. There was more trouble to be derived from trying to deal with them than from letting them find their own way.

I would like to suggest one more reason why Stalin had such limited expectations of the activities of the Communist Parties of Central Europe (I am using the word limited in reference to Western fears and apprehensions). Here I think that Stalin was very much the victim of his own political history, which he translated into an ideology. In fact most people who come from nowhere and become great men believe they have discovered universal political wisdom; it would be difficult for them to believe anything else. Stalin thought he knew all about history because he thought he knew all about the Russian Revolution; although his views may not coincide with ours, they very much influenced his view toward Central Europe. To put it in his language, he did not believe a revolutionary situation existed in Central Europe. After all, he was in the underground of the Bolshevik Party in 1915 and 1916. Although by now the view may have changed, I think that in the middle of World War II most top-level Russian Communists, including Stalin, believed the Russian Revolution had been led by the proletariat. I do not think they believed—as some of us did—that in February the Russian government fell apart because of the blows of the war and that the coup d'etat of October was consolidated by two years of civil war during which the army and the police were created. I think they really believed that in some mystical way (and anyone who believes in myths about his own history has to be mystical) the proletariat were the dominant force in 1917. If you looked around Eastern Europe and at the history of these Communist Parties between the two wars, with the exception perhaps of Czechoslovakia how could you believe that the proletariat was a dominant class and that the vanguard in those countries counted, when Stalin could pay them, or withhold payment, could give life or could withhold it? How could he respect people over whom he had so much power? The remark that Stalin made to Ambassador Bohlen during the war was revealing. He said to Bohlen that the German proletariat was a great disappointment during the war because they were Nazis, of course. I think that Stalin really believed that his vision of the history of the Russian Revolution applied to Central Europe in 1943. And if that reading is valid then it should be clear that there was no possibility that Communist Parties could be in a position to take power. This, I think, represents quite a change from 1939 when, judging from the discussions in the Party Congress, there was an anticipation that the next world war would produce the kind of social upheaval in Western European countries that occurred in Russia in 1917. By the middle of the war Stalin had given up that hope.

I have not answered the question of what the Russians were up to, and what were their aims. I think that like most historical questions, we will have to deal with it in this general way even when we have much more information than we have now.

3. Richard Löwenthal

Prof. Mastny's very stimulating study has, in my view, two great merits. One of them has been repeatedly mentioned, namely that he has gone to the new source materials recently published in Eastern Europe. I have not as yet had the advantage of studying these publications, and I am grateful to him for drawing our attention to them. The other great merit is that he has focused on the year 1943. I have always felt that the so-called revisionist American historians, in moving the date of the origins of the Cold War from

---

Richard Löwenthal is Professor of International Relations at Free University, Berlin, Federal Republic of Germany.

1947 to 1945 had not gone far enough, and that the real origin of the conflict was a grave crisis of confidence among the Allies that occurred in 1943.

Beyond this point, however, I find myself in disagreement with Prof. Mastny's interpretation. Permit me to begin not with Communist Party evidence but with Prof. Mastny's view of the origin of the partition of Europe, of the role of the concepts of the Western powers for postwar Europe, and of the alternatives to its partition into spheres of influence.

Prof. Mastny seems to take it for granted that the concept of spheres of influence is morally reprehensible, and I agree with Mr. Campbell that this is in keeping with the tradition of most American political thinking during the war. I am not in that tradition; I believe that there is really no alternative to spheres of influence. I do not mean this in the sense of rigidly controlled empires, as the Soviets understood it, for that is not a natural thing in world affairs. But great-power spheres of influence, in the sense of regional differences between who has influence where, seem to be a normal fact of international life. The opposite concept, advocated above all by Secretary of State Cordell Hull during the war, that after the war there should emerge some form of condominium of the great powers in Europe, supervised by the United Nations, which would insure that there would be no such wicked thing as spheres of influence, has always appeared to me utterly vague and woolly. What I should reproach the Western powers with is not that they agreed to spheres of influence but that they did not take sufficient care to see that the borders of the spheres of influence came to lie further east.

In fact, the actual spheres of influence were determined more by military events than by diplomatic negotiations. The major controversy over military strategy among the Western Allies during the war was due to the fact that Churchill was convinced of the inevitability of spheres of influence. I believe he never seriously entertained the idea that a regional confederation in Eastern Europe could be an actual alternative to spheres of influence, as Prof. Mastny seems to believe.

There were basically three possibilities in my view. Either there would be a peace with Hitler's Germany such as the Russians had at one time tried to get, or with an alternative Germany before Germany was utterly destroyed, which would still leave some core of German power in the center of Europe; or Germany would be destroyed and a new structure created in its place—whether a regional confederation or something else—that would necessarily be under the influence of either the Western powers or Russia. The regional confederation in East Central Europe that Churchill envisaged would have constituted a formidable Western sphere of influence, and it was very natural that the Russians opposed it.

SPHERES OF INFLUENCE

Now to Soviet war aims. In my opinion, Stalin never had the slightest doubt that he wanted to push his sphere of power as far west as possible. I do not think he had the kind of concept in mind that Prof. Mastny outlines, of keeping every European country weak by having Communists in their bellies, so to speak, through national-front coalitions. I think he wanted very much more than that, particularly in the countries that were closest to the Soviet Union. I do not think that he had committed himself in advance as to how far his sphere would extend, because he knew that this depended on the course of the war; and in early 1943 he did not know when the Western Allies would land. He also did not know how much blood it would still cost him to get rid of the Germans. After all, the main motivation of his bid for a separate peace with Hitler and of his second bid for a possible separate peace with the German Army by means of the National Committee for a Free Germany and the League of German Officers was to drive the Germans out of his country with a minimum expenditure of blood, strength, and destruction; for that he was willing to pay the price of leaving some kind of Germany intact. Thus the whole question of how soon the war would end and at what frontiers the armies would then stand was entirely undecided in early 1943, and therefore Stalin could not then have, in my opinion, a clear view as to how far his sphere would extend.

However, Stalin was extremely clear that he was not going to accept the Polish government-in-exile in London, even before the Katyn affair led to an open break with it. Starting in January 1943, Stalin made deliberate preparations for an alternative to the Polish government-in-exile in London. The Union of Polish Patriots has been mentioned by Mr. Campbell. At the same time, he had the Krajowa Rada Narodowa set up in Poland as a counter organization to the government-in-exile in London. Third, there was the creation of the army corps of General Berling as an alternative to the army of General Anders. Prof. Mastny quotes documents that the Polish Communists complained about being pressured to have better relations with the underground working for the London government. I do not know what the date of this document is, but I would venture a guess that, unlike the Yugoslavs, who were pressured by Stalin to arrive at an agreement with their government-in-exile in London, the Polish Communists were mainly pressured to try to wean the non-Communist underground from the London government. This, because it was quite clear to Stalin that the Polish government-in-exile was not going to accept the Soviet frontier established by the agreement reached by Stalin and Hitler on which the Soviet Union had determined to insist.

Further, the meaning of "National Front" for the Soviets in occupied Europe was much more ambiguous than Prof. Mastny has presented it. They were, in the first stage, again as Mr. Campbell has said, to be used to fight the Germans, and here the broadest possible front was desired. But, at the same time, Stalin's push for a more independent policy of the Communist movements in these fronts began early in the spring of 1943. The French Communists started an attack on the allegedly <u>attentiste</u> strategy of General De Gaulle, and began a push forward for a leading role in the National Council of the French Resistance. At the same time, the Greek Communists began to crack down on all non-Communist resistance groups. Thus it can be seen that, as early as the spring of 1943, Stalin, while still formally adhering to the concept of the National Front, started to push the Communists toward assuming a more independent stance with a view to furthering his postwar aims, and he did so in an atmosphere of crisis in his relations with the Allies that had just begun to develop.

Finally, I would suggest that the dissolution of the Comintern had its meaning precisely in that context. The dissolution of the Comintern did not take place at a time of harmony in relations with the Western Allies. It took place after Katyn in May 1943, and it was directly connected, in my view, with a kind of swarming out of exiled Communist leaders to the West. It was at that time that Andre Marty went to Algiers to lead a more active Communist policy in the French underground. This was in accordance with a general policy of permitting the Communist parties to take a more offensive line in every sense of the term. They had to do this on their own initiative, since the Soviet Union itself did not want to take public responsibility for this offensive line. Thus the dissolution of the Comintern was not simply a concession to the Western allies, and was not merely intended for propaganda purposes. I agree with Prof. Mastny on that. It was, rather, a change in the type of division of labor between the Soviet Union and the national Communist parties. I also agree with him that the book by Jesús Hernández is by far the best source for inside information that we have on this.

Let me sum up what I have tried to say. I think that the Russians had a natural commitment to a policy of spheres of influence because, as realistic politicians, they never believed in any viable alternative. A specific Soviet postwar program, however, had to await developments of the course of the war and the movement of armies. However, beginning with the spring of 1943 the Soviets embarked on a more independent European policy as part of the crisis of confidence in their relations with the Western powers.

4. Jovan Marjanovic

As a historian, I feel obliged to state that Prof. Mastny's study has relied mainly on secondary sources, as Prof. Mastny himself mentioned. I am quite aware of the fact this this is not his fault, and

I also regret that the primary documents concerning foreign policies of the Soviet Union, England, and the United States during World War II are still classified and therefore not available to scholars. British Foreign Office documents will be declassified in January 1972, but no one knows when we will have an opportunity to consult Soviet documents, which are the most important sources for the theme under discussion. In spite of these problems I appreciate Prof. Mastny's report, which very bravely draws attention to many complex and interesting problems in the history of World War II and especially of the Soviet war aims in 1943.

Prof. Mastny's conclusions, since made without the benefit of primary, and especially primary Soviet sources, are, in my opinion, one-sided. However, I appreciate his objectivity as reflected in his variegated approach to different Soviet actions and measures during 1943, especially with respect to Czechoslovakia and Poland. It is helpful and even necessary to draw these kinds of conclusions even before access to Soviet sources is granted, for there could be a very long wait. For example, Yugoslav historians up to now have had no opportunity to consult all Russian sources on the Serbian uprising of 1804-12!

I would like to comment on three points in this analysis. First, the opening of a second front in the Balkans; second, the National Front; and third, the meaning for the Soviet Union of the opening of the second front on the Atlantic shore. I am in full agreement with Prof. Mastny's statement concerning British intentions to open a new front in the Balkan Peninsula. This is a very important question in the European history of World War II. You should be aware of the two standpoints in the historiography of World War II on this question. The majority of British historians claim that Churchill and British Army Headquarters never had plans for a landing in the Balkan peninsula, on the Adriatic coast in particular. The second viewpoint, held by a great number of American historians, and Matlov in particular, has come up with a good deal of evidence on British intentions to open a second front throughout the Balkan Peninsula. Let me mention Alexander Voigt's book Pax Britannica in which he refers to the Salonika-Belgrade-Budapest-Warsaw line, which was a strategy to prevent the advance of the Red Army into Central Europe. I assume that you know of Churchill's intentions after the surrender of Italy to advance through the Ljubljana Gap in the direction of Vienna and Prague. I can assure you that these British intentions played a very

---

Jovan Marjanovic is Professor of History at the University of Belgrade.

great role in the behavior of the Mihailovic and Chetnik groups, but in my opinion Prof. Mastny does not sufficiently establish the connection between British intentions to open a second front in the Balkans on the one hand, and Soviet war aims with respect to Central Europe in 1943 on the other.

In reading Prof. Mastny's study concerning the National Front, I again have the impression of a one-sided viewpoint. One can be in full agreement with his statement that the Communists intended through the Popular Front to come to power in some Central European countries. But there is evidence that the combined force of anti-fascist groups against German occupying forces was very useful. The idea of a Popular Front was conceived, as I well know, in 1935 at the Seventh Comintern Congress. Unfortunately we do not have serious monographs about the Popular Fronts in Spain, France, and other countries in the prewar period, a subject that deserves careful research. It is not enough to say that the Popular Front and the National Front were only tools of Communist strategy to take control of different countries and different peoples; one should also take into consideration the effectiveness of the National Front strategy in the resistance movements of different European countries. I am aware of the fact that this is a very controversial problem, but may I ask what historical problem is not controversial?

Lastly, I would like to comment on the Soviet request to open a second front on the Atlantic. On this point I am in full agreement with Prof. Löwenthal. Prof. Mastny underestimates the extent of casualties on the Soviet Eastern front. In demanding the opening of a second front, Stalin's primary aim was to limit the number of Soviet casualties, already enormous, by holding down a number of German divisions on the Western front, thus easing the position of the Soviet Army on the Eastern front. I am conscious of the fact that along with its primary aim of smashing the Nazi state, the Soviet leadership had certain other war aims, but I view these aims as having been secondary in 1943. I also think, in all fairness, it must be stated that Soviet war aims during the war accommodated to prevailing circumstances and I would ask Prof. Mastny to explain how these accommodations were made.

5. Henry L. Roberts

I will limit my comments to a couple of methodological and conceptual problems in Professor Mastny's study. On the conceptual

---

Henry L. Roberts is Professor of History at Dartmouth College, Hanover, N.H.

SPHERES OF INFLUENCE

side, I found some difficulty in coming to grips with his terms, especially those relating to the shape of post-Hitlerian Europe and of Russia's intended role in it. There are five possibilities that emerge through the text in a somewhat kaleidoscopic fashion; some of these are given rather short shrift, while others are made central. He refers to "the lofty principles of the Atlantic Charter" but quickly dismisses the Charter as not being a serious possibility. The possibility of a great social upheaval, in the form of a massive popular revolution, flickers in and out, and here I think he is correct in saying that this was not central to Stalin's thought.

But there are three more serious possibilities within the frame of this study. One is the prospect of some type of European integration, federation, or confederation, arising out of the collapse of the Hitlerian Empire, advocated principally by Churchill to provide some kind of viable structure for Europe following the war. The second is the conscious partitioning, or the natural development, of spheres of influence throughout Europe between Eastern and Western powers. The third is the possibility of Soviet hegemony on the continent as a whole. It is very hard to relate these terms logically to one another, and it seems to me quite evident from the exposition that the theme of confederation or federation proposed by Churchill was advanced with the clear purpose of holding Russia back at least to its frontiers of 1940. If you are supporting a Polish-Czech federation as an independent entity, for example, the implication clearly is that this would mean that Soviet influence would be stopped at its frontier, wherever that might be drawn. On the question of the Soviet position on spheres of influence as against hegemony, on the whole Prof. Mastny suggests that the Soviets in this period were not interested in the idea of spheres of influence but favored hegemony, whereas, increasingly, the Americans and the British tended to drift away from the notion of Central European federations and toward a division into spheres of influence. But here again, as Prof. Löwenthal and Mr. Campbell have pointed out, these are not altogether distinct possibilities. In particular, it is not clear to me whether Prof. Mastny, in speaking of hegemony, means hegemony over Central and Eastern Europe, as he puts it in some places; or a less limited hegemony, conceivably over the continent as a whole; or the possibility, if one may refer to the Mackinder domino theory, that the former implies the latter, that hegemony over Eastern Europe implies hegemony over Central Europe, which in turn implies hegemony over Europe as a whole. In this case a sphere of influence could also point to hegemony over the whole of Europe. We simply have to face the old problem, common to all power politics relating to spheres and hegemony, that one man's teeter is another's totter.

This leads to a second question, a methodological one, about the evidence put forward regarding Soviet interest in the direction of hegemony as against partitioning or spheres of influence. As has been pointed out, the problem of obtaining evidence is a tough one. I had a slightly uncomfortable feeling, however, that by the end of the study the notion of a specific Soviet design for continental hegemony had to some extent become reinforced through repetition rather than accumulated evidence.

Prof. Mastny does indicate that, as of 1943, Russia was still very much occupied with the war, with Hitler's armies still deep in the heart of Russia, and that the first move onto the European continent was made by the Western Allies with the invasion of Sicily. At this point he stresses the fact that Russia seemed to be very remote from Central Europe, whereas the Western powers were beginning to move in. There were, to be sure, all the problems and uncertainties of the second front, specifically where it would be opened, how soon, and how fast it would advance, but I find the view of a Russian expectation that the Western powers could not attempt to fill the vacuum resulting from the extinction of German power very unpersuasive indeed.

Finally, one point that emerges periodically relates to the possibilities, in 1943, of Russia reaching some type of accommodation or armistice with Germany. My comment here is simply that the definition of what is involved makes a great deal of difference. Does it mean a specific arrangement or armistice with Hitler while he is still in power? An approach to military, conservative, or other possible opposition groups in conjunction with the disappearance of Hitler, one way or another, from power? Or the remote hope of a massive upheaval? Certainly, decisive to any serious prospect is whether this kind of arrangement could be made before or only after Hitler was ousted from power.

CHAPTER 5

THE NATIONAL QUESTION AND THE POLITICAL SYSTEMS OF EASTERN EUROPE

Paul Shoup

The purpose of this study is to consider the impact of nationality problems on the political institutions of Eastern Europe. The decision to undertake such work is based on the fact that the topic, although not a new one, has seldom been approached in a methodical fashion. The discussion that follows, as a consequence, brings together many disparate elements: it includes consideration of both national minorities and multinational states; it is concerned both with the impact of nationalities on the events of 1956 and the emergence of federal systems in Yugoslavia and Czechoslovakia; and it deals briefly with the interwar period as well as the period of Communist rule.

While it is not the intention to enter into a lengthy theoretical analysis of the task we are engaged in, several points of clarification are in order.

The first concerns the way in which we understand our subject; that is, what we mean by the interrelationship between political development and the national question. We are all well aware that the fate of Eastern European governments has been tied to nationalities disputes; in an extreme case, such as Czechoslovakia in 1938, such a situation has resulted in a change in the nature of the political system itself (the replacement of the democratic parties with the "Party of National Solidarity" and the adoption of a quasi-federal system under the terms of the Zilina agreement). Where such a dramatic change does not seem likely, as in the case in Eastern Europe

---

Paul Shoup is Professor of Government and Foreign Affairs at the University of Virginia, Charlottesville.

today, the problem of the nationalities* or minorities is commonly viewed in the context of the "subversion" of Communist authority, or the "triumph" of nationalism over Communism.

The intention is to view the national question in a broader perspective. Somewhat loosely, we might consider this as an attempt to analyze the systemic interactions of politics and the national question or, simply, the long-term effects of the national question on the political institutions and political practices of Eastern Europe. When we say that our subject has not been treated in a methodical way, it is this type of relationship we have in mind.

An effort of this kind would not have been undertaken if we did not feel it could be productive and shed some light on conditions in Eastern Europe. It will become clear that we feel that interesting connections do exist between nationality problems and political development. One might wish to ask, for example, why "revisionist" or "liberal" Communism has emerged in its most complete form in the two multinational states of Eastern Europe.** Was there a connection in these cases between liberalizing trends and nationality relationships? In attempting to deal with this question, further, we have found it worthwhile to consider broader issues concerning the relationship between the national question in the multinational states of Eastern Europe today (Yugoslavia and Czechoslovakia) and in the developing nations of the non-Communist world. Comments on the notion of "manipulative federalism" reflect this broader concern.

Speculative hypotheses are nevertheless best discussed within the context of concrete historical situations. Since we believe the national question has great continuity in Eastern Europe, we have not hesitated to allude to events taking place in the interwar period, as well as to acquaint the reader with the most essential aspects of the recent national crisis in Yugoslavia (not well-known outside of Yugoslavia itself, but of great importance for Eastern Europe), and the problem

---

*For the sake of convenience, the term "nationalities" will be used to refer to the Slav nationalities of Czechoslovakia and Yugoslavia, the two multinational states considered in our account.

**As so stated, the question is loaded somewhat to exclude the events preceding the revolution in Hungary in 1956, and assumes that the post-1968 developments in Czechoslovakia, because they were the result of Soviet intervention, do not constitute the natural outcome of the system that was being developed in the summer of 1968. The reader is not asked to accept these assumptions as indisputable, but to consider them for the sake of the arguments that follow.

THE NATIONAL QUESTION

of the Slovaks in Czechoslovakia at the time of the Czech "spring" (a subject which is indeed very familiar to many of those who will read this study).

Several remarks on the scope and character of the national question in Eastern Europe are in order at this point. We must recognize the fact that in the period under consideration the scope of the national question has undergone considerable change. In the interwar period the majority of Eastern European states had larger minority populations than they do now. And there is no doubt that the character of the national question in the interwar period was much more complex than it is now. It involved, for example, problems of social classes to a much greater degree than today. It reflected, further, a much more complex historical situation, and it embodied a much greater range of clashing political philosophies. Finally, the overriding question of the interwar period was security, and the national question impinged on this concern to a much greater extent then than at the present time.

There is nevertheless the possibility that the national question has had a somewhat greater impact on the political institutions of Eastern Europe after World War II than before. Several factors have been at work in the postwar period that have tended to enhance the impact of the national question in those states where the problem could still be said to exist to a measurable degree. One such factor has been the recognition of the multinational character of Yugoslavia and Czechoslovakia by the postwar regimes. One should not consider this simply a Communist maneuver; on the contrary, this policy reflected a change in thinking that was already at work before the war, a change that led to the discrediting of the notion of the existence of a Czechoslovak or Yugoslav nation and that the Communist regimes could not, even when they wished to, reverse. With the recognition as distinct nationalities of the Macedonians, Slovaks, and Montenegrins, in addition to the Serbs, Czechs, Croats and Slovenes, came a whole new set of problems with which we shall be deeply concerned in this study.

A second factor we would like to stress in respect to the postwar national question is the dynamic nature of the political systems of Eastern Europe. This dynamism derived from two sources: the revolutionary nature of the governments, which created new opportunities for rising elites, and the need for constant reform, stemming from the excesses of totalitarian rule. These changes have been accompanied by social and economic transformations that have had a deep impact on the national question, encouraging the emergence of new national elites, creating an awareness of national cultures, and stimulating economic competition as well as rivalry for investment funds among regional governments. We may point to one Slav nationality—the Slovaks—and one large minority—the Albanians in Yugoslavia—as outstanding examples of groups caught up in this kind of change.

Naturally this political and social dynamism improves the chances that the national question will have some impact on political institutions, either when the process of reform gets under way from above, or the forces of social change and elite development press on the government from below.

We would also like, in these introductory remarks, to comment briefly on what remains unchanging, in our view, in the national question in Eastern Europe.

Clearly one constant thread in the evolution of the national question has been the highly developed historical sense and the stress on the continuity of national development that permeates the thinking of national groups. In this connection we may note that one quality that distinguishes the Eastern European attitude from that of regional groups in underdeveloped countries is the sense of belonging to a "nation," by which is meant a group with a historical personality, as well as a distinct ethnic or cultural identity. Today, as in the past, the defense of the reputation of the "nation," no less than the protection of the rights of the individual, provide a focus for nationalism in Eastern Europe.

The Eastern European nationality problem has also remained largely unchanged over the years in respect to the emphasis placed on communal solidarity, or ethnicity; what Macartney called "personal nationalism."[1] In this respect Eastern European national feelings can be said to differ from national feelings in the West, but resemble the nationalism of emerging groups in the developing countries.

One additional point should be made in reference to the problems of the minorities. As has been pointed out,[2] European minorities are distinguished from the population around them not only by ethnic criteria but by the fact that they are linked, by the bond of nationality, to a nation-state in Europe outside that country in which they reside.*
This was of immense importance in the interwar period, when the problem of the "national" minorities sprang not primarily from the fact that the new nation states were still ethnically heterogeneous, but because every minority was, as it were, the representative of a nearby European state, a foreign power that was more often than not a

---

*In Eastern Europe there are, as we know, "nonnational" minorities, such as Gypsies, Vlachs, and perhaps Jews that do not fit this criterion.

threat to the national security of the country, even when the problem of irredenta was not immediately at issue.*

Menzel, in the work just cited, has noted that although this structural feature of the minority problem in Europe remains unchanged, its significance in Western Europe has altered because of increased contacts among nations and decreasing national rivalries, as well as the disappearance of the problem of national security. Eastern Europe would also like to reach this stage, and certain significant changes have taken place, especially in respect to the problem of security. Nevertheless, her minority problems have not been "modernized," as it were, along the Western European model, to the point where they are of secondary importance. This point will be elaborated as the discussion proceeds.

We would like to close these introductory comments with a few observations on the national question in the interwar period.

The national question was a burden for the interwar governments in innumerable ways: it posed the constant threat of separatism; it encouraged political protest and was a spawning ground for radical movements; and, of course, it slowed the process of integration and assimilation of territories acquired by the new states as a result of the Versailles settlements. As Erwin Viefhaus observed in his monograph on the minority question,[3] the interwar regimes faced the multiple burden of consolidating their rule, developing democratic institutions, and finding a solution to their nationalities problems. With the exception of Czechoslovakia, these tasks proved beyond the strength and skills of the governments of the time. The central governments, backed by the dominant national group and in control of the bureaucracy and army, were able to prevail in the short run but were never strong enough to assimilate the minorities or Slav nationalities ranged against them. The minorities and discontented nationalities could never gain control of the central governments, and were in many cases deprived of privileged positions they had enjoyed before the war.

The issue of decentralization and regional autonomy was debated back and forth for a decade after the war, but little progress was

---

*Of course there were important differences among the minority groups. At one extreme there were what Macartney referred to as the "frontier" nationalities. At the other were the "loyal" minorities: the Germans and the Baltic states, Hungary and Rumania, and the Czechoslovak and Slovak minorities in Yugoslavia.

made toward real reform.* With the collapse of parliamentary government and the rise of international tensions in the 1930s, the ability of the East European governments to survive any experiment in the devolution of power was open to question. Internally weak, and threatened from without, the only course open to governments of Eastern Europe was to rely on the existing bureaucracies and those national elites that had a stake in the maintenance of the system. By the mid-1930s this trend reached its highest point of development; most local administrations were organized directly under the Ministry of the Interior within a dozen or so large provinces over which the governments could exert direct control.

The trend in Yugoslavia was broken by the Sporazum of 1939 that granted Croatia autonomy. It is possible that this agreement could have led to the wide devolution of the powers of the central government in Yugoslavia (there was talk of giving the remaining banovina autonomy when Peter came of age in 1941). Nevertheless the immediate aim of the agreement was to strengthen the central government by granting special favors to the Croats. The granting of autonomy to one area did not therefore solve, once and for all, the problem of the central government and its relationship with the dominant nationality, or the question of whether central government powers could in fact be divided and shared, in some type of federal system, with the provinces. Suspicions of the central government— based not on a belief in the merits of decentralization, but on a fear of exploitation by the dominant nationality—lived on and continued to play a major role in postwar political attitudes.

The political life of the period reflected the turbulence created by the national question. The national controversy was directly responsible for the collapse of parliamentary government in Yugoslavia and encouraged the emergence of authoritarian governments in Poland and Romania. At the same time the actions of the minority or regional parties often served to encourage the governments of the Eastern European states to avoid giving the national question the

---

*Autonomy was recognized only in the case of the provincial government in Silesia. In Rumania a bill was introduced in 1929 by the Maniu government to restore the historical provinces abolished by the administrative system introduced by the Averescu government in 1922. The bill, which also envisaged self-government in the provinces, did not survive the National Peasant government. In Yugoslavia the oblast system, meant to aid in the centralization of administration, was introduced in 1922, its implementation was halted by the Davidovic government in 1924, and then finally implemented by the Radicals in 1925.

serious attention it deserved. Minority parties found it difficult to
form united fronts and were splintered into numerous competing
parties along regional and ideological lines. By and large each group
was content to seek concessions for itself and disregard the remaining minorities; as a result the governments found it relatively easy
to entice minority parties into agreements or pacts (the "Bled Agreement" between the Slovene Populists and the Radical Democratic
Coalition in Yugoslavia in 1927, or the "Ciucea Pact" between the
Magyar Party and General Averescu in 1923) that gave the regime the
margin of political support it needed to put off major reforms. The
promulgation of the Vidovdan constitution in Yugoslavia with the help
of the Moslem Party—in return for which the Moslem landowners
received more favorable compensation during the course of land
reform—was a particularly flagrant case of this kind. The pact
between the minority parties and the government of the colonels in
Poland prior to the 1935 elections also illustrates the way in which
the actions of the minority parties helped to sustain the very governments most hostile to real reform.*

The political systems of the interwar period nevertheless did,
in certain cases, show themselves to be well adapted to dealing with
the national question. Given the necessary amount of goodwill, it was
possible for some of the governments of the time to work out policies
for dealing with the minority question that still stand as models of
toleration and constructive collaboration. This holds true particularly
for the minority policy of the Estonian government, developed in cooperation with the German minority, that regularized minority rights
in the Cultural Autonomy Law of 1926. Rudolf Brandsch, a deputy of
the German Party, cooperated with the Maniu government in an attempt, in the end unsuccessful, to draw up a comprehensive minority
statute for Romania.[4] Czech legislation in the interwar period was
a model of its kind, although it never went to the extent of recognizing
corporate rights of minorities, as did the Estonian legislation.

These acts still represent a model toward which the minorities
of Eastern Europe aspire, especially in respect to the enactment of
comprehensive statutes governing the rights of the minorities, statutes
that would provide corporate as well as individual guarantees. Although this experience in collaboration was limited in scope, it points
to the natural alliance between reforming elements and national

---

*As a result of this pact, and the boycott of the elections of
1935 by the major Polish parties, the percentage of electorate voting
in the Eastern provinces was, for the first time, higher than the percentage voting in the central provinces.

groups interested in securing basic rights, an alliance we shall see emerge in the postwar period.

MINORITIES AND SMALLER NATIONAL GROUPS

Our account of the national question after World War II will begin by considering the policies pursued by the Communists toward minorities and the smaller Slav nationalities, and then take up the problem of how the national question was reflected in the development of the political systems themselves.

The thrust of the Communist revolutions was, first and foremost, toward assimilation and control of the nationalities and national minorities in Eastern Europe. The pressure for assimilation and control had several origins. One lay in the nature of the totalitarian system itself, which worked in a multitude of ways to reduce the minorities and other national groups to the status of undifferentiated individuals within the new social and political order. On the ideological level, the issue of national rights was preempted by Communist propaganda, which claimed to have ended the discrimination practiced by the prewar regimes. In many instances administrative redistricting destroyed old regional frontiers, while the party recruited local cadres as a means of penetrating and controlling national groups. In order to prevent local nationalism from infecting the party, the Communist regimes purged local party organizations of persons suspected of "bourgeois nationalism," or, as was frequently practiced in Yugoslavia in the 1950s, recruited regional party leaders for service in the capital where they quickly lost their regional ties. Most important, perhaps, the Communist regimes relied heavily on the secret police, especially in dealing with the minorities. The pervasive fear that the totalitarian system generated in Eastern Europe was felt with special intensity and with demoralizing effect among minority groups.

These pressures were made even more difficult to bear by the almost total isolation of the minorities after the war, and in the case of several groups—the German minority throughout Eastern Europe, the Hungarians in Czechoslovakia until 1948—the deprivation of all legal rights. In addition, the Communist regimes often chose to ignore the existence of discriminatory practices at the local level in order to placate the national feelings of the dominant group in the region in question. This tolerant attitude permitted, for example, discrimination

THE NATIONAL QUESTION 129

against the Croats in Bosnia-Herzegovina to continue long after the war.* The indifference of local authorities also played a great role in the persistence of discrimination against the White Russian element left in Bialystok province in Poland, and, although the picture is complicated by the campaign against Slovak bourgeois nationalism in the 1950s, in the discrimination experienced by the Hungarians in Slovakia.

Finally, it should be noted that many of the minorities in Eastern Europe simply vanished from view by virtue of not being reported in national statistics or mentioned in the news media. While this was not the case in Yugoslavia and Romania, all minorities "disappeared" in this fashion from Poland until an article by J. Sieklerska in Nowe drogi, in 1956, gave data as to their number and whereabouts.[5] The Hungarian census of 1949 gave figures that all but denied the presence of minorities in that country.[6] Data on nationalities in the Bulgarian censuses showed considerable variations.[7] This lack of information did not necessarily mean that an effort was being made to deny the minorities their national identity,** as had occurred before the war, since data on all aspects of the Eastern European populations was scarce during the Stalinist period. The effect of this and of the other measures just listed was, nevertheless, to create a climate that was overwhelmingly "assimilationist" and, as we know, some members of the minority groups did attempt to change their nationality.***

At the same time the advent of the Communists to power was not followed by the rapid assimilation—or even successful integration— of the national minorities. Minority national groups remained by and large intact. The Slav nationalities of Yugoslavia and Czechoslovakia enjoyed even greater recognition than in the interwar years.

While the reasons for this differ from country to country, and are not strictly comparable in the case of the minorities and the Slav nationalities, several general factors may be suggested as important

---

*The downfall of Rankovic and the disgrace of Colakovic, his ally, in 1966 ended this period of discrimination against the Croats.

**In the case of the Pirin Macedonians, the reverse was true: we know that great pressure was exerted on the Bulgarian population of the region to declare itself Macedonian. Subsequent failure to publish the data reflect, it is true, a change in Bulgarian policy toward this group.

**For assimilationist pressures against the German minority in Czechoslovakia, see below.

in contributing to group cohesiveness in the face of assimilationist pressures. First, and extremely important in understanding the persistence of the national question after the war, a majority of the minority groups (Germans, Hungarians, Ukrainians and Albanians) were considered to have collaborated during the war and, as a consequence, were mistreated and then isolated politically by the Communists. The massacre of the Albanians in Kosovo in the winter of 1944-45, the hasty and brutal transfer of the Ukrainian minority from the region of the Bieszczed mountains to Western Poland, and the temporary transfer of the Hungarian minority in Slovakia to the former Sudeten regions, all served to deepen already existing animosities and to isolate the minorities in question from the rest of the population.

Second, there were occasions on which the Communists found it in their interest to make concessions to national groups. This was especially true of the Slav nationalities who were loyal to the Communists, such as the Serbs in Croatia and, for a time, the Hungarian minority in Romania.* Although there were exceptions, the period 1950-53 was one of increasing recognition of certain basic needs of the minority groups in Eastern Europe, including the passage of basic legislation dealing with minority schools (at the primary level) and cultural organizations.[8]

Finally, we must remind ourselves that Communist doctrine did not, in principle, approve of assimilation as a solution to the national question. In the case of the Slav nationalities of Czechoslovakia and Yugoslavia, the stress, immediately after the war, fell on the national distinctiveness of the Slovaks, the Macedonians, and the Montenegrins, all groups previously associated with either the Czechs or the Serbs. We shall see that this policy was by no means consistent and that in the late 1950s there was a strong trend toward assimilation throughout the area.[9] But beneath these shifts, what was significant was the fact that Communist ideology and propaganda in principle identified the new postwar Communist era and the new Communist society with the realization of national, as well as class, rights. Although the use of national cadre was by no means assured in minority regions and areas with minorities often did not receive economic assistance,[10] some consideration was usually given to meeting minority needs where possible, and the smaller Slav nationalities benefited greatly from these policies.

As a consequence, the nationalities of Eastern Europe preserved their identity, even though the national question itself did not attract a great deal of attention. Now, two and a half decades after the war,

---

*The case of the Hungarians in discussed below.

the situation has changed dramatically and national problems are again the focus of attention. Three factors have played a role in this situation. One is the appearance of revisionist critiques of Stalinist practices, with the attendant airing of national grievances and the partial admission by Communist regimes of the injustices perpetrated against the minorities after the war. A second consideration has been the reemergence of the national question as an issue affecting national security—a development observable as early as the Tito-Stalin split in 1948, but especially evident during and after the invasion of Czechoslovakia in 1968. Third, one can point to changes taking place in the political systems of Eastern Europe as a result of which the Communist regimes have become less monolithic and more susceptible to centrifugal forces—economic, political, or otherwise—rooted in national differences.

It seems wise, in light of the changes that have taken place in the importance of the national question, to single out the Stalinist period of totalitarian rule and speak briefly of the situation at that time, before getting into the more complex developments of recent years. The extraordinary importance of the national question in Yugoslavia and Czechoslovakia makes it necessary to treat these countries in separate sections, one dealing with the evolution of political and national problems, the other with the federal systems of the two countries.

The totalitarian regimes of postwar Eastern Europe, although largely imposed from without, were powerful, revolutionary political systems, able to withstand, and even exploit, the many social, political, and national divisions that had weakened the prewar governments. In respect to the national question, the Communists were, therefore, acting from a position of strength. This was reflected in the actions of these regimes, when, upon consolidating power, they passed legislation that provided severe sanctions against those who, regardless of their national origins, were guilty of displaying nationalist sentiments. Such laws were by and large effective in eliminating clashes among national groups. Outwardly it seemed that the Communist regimes had successfully coped with the national problems of the region, and the Communists themselves were not slow to make this claim.

The totalitarian regimes of Eastern Europe nevertheless suffered from profound internal weaknesses, as time was to demonstrate, and these weaknesses were in certain respects related to the presence of minorities, or potentially "disloyal" Slav nationalities. For one thing, there was the ever increasing reliance that these regimes placed on terror, and the vicious circle that this created as the growing gap between the mass of the people and their regimes created the need for the use of still more force. Under these conditions, there was always the possibility that some group would rise up in protest and set off a major conflagration. Since the national minorities, especially, were hostile to the Communists, they were a potential threat to the Communist regimes despite their isolation and relative passivity. The same could be said of some of the Slav groups in Eastern Europe, above all the Croats in Yugoslavia.

The totalitarian regimes were also vulnerable because of the ferocity of inner-party power struggles, and the ever present danger that such struggles could lead to prolonged factional disputes. Such a development would open the door to the formation of factions along regional and national lines within the Party power structure. While such factions were not likely to include leaders of the minorities— few, if any, being in the top echelons of the Communist Parties outside of Romania—the power struggles in Yugoslavia and Czechoslovakia were always in danger of succumbing to such a pattern.

Finally, we may add that the totalitarian systems of Eastern Europe, for all their dynamism, were caught up in the problem of the discrepancy between theory and practice which had also plagued the interwar governments. In the case of the Communist regimes, this discrepancy extended to every aspect of the system's operation, including the national question. In this respect it is clear that whatever momentary advantage the Communists gained from quieting national passions after the war, failure to reach a lasting solution to the role of nationalities in Eastern Europe would seriously compromise these regimes, perhaps even more than the prewar governments, given the degree of Communist commitment to doing away with the national question once and for all.

The concrete impact of some of these general problems can now be examined in more detail. We shall focus on three issues: (1) the extent to which the national situation in Eastern Europe promoted the seizure of power and then facilitated the rapid consolidation of Communist rule; (2) the nature of the threat facing the totalitarian system as a result of the existence of disaffected national groups; and (3) the positive, or liberalizing, influence that national minorities have had on the Communist regimes in Eastern Europe.

In turning to the first of the above questions, it may be noted that there was once a feeling among certain Western observers that the Communists in Eastern European countries relied heavily on discontented nationalities in carrying out their take-overs, riding to power, as it were, on the coattails of national frustrations and animosities.[11] There were, of course, cases in which these considerations played a role in the Communist take-over of Eastern Europe. In Yugoslavia the powerful impetus given the Communists by the failure of earlier regimes to solve the national question was reenforced by certain sociological and political phenomena associated with the partisan wars, namely the recruitment of great numbers of cadre from rural areas. These were in a large part drawn from national groups—especially the Montenegrins—who had not previously been a part of the ruling bureaucratic caste. The appearance of these peoples in the urban bastions of the old order, in the winter and spring of 1944-45, was a cultural and political shock of the first order.

The vastly different situation in Romania and Poland, where the Communists had alienated patriotic national sentiment, led to the inclusion of representatives of the minorities, or persons of Jewish extraction, in the postwar Communist-dominated governments, and the favoring, usually in rather insignificant ways, of some of the minority groups themselves. In the Polish case, the Communist regime initially opposed manifestations of anti-Semitism in the Polish population and, as we know, a number of prominent Communist leaders were Jewish.[12] In Romania the postwar Communist government was, up to the late 1950s, composed to a significant degree of persons from outside the Old Kingdom, including members from the Hungarian minority.[13] (Vasile Luca was probably the most important Communist official in postwar Europe to have come from the ranks of one of the minorities.) For a time after the war the Hungarian section of the Romanian CP was relatively stronger than the Romanian, and it is to its influence that the granting of autonomous status to the Szekely region in 1952 has been attributed by some authors.[14]

We cannot judge exactly how important the presence of these non-Romanians and persons of Jewish background was in the development of Communism in Romania and Poland. It would clearly be the opposite of truth to suggest that the presence of such groups discouraged the rise of national communism—rather, it appears to have encouraged it. If, as seems to be the case, the Communists came to be regarded as an alien element in these two countries, they were to make every effort to correct this image later, in the 1960s, at the expense of the minorities themselves.

With these possible exceptions, therefore, the national minorities did not contribute to the consolidation of Communist rule in Eastern Europe. On the contrary, in the eyes of the Communist regimes, the minorities represented a potentially subversive element. The actual danger is hard to measure and involves several different types of considerations. On the one hand, the Communist regimes themselves, when faced with the possibility that the national minorities might be drawn into the Cominform dispute, acted with great severity; we know of how the Serbs in Hungary and Romania were evacuated from their villages along the Yugoslav border, and even a portion of the German Swabian minority was resettled in 1951 to the Baragan steppe region east of Bucharest.[15] One may venture a guess, nevertheless, that the danger these groups represented to the Soviet-bloc regimes in their struggle with Titoism was minimal and that the wholesale resettlement of minority groups occasioned by the Cominform dispute was an overreaction, one that helped create still greater feelings of alienation among the minorities involved. The same might be said of the less hysterical, but no less harsh, treatment of the Albanian minority by the Yugoslav government, especially during the height of the quarrel between Albania and Yugoslavia in the early 1960s.

In the course of events the threat to the Communist regimes of the 1950s did not prove to be external, but internal, the result of the systems' own excesses that provoked the protests and the revolts of 1956. In these events certain minorities were positioned to play a key role, not so much in demonstrations in large urban centers, but in border regions where they were potential "transmitters" of the mood of revolt from co-nationals who lived across the normally sealed boundaries that existed at the time between the East European countries. This was particularly true of two groups: the Poles of Czechoslovakia and the Hungarians of Romania.

The former case has been little discussed and, given the small size of the Polish minority in Czechoslovakia, the group was not a great danger to the Czech regime at the time of the October events in Poland. Nevertheless, the Prague government showed its concern and took steps to seal off the border.[16] The reaction of the Hungarians in Transylvania to the events in Hungary in 1956 is, in contrast, better known, and the possibility exists that this group could have helped light the "spark" of protest and rebellion in Romania.[17] Twelve years later, in connection with the Czech spring, the role of minorities as transmitters of heretical ideas across national boundaries became important once more. In this case, the Soviet Union reacted with alarm to the ferment going on in the Ukrainian minority in Czechoslovakia. One suspects that this alarm was not entirely unjustified, given the difference between the rights that the Ukrainians stood to win from the Dubcek regime and the reactionary nature of Soviet nationalities policy.[18]

These incidents, each different in respect to the size and location of the minority, the groups to which appeals were being directed, and the real dangers to the regimes involved, are a reminder that the national problem in Eastern Europe continued to be viewed after the war as posing a threat to the political order, albeit in a context that differed from the interwar situation. We must nevertheless keep in mind that the national minorities—as contrasted to the Slav nationalities in Yugoslavia and Czechoslovakia—have not been intimately associated with the great upheavals of Eastern Europe.

THE NATIONAL QUESTION							135

So far our account has emphasized the element of confrontation between the postwar Communist regimes on the one side, and the national minorities on the other. Was there not also a more positive aspect to this situation, one that developed out of the interaction of the minority populations with the surrounding population, and ultimately with the political system itself?

Undoubtedly such a dimension does exist to the minority question in Eastern Europe, although it must be admitted that the evidence itself is not easy to gather, and the total impact may seem small in comparison to other forces at work in the area. For one thing, the national minorities of Eastern Europe are still, taken as a whole, a social and economic force of some importance. The Stalinist regimes admitted this fact when they made efforts to gain the return of skilled laborers—Germans in particular—who fled the area at the close of the war.*

Secondly, the minorities in Romania and Yugoslavia have in recent years improved their position as a result of the continuing tensions between these two countries, on the one hand, and the Soviet Union on the other. This improvement represents a reversal of the pattern at work during the Cominform dispute, and also in the interwar period when international tensions were usually accompanied by acts of repression against the minorities. What has taken place is not a change in attitudes toward the minorities, but rather a change in roles, in which the minorities are no longer associated, because of their national sympathies, with one or another of the rivals in the power struggle in the area. Not wishing to see the Soviet Union exploit minority discontent, but hopeful that the minorities would be loyal in any conflict with the Soviet Union, the regimes of Yugoslavia and Romania have become interested in winning minority support. As a means of achieving this the governments in both countries have been willing to permit the minorities to improve their contacts with neighboring states; in Yugoslavia, this policy is officially incorporated into the Titoist ideology in the position that minorities in socialist systems should act as a "bridge" among nations.[19]

In the case of Romania the new policy holds out the possibility, at least, that the Hungarian minority may, as a result of its increased contacts with Hungary, transmit some of the ideas of the Hungarian approach to Communism to the Romanian decision-makers, although

---

*Thus for a time in Poland the Germans still in the country were denied all legal rights, but at the same time the government was promising to restore rights to those Germans who returned to the country from abroad.

to accomplish this, there would have to be improved representation
of the Hungarians in the Romanian party leadership.* The influence
the Albanians might have on Yugoslavia is, of course, hardly comparable to the Hungarians in Romania, but one would hope that in the
long run the Albanians, thanks to their improved contacts with Tirana,
will serve the function of a bridge between Yugoslavia and Albania.**

We are on surer ground in seeing some positive interactions
between the Communist political systems of Yugoslavia and Czechoslovakia and their Slav nationalities. Both countries, after all, in
addition to being multinational, have carried out extensive reforms,
and this has taken place despite obvious differences in the level of
economic development and the degree of democratic traditions that
have existed in the two countries.

At first glance there is a great deal that can be said against
the thesis that the process of liberalization in these two countries
should be linked to their multinational character and indeed, much of
what we have to say would be misinterpreted if it was taken to mean
that such a link must exist. There are Communist states that have
undertaken reforms that are not multinational (Poland, Hungary),
while the Soviet Union has apparently not been prompted by pronounced
multinational composition to liberalize its own political system.
Nevertheless, when viewed in terms of the ability of a Communist
system to reform itself from within, it does seem worthy of note
that the two multinational states of Eastern Europe have been most
successful and ventured the farthest. With this thought in mind,
we can plunge into the intricacies of the Yugoslav and Czech
reforms and their link to the national question.

---

*With one or two possible exceptions, there are at present no
persons of minority background in leading Romanian party bodies.
The ratio of Hungarians in the party is 8.4%, the same as the percentage of Hungarians in the population.

**At the moment the Yugoslavs continue to encourage this link,
despite growing difficulties with the Albanian minority. With the
most recent census showing the Albanians an overwhelming majority
in Kosovo, the Albanian Communists have begun to act as the "majority"
in the region. Serb technicians have been leaving the factories in
Kosovo in significant numbers since the riots of 1968. Most recently,
under the new constitutional arrangements for Yugoslavia (below),
the Kosovo delegation to the federal government refused to accept
the proposed five-year plan on the grounds that it did not provide
adequate development funds.

THE SPECIAL CASES OF YUGOSLAVIA
AND CZECHOSLOVAKIA

We shall begin with the case of Yugoslavia and, assuming some knowledge of the Titoist system on the part of the reader, focus at once on the rather complex developments that marked the evolution of the national problem and the emergence of a liberal form of Communism in the country.

Although events in Yugoslavia have not always fitted into a neat pattern, it is possible to speak of several more or less clearly defined periods in the evolution of the Yugoslav system that help clarify the relationship between politics and the national question.*

The first such period extended from the middle to the late 1950s, a time when the external danger to Yugoslavia, represented by the Cominform, had diminished and the country was entering into a period of rapid economic growth. This was a time of decentralization and party reform, followed by partial reconsolidation of the power of the central government after organs of local government proved unable to cope with their new responsibilities. Although the first signs of controversy over national relations had already made their appearance— the struggle between the developed and underdeveloped republics dates from this time—the view prevailed that Yugoslavia was entering into a new era shaped by self-management relations and that national differences would gradually grow less and less important, finally to be overshadowed completely by the self-management system and its socialist principles.[20] From this time (1955) date efforts to integrate the minorities into Slav schools, and the closing down of the cultural societies of the Hungarian and Romanian minorities in the Vojvodina.

In 1958 Edvard Kardelj gave this approach to the nationality question an ideological justification in his work, Razvoj slovenackog nacionalnog pitanja. Without going into Kardelj's theory in detail, we may note that it displayed several parallels with Czech "assimilationist" doctrines of the same period,[21] but reflected Yugoslav conditions and Yugoslav experiences, especially in categorically rejecting any form of assimilation of the national cultures in Yugoslavia. Kardelj did raise the possibility that a new socialist consciousness would develop in Yugoslavia and, in this connection, spoke of the emergence

---

*We omit from the discussion reference to problems arising prior to the advent of reform in the 1950s.

of a feeling of "Yugoslavianism"—Jugoslovenstvo—as a result of the growth of the new socialist system.

The policies of the 1950s demonstrate the manner in which the thrust of reform, in the economy and society, was initially directed toward reducing national differences and eventually even replacing the federal system with communal self-government. The fact that this policy was pursued at exactly the same time as the assimilationist policy in Czechoslovakia may have been fortuitous, or may have reflected the fact that in both countries a reaction against Stalinist policy led to stress on national unity over national, and minority, rights. Although it is commonly thought that pressure to create an integral Yugoslavia was a reactionary idea encouraged by Rankovic, it in fact was a product of liberal forces, later to be repudiated by these very same elements when it became necessary to rally the nationalist forces of Croatia and Slovenia against Rankovic and his Serb contingent.

The policy of integrating the Yugoslav nationalities under a new socialist system of self-management relationships failed. Several factors help account for this: the rise of powerful localistic forces as a result of economic decentralization and the emergence of the struggle between the developed and the underdeveloped republics over investment funds; the struggle for power that began to preoccupy the top Party leadership; and last, but not least, a strong, at times violent, reaction against the notion that the development of socialism in Yugoslavia would lead to the creation of a new Yugoslav nation existing side by side with the nations represented by the five major Slav nationalities. The emergence of these divisive factors led to what we might call Yugoslavia's first "Time of Troubles" between 1962 and 1966. The period was ushered in by the 4th plenum of the League of Communists, at which Rankovic prevailed over his rivals, and ended with the 4th, Brioni, plenum, at which Rankovic was removed from the Yugoslav party leadership. The defeat of Rankovic marked a victory not only for the liberal faction in favor of economic reform, but a triumph for regional interests in the advanced republics who stood to gain by implementation of the new economic policy. These same forces, concentrated in Slovenia and Croatia, played a major role in a second period of great political and economic turmoil that commenced in earnest in 1969 and continued through 1971.

The reasons for the most recent crisis lie in a complex of factors. Slovenia and Croatia discovered that Serbia, supported by the underdeveloped republics, could outvote the two advanced republics in the federal government on matters considered crucial to the latter's interests (devaluation of the dinar, for example),* while, quite contrary to the expectations of the two advanced republics, the new economic system added to the economic power of Belgrade—and thus of the Serbs—by encouraging the growth of large trading organizations (the export-import companies) in the capital. The Croats and Slovenes also attacked the power of the Yugoslav banks located in Belgrade (although a major share of the assets of these banks was divided among the republics in 1969) utilizing this campaign as a starting point for demands that the assets of the funds accumulated by the federal government over the years should be distributed among the republics.

We shall not try to describe in detail the controversies that ensued; not only are they complex beyond belief, but they were accompanied by such an outpouring of materials that scholars will undoubtedly be analyzing them for many years to come. In 1969 Slovenia, outvoted in the Federal Executive Council over what seemed an issue of less than major importance concerning the allocation of international aid for road building in Yugoslavia, gave vent to her deep discontent in a wave of criticism, unprecedented in Slovenia up to that time, of the actions of the federal government.[22] At the end of the year it was Croatia's turn to become outraged over criticism directed against the nationalistic views of Matica Hrvatska (but, in actuality, against the nationalism of the Croatian Communists themselves) launched by Milos Zanko in Borba.[23] Ostensibly a Croatian delegate to the Federal Assembly, Zanko had allied himself with the opponents of Croatia in Belgrade. At the 10th plenum of the Croatian Central Committee, which met in early 1970, Zanko was recalled and lost his party and government posts. The plenum, which is now considered a turning point in the history of the Croatian party, marked the beginning of a period in which the Croatian League of Communists assumed a more and more nationalistic posture in its dealings with Belgrade, as well as in domestic, Croatian, affairs. One very visible consequence of this development was an increase of tensions between Serbs and Croats, marked by quarrels over issues long associated with the national problem: the language question, the problem of the Serbs in Croatia, reputed demonstrations by Ustasi in Croatia, and even that old staple of nationalities disputes in Eastern Europe, the

---

*Croatia and Slovenia could also block steps from being taken that were contrary to their interests, as the prolonged delay in refunding the program for aid to underdeveloped regions in 1970 demonstrated.

administration of the federal census.* These national quarrels between Serbs and Croats broadened, in the course of 1970 and 1971, to include other groups with their own special grievances—Macedonians, Montenegrins, and, of course, Albanians.[24]

This national crisis reached its height in the winter and spring of 1970-71. In the fall the federal government found itself deadlocked over the issue of how to deal with the worsening economic situation; the Croats and the Slovenes were asking for fundamental reforms in the federal structure but were blocked in their demands by Serbia.** The result was a governmental "crisis of confidence" in the fall,*** from which the Communists were able to extract themselves through the adoption of constitutional reforms. Without going further into the matter at this point, we may note that these amendments involved the creation of a collective presidency to exercise governmental power

---

*We cannot go into details concerning these disputes. We may note in respect to the census controversy that Point 10 of the directives issued by the federal statistical office for the conduct of the 1971 census permitted a person to identify himself by his region of origin, e.g., as a Dalmatian rather than a Croat. Croatia demanded postponement of the census, although Serbian comment suggested the regional affiliation was merely a residual category—as was the category of "Yugoslav"—without nationality implications. Federal officials finally ruled that each republic was free to omit the question. The matter was extensively discussed in the Belgrade and Zagreb press during the month of February 1971.

**A major turning point in the crisis came when the Serbian National Assembly agreed to the devolution of the economic powers of the federal government. This decision was made easier for the Serbs, it may be noted, by the relative prosperity of Serbia and the strength of her industrial sector, as well as the wealth of her commercial firms.

***When it proved impossible to gain approval of austerity measures to end the drain on the balance of payments and to curb inflation, one minister resigned and the Chairman of the Executive Council, Mitja Ribicic, threatened to make adoption of his program a question of confidence. Ribicic favored a program which put off devaluation; this solution was not acceptable to Croatia, however, and when a Croatian advocate of devaluation was installed in the FEC, followed by devaluation in the spring, the crisis temporarily ended.

THE NATIONAL QUESTION

after Tito retires, the devolution of a wide range of central government powers to the republics, and the division of the assets of most of the funds of the federal government among the republics. Agreement over these changes among the Republic party leaders early in 1971 temporarily eased the crisis, but the publication of the amendments in March provoked a wave of criticism (from both Serbs and Croats) that did not end even with the promulgation of the amendments in June.* Nationalist manifestations spread in Croatia during the spring, especially among the students. Tito's direct intervention in the situation in July eased the situation. But prior to Tito's confrontation with the Croats, Miko Tripalo, the leader of the national faction in the Croatian party, had been drawing crowds of thousands to hear and applaud his nationalistically tinged speeches.

Focusing on the dynamics of Yugoslav developments, that is, the forces that have combined to produce the present situation, in order to suggest ways in which this controversy in the field of national relations influenced the development of the Titoist political system, we may begin by pointing out that the struggle for national rights was bound up from an early date with the problem of reform of the Stalinist system. We see evidence of this briefly in the mid-1950s, in the debate held among Yugoslav constitutional lawyers over the true nature of the Yugoslav federal system,[25] as well as in the debates over "Jugoslovenstvo" in the early 1960s, and the tying of this view, in part erroneously, to the machinations of Rankovic and his conservative supporters. The campaign to improve minority rights in the late 1960s was also—as we have seen—closely associated with the struggle to end the influence of the conservatives, and more specifically of the secret police, in Yugoslav life.

There are good reasons to question, however, whether the federal system that Yugoslavia put into effect springs directly from the reforming spirit of the Titoist system. While <u>decentralization</u> was, from the start, an essential part of the Titoist approach to the elimination of Stalinist bureaucratic practices, the idea of giving powers to the <u>republics</u> was frowned upon. The general feeling among the ideological spokesmen for the Titoist system in the 1950s was that republic autonomy would simply recreate bureaucratic relations at the republic level. This view, it might be noted, seemed to be borne out by the experience with decentralization in the early 1950s. The struggle to have the republics "legitimized" began in earnest with the attack on Rankovic for reputedly wishing to do away with republics in Yugoslavia. It spread, in the following years, through

---

*For more on these criticisms, see next section.

recognition of the republics' right to have the final word concerning problems of regional economic development.* Following this there emerged a struggle over the right of the republics to veto decisions of the federal government contrary to republic interests (the so-called "imperative mandate").** Finally, in the past several years, the issue was squarely joined over whether the republics or the federal government were, in principle, to be the primary focus of governmental power in Yugoslavia. In theory, at least, the republics won the struggle. It bears repeating, however, that this was accomplished not through a campaign to end the "abuses" of the existing federal system—abuses that could quite rightly be traced to the influence of the Stalinist approach to federalism—but rather in the context of a campaign against the powers of the federal bureaucracy <u>as such</u>, as well as against the banking-commercial complex located in Belgrade.

Our second point follows directly from what we have just said: one is surprised to note, given the depth of national feelings and national antagonisms in Yugoslavia, the degree to which the present conflict originated in purely elite concerns, only to spill over into the population at large. Elite problems, by and large, dictated the way in which the issues emerged and were finally resolved.

The implications of these points are certainly negative. They suggest that the recent reforms of the federal system are not so much the result of the application of Titoist principles of decentralization and self-management as the product of centrifugal forces originating within the Titoist system, the result of a clash of interests rather than a principled approach to the national problem.

---

*This point may be confusing. The republics were always granted the "right" to develop economically, but there was great reluctance to recognize anyone but the central government as ultimately responsible for how that growth was to be achieved. The change in tone is first obvious at the 8th Congress of the League of Communists in 1964.

**The "imperative mandate," championed by Croatia, would have permitted Croatia to give binding instructions to her delegation in the Chamber of Nationalities. The implication was that the delegation would use this power to block legislation contrary to Croatia's interests. The principle was not accepted, and this added to Croatia's resentment against the central government. In 1968 the Chamber of Nationalities was, however, given the right to pass on all legislation considered by the Federal Assembly. See next section.

THE NATIONAL QUESTION

We would like to close this brief account of the Yugoslav situation with reference to the party—more precisely, the way in which changes in party organization have reflected pressures for greater republic independence.

The League of Communists, like the federal administration, passed through periods of decentralization and recentralization in the 1950s and the early 1960s. The 8th Congress of the League of Communists, in 1964, produced the first change in the party statute that favored the independence of the republic parties, adopting the position that within the limits imposed by the principle of democratic centralism and the obligation to adhere to policies of the LCY, the republic parties would be able to develop their own independent policies. The disgrace of Rankovic led to a period of party reorganization and proposals for far-reaching reforms that ended with the adoption of a new party statute at the 9th Congress of the LCY in 1969. Under this statute a party "presidium" (really the old Central Committee) was to be chosen by the republics. The Executive Bureau, elected by the Presidium, became, in practice, a meeting place for the highest ranking party leaders from each of the republics, as well as several leaders not associated with any of the republics.* Leadership of the LCY was vested in the post of "President" of the LCY, but real power was retained by the Executive Bureau and its commissions.

Although there is very little material available on the discussions that have gone on within the Executive Bureau, the circumstantial evidence is overwhelming that the Bureau has frequently been deadlocked because of disputes among the republics. This situation, in turn, seems to have accelerated the general trend toward placing more decision-making responsibility in the hands of the government or, more precisely, the Federal Executive Council and the Federal Assembly, not only in respect to minor matters but also in the case of major policy decisions over which the republic Party leaders cannot agree. At the same time the Federal Executive Council, lacking strong political support from the Executive Bureau, has on numerous occasions found itself deadlocked, unable to agree on what policy should be pursued or, if successful in hammering out a policy, unable to enforce it on the republics. The controversy in the fall of 1970 over the introduction of austerity measures designed to curb inflation and

---

*But republic leaders could lose their republic ties and support as a result of participating in the Executive Bureau. This has clearly happened to Bakaric, once considered a spokesman for Croatian interests. While he has become more "Yugoslav" in his outlook, he has lost control over the Croatian party to Tripalo and others.

halt the deterioration in the balance of payments was not contrived to
make Yugoslavia appear more Western, but was a genuine governmental crisis brought on by the deterioration of the authority of the
central party and government organs.

It is interesting to note how the emergence of the republics as
key decision makers in the central party organs in Yugoslavia preceded
and, in a certain sense, made inevitable the decision to distribute the
powers of the central government among the republics. In an indirect
way, it can also be seen that disputes among the republics—insofar as
they did compel the party to abdicate some of its responsibilities to
government and legislative bodies—accelerated that broader trend
toward a reduction of party controls over Yugoslavia. This, then, is
one link that may be discerned between the course of the nationalities
dispute and the liberalization process in Yugoslavia. It fits into a
general pattern on which comment will be made at greater length.

In the case of Czechoslovakia—or to be more precise, the Czech
events of 1968—we find ourselves dealing with what appears to be a
clear-cut example of the impact of the national question on politics
and political institutions in the postwar period. We shall approach
the problem with a few general observations concerning the development of the Slovak question in postwar Czechoslovakia, and then move
directly into the events surrounding the summer of 1968.

The evolution of Communist policy toward the Slovaks after
World War II typified that trend that we have associated with totalitarian
rule—slow but persistent pressure for conformity, integration, and
eventually assimilation. We are familiar with the way in which the
rights of the National Council and the Board of Commissioners were
restricted by the constitution of 1948 and again, after concessions
to the Slovaks in 1956, in the constitution of 1960. The height of these
pressures was reached in the early 1960s, and was marked by the
introduction of Soviet theory on the "growing together" of the Czech
nationalities who, although they were still described as two distinct
national groups, were said to form one "national-political" (narodnopoliticke) community.[26] It was suggested that as the Slovaks gained
economic equality with the peoples of the Czech lands, the need for
separate Slovak organs would disappear entirely, leaving the Slovaks
with cultural autonomy as their only specifically national trait.

We know now that these pressures were not successful and, on
balance, probably helped to spur Slovak nationalism rather than encourage assimilationist trends. An idea of the difficulties that faced
the Czech party in making this assimilationist campaign credible is
suggested by the fact that one of the basic documents concerned with
recognition of Slovak national rights—the Banska Bystrica program
of 1937—was written by Siroky. The document was reprinted in 1952
and widely circulated at a time that Siroky was a leading representative
of the "centralist" camp in Prague.[27]

THE NATIONAL QUESTION

The campaign against bourgeois nationalism—beginning with the arrest of Clementis, Husak and Novomesky in 1950—provided a second issue around which national grievances could build. The efforts of the Slovak party to rehabilitate the men arrested during the campaign and to remove from power those responsible for the arrests helped set in motion the forces that brought the liberals to power in 1968, while at the same time stimulating nationalism among the Slovak Communists.*

Finally, brief reference should be made to the economic grievances of the Slovaks. In respect to economic growth, the Slovak experience was far from unsatisfactory during the Stalinist period. The rule between 1948 and 1966 seemed to be that Slovakia would receive a percentage of investments about equal to her share in the population.[28] This was sufficient to start Slovakia on her way to rapid economic development after the war; not only did industry grow at a faster rate than in the Czech lands, but agricultural productivity, which experienced a drop in the Czech regions in comparison to prewar levels, rose in Slovakia.[29] Slovakia was also aided economically by internal migrations that brought Czech experts to Slovakia and saw surplus Slovak labor find employment in Czech lands.[30] This sort of internal migration was much greater than in Yugoslavia.

Control over investments earmarked for Slovakia was exercised mainly by the ministries in Prague, however. The idea of a "Slovak" economy received a particularly hard blow in the administrative reform of 1960, which, on the one hand, reorganized the country into ten large provinces and, on the other, eliminated many of the Slovak regional organs of administration, including the Slovak statistical office, the Slovak Social Security Office, and the offices of the Commissioners for Construction, Trade, Transportation, and Interior.

---

*It is tempting to see a parallel between the success of the Slovaks in gaining the removal of Bacilek as First Secretary of the Slovak party in 1963 and the recall of Zanko by the Croatian party in 1969. In both cases what was in part at stake was the right of the provincial party to hold its leaders responsible for their actions. Winning the battle, the provincial party gained, in theory, some power over its representatives in the central government. While this seems to be what happened at the Croatian plenum of 1969, the success of the Slovaks in 1963 did not lead to Slovak control of its own party leadership, much less control over those representing it in Prague. Nevertheless, in both cases, the successful outcome of the struggle put the center on notice that it could no longer disregard provincial party interests.

Also, it should be noted that the Slovaks, fired by their own nationalism and the promises of Prague that the goal of Slovak economic development was "equality" with the Czech lands, began to view any discrepancy between the Czechs and the Slovaks in respect to wages, housing, and so forth as a failure to provide Slovakia with sufficient economic aid. By 1962 one can see Slovak economists not only arguing for equality but reexamining the concept in a way that brought into question some of the claims for progress in this field made by the Prague government.[31]

The fact that the Slovaks played a role in bringing about the downfall of Novotny in 1968 is widely accepted. But certainly, if we may fall back on the case of Yugoslavia, the meetings of the Czech Party were not comparable to those of the League of Communists, in which national factions openly confronted one another. We are told that in the Presidium, an almost equal number of Slovaks were lined up on the side of the Novotny faction, on the one hand, and the Dubcek faction, on the other. According to several accounts,[32] the key vote of 5-5 in the Presidium in December saw Chudik (the most notorious of the Slovak centralists since the removal of Bacilek and Siroky) and Lenart side with Novotny; Dubcek, on the other hand, had the support of the Czech centrist Jiri Hendrych.

Existing accounts do not make entirely clear how great a role the demands of the Slovaks played in the debate leading to Novotny's ouster. We can, indeed, judge what Slovak economic grievances were from the speech of Dubcek in September 1967 that dealt with Slovakia's economic problems under the new economic system,* as well as from Slovak demands made before and after this time for increased governmental autonomy.** If, as has been suggested,[33] Novotny accused Dubcek of "bourgeois nationalism" at the September 1967 CC plenum, and this helped turn the Slovak members of the Central Committee to Dubcek's side, then the debate over Slovak grievances must have shared the spotlight equally with the issue of economic reform and the need to end the abuses associated with Novotny's rule.

Above and beyond the question of the precise role of the Slovaks in the events surrounding Novotny's downfall lies the problem of the motives of those who gave their support to Dubcek. For our purposes it is especially interesting to determine whether sympathy for the liberals' cause or narrow nationalist considerations predominated in the thinking of the Slovaks. Lacking detailed knowledge of the Slovak

---

*The speech is discussed below.

**Discussed below.

position, it would be presumptions for us to try to solve this question. We may assume that the Slovaks, like the Czechs, were deeply divided over the issue of reform and argued its merits without regard to national interest. On the other hand it also seems reasonable to assume that Slovak opposition to Novotny was deeply influenced by the conviction that he and his government were irrevocably hostile to the Slovaks and their interests, and that the era of reform and liberalism was welcomed as an opportunity to affirm Slovak rights.

That this was the attitude of the Slovak Communists seems borne out by the fact that the downfall of Novotny was used by the Slovaks to press economic demands and to gain constitutional revisions that would create a federal Czechoslovak state. Dubcek's speech of September echoed the concerns of Slovak economists over the falling rate of investment in Slovakia (in 1967 the rate of increase of investments in Slovakia was for the first time lower than for the country as a whole), the need to develop underdeveloped regions in Slovakia, and the importance of ending the migration of Slovak labor to the Czech lands.[34] Slovak economic demands were again voiced at a meeting of the Slovak Central Committee in January 1968.[35]

For the Slovaks, these demands were a question of economic justice and, as such, part of the atmosphere of reform associated with the Czech spring. At the same time the Slovak position reflected concern that implementation of economic reforms (the NEM) would be contrary to their interests. In order to prevent or neutralize its effects, the Slovaks not only demanded greater economic assistance from the central government, but greater control over their own economy to be achieved through the introduction of a federal system. Not only conservatives, but liberal economists (among them the Slovak economist Löbl) saw a danger in this, warning that what the Slovaks sought in order to protect their economy from the effects of the NEM would create two separate economies and lead to the mistake of replacing the Prague bureaucracy with a Slovak one.[36] These issues were thrashed out by Czech and Slovak economists at a conference held in Bratislava in April; the meeting's "Draft Proposals" were a fascinating melange of political and economic principles in which the idea of the NEM coexisted uneasily with the national and developmental outlook of the Slovaks.[37]

The second main objective of the Slovaks was the creation of a federal system, to be made possible through recognition of the principle of "symmetry." This principle was endorsed in the Action Program (adopted in April) that also set out a list of reforms aimed at recognizing Slovak autonomy.[38] Local government organs were to be placed under control of the Slovak government; Slovak organs of internal affairs were to be created, with full authority; the Slovaks were to be permitted to draft their own economic plan and budget;

Slovak representation in the central government was to be assured
through placing State Secretaries in the ministries, and a proportional
share of the posts in the central government were to be in Slovak
hands. Finally, in "constitutional matters concerning the relations
between Czechs and Slovaks and the constitutional position of Slovakia,"
decisions by majority rule were to be forbidden. In these points the
Action Program set down in a concise fashion the basic elements of
the new federalism. The plan coincided rather closely, it might be
noted, with practice in Yugoslavia at the time; that is, after 1968
and before the 1971 constitutional revisions.

Even at the time these principles were being laid down, Slovaks
writing on the subject of the new federal system were making suggestions for what would have amounted to a confederation, or even
an alliance, between the two parts of Czechoslovakia. In these schemes
Slovakia would act as an independent republic and only a minimum of
powers would be retained by the federal government.[39] In July, Husak
revealed that the Slovaks had been asking for "parity"—equal votes
for the two national groups in any future national assembly—and that
this demand had been rejected by the Czechs.* In this way the issue
of federalism and what it was to represent was fully joined, and differences between the Slovaks and the Czechs began to emerge.

The issue of parity was initially resolved in favor of the Slovaks;
shortly after Husak's public airing of Czech-Slovak differences, the
Presidium of the Czech CP took the position that the Slovaks should
not be outvoted in the new national assembly. The differences between
the Czechs and Slovaks were not fully resolved, however, by the time
of the Soviet invasion, and the two sides continued to be at odds until
early October, when a compromise was reached in order to allow
the adoption of the law on the federation on October 27.** Although
Czech and Slovak views were sometimes wide apart, one gets the
impression that their differences were resolved without grave difficulties, and that the negotiations, while dealing with matters of
fundamental importance for all concerned, did not occasion as much
controversy as the bargaining preceding the adoption of the constitutional amendments in Yugoslavia. On the other hand, the relative
ease with which the law of October 27 was passed may reflect the

---

*Husak made his statement at a party conference in Bratislava,
July 11, 1968.

**At issue were the economic powers of the federal ministries,
and, of course, the question of parity. The Slovaks wished to see
parity apply to all questions coming before the national assembly.

THE NATIONAL QUESTION

unusual circumstances of the time rather than a meeting of the minds between Czechs and Slovaks over the federal system.[40]

There will always be questions concerning the Slovak role in the Czech spring. There is a danger, in attempting to deal with this issue, that national roles will be assigned to actors in this drama who were not acting out of national motives. Nevertheless, the alliance between Dubcek and the Slovak Communists was a crucial factor for the survival of the liberal regime. Slovak interests were in certain ways endangered by the reforms, and conservatives, well aware of this fact, hoped to swing the Slovak party to their side. The Slovak Communists nevertheless endorsed the Dubcek program—including the NEM—on the understanding that they would be given their long-hoped-for federal system. Thus the implementation of the program of reform and the creation of a federal Czechoslovakia were inextricably linked.

We can only speculate how well such a system would have functioned if it was implemented and whether, as the liberals feared, the introduction of federalism would have delayed democratization in Slovakia. The invaluable "Report on the Current Political Situation," prepared by the Central Committee of the Czech CP shortly before the Soviet invasion, saw the introduction of the federal system as an important step in the liberalization of the bureaucracy, at least in the Czech lands. In the words of the report:

> Another element is represented by those who disassociated themselves from the pre-January policies but who, in subsequent developments have emerged as retarding factors as far as the realization of the Party's Action Program is concerned. . . . The federal reform of the state and its agencies will mark the complete destruction of these forces. In this context it is necessary to point out the difference between the Czech Lands and Slovakia, arising from the fact that entirely new institutions will be formed in the Czech Lands, while the institutions in Slovakia will only be reformed and restructured.[41]

At the same time, the report spoke of disintegrative and particularistic tendencies that were already growing in the country:

> The guiding economic system is faced with an inner economic reconstruction and change and is at the same time faced with fundamental federal change which will deeply affect all of the economic management systems; it is faced with many disintegrating tendencies linked with economic as well as federative processes which will

result in great demands upon the financial resources of the republic. It must be expected that in the present state of fragmentation in central economic management, basic and powerful social procedures will be manifest more and more, as well as branch, local and national interests which will lead to wage, social and investment demands.

The trends to which the report refers would have been augmented by another aspect of the Dubcek program: reform of the Communist Party. This involved the creation of a "symmetric" party through the setting up of a Czech CP parallel to the Slovak party organization. In addition, under the provisions of the draft party statute published August 10, the republic party organizations were under certain circumstances to enjoy the right of veto over the decisions of the Central Committee; that is, a majority of delegates of both republics would be required in a vote in the Central Committee affecting the "existence, sovereignty, or key national interests" of the republic.[42] To the best of our knowledge, this provision is unique in the history of Communist Party statutes. It suggests that in Czechoslovakia, as well as Yugoslavia, "federalization" of the party was destined to play an important role in the process of the devolution of powers initiated as a consequence of reform.

This study is not concerned with the events following the Soviet invasion; we know that the federal system has been emasculated and today exists only on paper, returning Czechoslovakia to her pre-1968 condition.* Rather than speculating on that situation further, we turn to a comparison of the Yugoslav and Czech situations.

We are struck, first of all, by how different the main actors appear to be in each case. Croatia and Slovenia—the prime forces for change in Yugoslavia—are the most advanced republics, as well as being most consistently associated with the cause of the liberalization. They have been powerful influences in the postwar governments of Yugoslavia, even when finding themselves in competition with Serbia. Slovakia in the 1960s found herself in more or less the opposite position: underdeveloped, less liberal than the Czech lands, and certainly not the equal of the Czechs in population or economic power.

---

*A law passed December 20, 1970, abolished the office of State Secretary and replaced separate Czech and Slovak citizenship with Czechoslovak citizenship.

And yet, when these more obvious differences are put to one
side, a basic parallel can be established in the manner in which the
Communist Parties in these republics, or provinces, in the course of
seeking recognition of certain national interests, provided critical
organizational support to the liberal forces of both countries.

Deciding whether this alliance was one of convenience, or
reflected a real sympathy for the liberal cause, can be difficult, and
raises the broader problem of how liberal or reform values came to
be associated with one province—or republic—but not with another.
The point was much discussed in the case of Slovakia, whose slow
response to the reform movement was attributed to her less advanced
social and economic status, her lack of a democratic tradition, and
her dependence on the central government in the past. These criticisms
do not seem completely justified in light of Slovakia's role in initiating
the attacks on the Novotny regime in 1963. In 1968, however, the difference in the degree of democratization of the Czech lands and
Slovakia was quite real and a source of concern to the reformers.

No such clear-cut differences in outlook exist between the main
actors in the Yugoslav national controversy. When one compares
Serbia, on the one hand, with Croatia and Slovenia, on the other, conservative forces appear to have been stronger in Serbia, but liberals
can be found in both camps. The revisionist philosophers have been
more influential in Croatia, the student protest movement in Serbia.
If one contrasts Slovenia and Croatia with the underdeveloped republics,
however, the dichotomy in political attitudes begins to emerge more
clearly. Although the problem is not discussed in Yugoslavia, there
does seem to be a "lag" in the liberalization process, particularly
noticeable in Montenegro, but also true for the "South" as a whole.*

The north-south dichotomy in political values in Yugoslavia
therefore corresponds in a rough way to the west-east dichotomy in
Czechoslovakia. This suggests that an essential precondition for
the emergence of liberal Communist regimes in these countries was
the presence of democratizing trends in the <u>dominant</u> political regions
that, at crucial moments, allied themselves with regional national
movements in order to overcome the power of what we might call
"native conservatives"—Novotny, Rankovic—themselves products of
the dominant, or more powerful, ethnic group.**

---

*That is, Macedonia, Kosovo, Montenegro, and—although not
really in the South—Bosnia Herzegovina.

**The model might not seem to apply to Yugoslavia because it
was not the underdeveloped republics that allied themselves with

Such broad-gauge generalizations are easily open to criticism, and we suggest some refinements and reservations in the conclusions of this study. Nevertheless, such an approach does serve to suggest the importance of a coincidence of elite interests between national elements and the reform movement for the emergence of liberal Communist regimes, and the fact that under certain conditions, this may be easier to achieve in a multinational state than in one in which politics is the province of one dominating nationality. It is equally true, however, that such a coincidence of interests may be a passing phase, destroyed by the process of liberalization itself. We have seen how NEM promised to create difficulties for Slovakia, and what was still a cloud on the horizon in the Slovak case has become a grim reality in Yugoslavia, where rates of growth in the underdeveloped republics have been dangerously low since the system of "market socialism" was introduced. Only large loans from the developed areas of the country have prevented this situation from deteriorating into a full-fledged economic disaster.

It may be, nevertheless, that the alliance between reformers and nationalists has not been merely one of momentary convenience, but has been influenced by more basic considerations.

One such consideration would be economic, derived from the fact that federal systems in both Yugoslavia and Czechoslovakia probably could not have been introduced under command-economy methods. There are several reasons for this, the most obvious being the impossibility of satisfying even minimum demands for regional economic autonomy under the system of economic ministries and branch trusts that characterize the command economy. Thus, a region such as Slovakia may be forced into the realization that the economic reforms advocated by liberal forces, despite their possibly adverse results on the local economy, are a prerequisite for the successful functioning of a federal system.

A second factor that would promote an alliance between the nationalist movement and the liberal reformers would be the assumption, on the part of the former group, that a liberal Communist regime would include the redress of national grievances in its program for creating a more humane socialism. This consideration certainly played a role in determining the Slovak attitude toward the Dubcek regime, and, in a more roundabout way, in the thinking of the Croats and the Slovenes.

Croatia and Slovenia. Here, however, the Serb-Croat struggle can be seen as a force that delivered the nationalists in Croatia into the hands of the liberals.

The Yugoslav case suggests one further set of generalizations concerning the emergence of more democratic regimes in multinational Communist states. This concerns not the interaction between reformers and nationalists, but the effects of the intense clash of interests within the narrow circle of the ruling Communist elite, characteristic of the period of emerging federalism in a system that has adopted a semimarket economy and other liberal reforms. If the state is to survive, "elite restraint" must become the order of the day; the rights of the "minority" must be respected and even acceded to when problems fundamental to the national interest (that is, the interest of republics) are at stake. The term "loyal opposition" becomes, under these circumstances, more comprehensible and acceptable, and, finally, even constitutional restraints, including the division of powers under a federal system, seem necessary if not welcome.

No one would claim that events in Yugoslavia have exactly followed this course. But, as an element in the overall pattern of evolution and change away from the totalitarian system, the process of learning to accept minority views and of being bound by constitutional procedures is important and is not really brought into consideration in existing theories concerning the growth of pluralism or the effects of economic reform on Communist systems.*

Given the disruptive effects of nationality disputes in Eastern Europe in the past, the thesis that today such conflicts encourage "constitutionalism" would seem to require further explanation. If the argument has some merit, it might be asked, what has changed between the nature of nationality conflicts today and those of the past? An effort will be made to suggest some answers to this question in our conclusions. First, however, we shall turn to the federal systems to see in what way they relate to our observations concerning the impact of the national question on the political institutions of Eastern Europe.

FEDERAL SYSTEMS IN EASTERN EUROPE

The federal systems introduced by the Czechs and the Yugoslavs constitute the most visible and dramatic impact of the national question on the political institutions of postwar Eastern Europe. We have considered the events that led up to adoption of these federal systems

---

*See final section for reference to Friedrich's theories of opposition in federal systems.

in the preceding section. At this point we would like to concentrate on the character of the systems themselves.

We must warn the reader of the preliminary nature of this analysis. We are concerned here with the more obvious features of these two systems discernible in the amendments of 1971 to the Yugoslav constitution and the Law of October 27, 1968, that created the Czech federal structure. A more comprehensive comparison would have to take into account supporting legislation and decrees dealing with the administrative system, the organization of the economy, the judicial system, and so forth. In the case of Yugoslavia the republic constitutions, when they are promulgated, will be of great importance in determining the character of the federal system.

The Yugoslav case may be considered first. The constitution of 1963 had provided the rudiments of a federal system. Under its provisions a Council of Nationalities represented the republics in the Federal Assembly; the republics enjoyed residual legislative powers and were permitted—at least in theory—to complete "basic" or "general" laws adopted by the Federal Assembly. Amendments to the constitution passed after the downfall of Rankovic in 1966 increased the powers of the Council of Nationalities* without altering the basic nature of the system.** Fundamentally the country was governed by a unitary form of government,*** partially "federalized" by virtue of the growing weight of the republics in the decision-making organs of the central government and the devolution to the republics of certain powers, such as control over the secret police and regional economic planning.

---

*Amendment IX, approved December 1968, provided that all legislation approved by the Federal Assembly had to be approved by the Council of Nationalities. This was in fact a return to the provisions of the 1946 constitution, which had been dropped in the constitutional amendments of 1953.

**With the failure of the campaign to impose the "imperative mandate" on the Federal Assembly, the efforts of the Croats to gain a veto turned to the executive branch, with results we shall describe below. The veto power of the Council of Nationalities was never formally invoked between 1968 and 1971.

***It was notorious, for example, that basic laws were passed in such detail that the republic governments had no opportunity to complete them.

THE NATIONAL QUESTION

In the discussion of the constitutional reforms that took place during the course of 1970 and the spring of 1971, the official position was that existing relations between the federal government and the republics would be basically altered, leaving the central government with only those responsibilities essential for the preservation of the federation and the political and economic order. This meant that the powers of the federal government were to be restricted to four areas: national defense, international relations, preservation of the unity of the Yugoslav market, and "protecting the foundations of the socialist system."[43]

The constitutional amendments provide a confirmation of the federal government's rights in these areas.[44] In matters of defense, state security, foreign affairs, economic relations with foreign countries, protection of the unity of the market, and protection of Yugoslav citizens working abroad, the central government has the right to pass legislation without consulting the republics and enjoys the right to utilize federal administrative organs in carrying out these decisions.

In addition, the Federal Assembly is empowered to legislate on a broad range of subjects of all-Yugoslav importance. The distinction between "exclusive," "basic," and "general" legislation is abolished. Such is the scope of the matters on which the Assembly can act that the principle of residual powers to the republics is rendered almost meaningless.

The first fact that emerges, therefore, is the potential power of the central government under the new system. The second is the degree to which the constitutional amendments assure that it is the <u>republics</u> that will control the system, administer it, and, if necessary, block its operation. Republic control is achieved in several ways. First, the Presidency is to have a dominant voice in the legislative and executive process and may act to initiate emergency legislation when the coordinating principles envisaged under Amendment 33 break down.* Members of the Presidency are chosen by the republics and the two autonomous provinces (three delegates from each of the

---

*Under Amendment 33, which provides that if agreement is not reached among the republics, the Federal Executive Council can propose to the Presidency that a law be passed to regulate, temporarily, the matter in question. Complex provisions are set out for the Presidency in its dealings with the Federal Assembly, allowing the Presidency to propose laws to the Assembly. If they cannot agree, the Presidency can dissolve the Assembly. In addition, the Presidency controls three new councils responsible for formulating government policy on defense, security, and foreign affairs.

former, two from each of the latter). Second, the personnel of federal offices are to be drawn from the republics—presumably in some ratio reflecting republic population. Third, and most interesting, Amendment 33 introduces the "coordinating principle." Under the provisions of this amendment, assent of all republics and provincial governments must be obtained before the federal government can act on a wide range of issues dealing with economic policy, including the basic elements of the social plan, the foreign exchange system, foreign trade and credit relations with foreign countries, customs, aid to underdeveloped regions, turnover tax rates, and financing of the activities of the federation. In cases of emergency or of deadlock among the republics, the coordinating procedure may nevertheless be bypassed by the Presidency.*

The taxing power of the federal government has been drastically curbed, at least on paper, by the new amendments. The only taxes that the government will collect directly will be customs and administrative fees. The bulk of the income of the federal government will be derived from the turnover tax, administered by the republics and then contributed to the federal government.** Other provisions assure that enterprises contributing funds to the commercial firms and banks located in Belgrade will have greater control over their investments, and over profits.*** The Yugoslav National Bank is retained, but its board is to be made up of persons chosen by the republics. The members of the enlarged constitutional court are also to be chosen by the republics; since 1963 the court has had the power of judicial review, and this remains unchanged. No changes have been made, for the moment, in the Federal Assembly or the basic mode of operation of the Federal Executive Council—the government—although a new round of constitutional amendments may alter these institutions as well, eliminating popular representation in the Assembly entirely and replacing it with delegations from the republics.

---

*In the draft constitutional amendments a unanimous vote of the Presidency was required to end deadlocks precipitated by a breakdown of the coordinating principle. This requirement was omitted in the final version of the amendments.

**The rate will, however, be determined by the federal government, thus preserving the unity of the market. There is also provision for federal control over republic and local government tax revenues in emergency situations.

***Amendments 21 through 23.

THE NATIONAL QUESTION 157

Taken as a whole, the constitutional amendments constitute a remarkable document that signals a sharp departure from the theory, if not the practice, of Yugoslav federalism up to this point. But the amendments are also remarkably ambiguous and leave many questions unanswered concerning the nature of the system that has just been put into operation.

It should be noted that the amendments write into the constitution what has been, to a large extent, existing practice. The veto power given the republics by virtue of the "coordinating principle" reflects a right that apparently became part of unwritten constitutional practice in Yugoslavia prior to 1971. Seen in this light, the addition of provisions for breaking deadlocks in the government through the intervention of the Presidency strengthens the hand of the central government. In addition, the peculiar nature of these changes—amendments to a constitution already overburdened with revisions—casts some doubt on how the new system will operate. In their present form the amendments could be enforced in the courts only with great difficulty, owing to their complexity, ambiguity, and length. Clearly we are dealing here with a set of political agreements arrived at among the leaders of the republics, put in constitutional form so that they cannot easily be repudiated.

The power of the republics is nevertheless assured through the presence of republic representatives in all organs of the executive branch.* The priority of federal laws that prevailed in the old system as a result of the existence of "basic" and "general" legislation, which always took precedence over republic statutes, is now abolished. The administration of federal legislation and the collection of federal revenues will be up to the individual republics. Finally, there is no limit to the subjects on which the republics can legislate, with the exception of the "exclusive" powers granted the federal government under Amendment 31.

We shall return to the problems of what the new Yugoslav system hopes to achieve and the degree to which it departs from past unitary practice after examining the basic provisions of the Czech federal system. The discussion that follows is based on the law of October 27.[45] Legislation that supplemented the law, or subsequently limited it, is with one or two exceptions not considered.**

---

*Members of the Presidency are chosen by the republic assemblies for five-year terms (one member of the republic delegation is President of the republic assembly). But in Yugoslav practice a person can easily be recalled from a political post.

**Note the law passed the same day on citizenship; the law dealing

The law accepted the view that the new federal system should be based on the symmetric model and also that a system of modified "parity" should be employed. On the latter point it was provided that there would be a bicameral legislature made up of the Chamber of the People and the Chamber of Nations. The uncertainty that prevailed up to the moment of the promulgation of the law on the method of choosing the Chamber of Nations was resolved by stipulating that its members would be directly elected, rather than chosen by the republics (Article 31). The question of parity was solved in a complex and novel fashion; the Chamber of Nations was to give its approval to all legislation. The approval of the republic delegations to the Chamber was reserved for two types of situations. The first (Article 41) concerned the election of the President of the Republic, amendments to the constitution, and the declaration of war, and required that 3/5 of each republic delegation give its assent for the matter in question to be approved. The second (Article 42) concerned situations where a majority vote was forbidden ("zakaz majorizace"); in such cases the approval of a majority of each republic delegation was necessary. Areas of federal competence in which the principle of "Prohibited Majorities" applied included laws on citizenship; middle-range federal economic plans; bills governing the tax system, the budgetary system, and the system of federal funds; laws on currency and banks; laws dealing with foreign economic relations and the organization of economic enterprises; laws dealing with the setting up of federal organs of government; and so on. In all cases, the legislation in question was concerned with establishing basic principles in the economy, government administration, planning, foreign trade, and the like. The same principle was to operate in the Presidium of the Federal Assembly when it was exercising powers of the Assembly (Article 67). Under Article 25, the republics obtained the right to be consulted concerning international treaties negotiated by the federal government that would touch on areas of joint or shared competence.

The division of powers between the federal authorities and the republics was accomplished in a more conventional fashion and relied heavily on the distinction between general legislation and detailed (republic) legislation that figured so prominently in Yugoslav theory (general, basic, and exclusive laws) prior to 1971. The constitutional law laid out the sphere of "exclusive" federal powers much in the way

---

with the Ministry of the Interior, passed December 19; and the law of December 20, 1970, that altered the federal system by abrogating the post of State Secretary and repealing the law dealing with citizenship—that is, abrogating republic citizenship.

the Yugoslavs were to do, although what fell into this realm was not identical in both cases. These were limited, under Article 7 of the Czech law, to defense, foreign policy, federal financial reserves, defense of the federal constitution, and control over the activities of federal organs. Lengthy provisions were made for the sharing of powers between republic and federal authorities. Articles 10 through 28 dealt with separate spheres of domestic activity, spelling out how the Federal Assembly was to establish basic policies, leaving the republics to fill in the details with their own legislation. It was, as we have noted, a system of general federal legislation that might or might not leave certain areas for republic normative action. Article 107, which enumerated the powers of the republic assemblies, gave the impression that the republics were not expected to exercise great legislative initiative; the duties of the assemblies specifically mentioned were unimposing and reminded one of the powers customarily granted autonomous regions in other Communist constitutions (adoption of one's own budget and economic plan). Article 9 did provide that residual powers would rest with the republics.

The federal administration was given the power to act in carrying out laws in the field of exclusive federal competency and also in the area of shared powers (Article 81). This, then, differed from the Yugoslav solution of 1971, in which the federal administration was restricted to areas of exclusive federal competency. To assure adequate national representation in the running of the federal administration, provision was made for the post of Secretary of State. The incumbent would fulfill the function of deputy minister and be a member of the government; he would be Czech if the minister was Slovak and vice versa. Federal committees, which would supervise areas of republic concern, were to be made up of equal numbers of Czechs and Slovaks; if one delegation objected to the committee's decisions, they could be brought to the attention of the government. The constitutional court established in the law was to have the right to pass on the constitutionality of federal laws and to solve conflicts in jurisdiction, in accordance with federal law, between republic and federal administrative bodies. Of the 12 court members, 6 were to be Slovak and 6 Czech. If the president of the court was Czech, the vice-president would have to be a Slovak, and vice versa.

Because the provisions of the October 27 law have not been adhered to in practice, the federal system that emerged from the Czech spring remains a largely theoretical design. Nevertheless the law of October 27 was not a theoretical exercise in constitution drafting; it was meant to be implemented. It is therefore valid to compare it with the Yugoslav amendments of 1971 and comment on the kind of relationships both systems were meant to embody.

Despite obvious differences there are certain common features in both systems: first, care is taken to protect the prerogatives of the central government in respect to foreign policy and defense; second, an attempt is made to formulate a policy of joint responsibility between the federal government and the republics for problems in the social and economic realm; third, care is taken to assure that the federal government contains representatives of the republics; and last, provision is made in both systems for gaining republic assent to basic legislation in areas considered most vital to the republics' interests.

What is striking is the manner in which the Yugoslav and Czech laws—very much in keeping with the history of the national question in Eastern Europe—reveal a deep distrust of the central government and bureaucracy. Obstacles must be created that will, at a minimum, block the actions of the federal authorities considered inimical to republic interests. And care is to be taken that no one national group gains any advantage over the rest. One feels, in examining these laws, that the disillusioned or impatient national elites, shut out of power before the war, have finally penetrated, if not conquered, the citadels of power and are asserting the right to be consulted before decisions affecting their vital interests are made.

Both cases also reveal that the bureaucratic and unitary approach to government is deeply entrenched. In both, care is taken to reassert the sovereign powers of the central authorities. What concrete powers are claimed for the federal government provides an interesting insight into the differences between the governments of Yugoslavia and Czechoslovakia; while both federal systems preserve the powers of the central government over foreign affairs and defense, the Yugoslav amendments include the realm of state security—a recentralization of powers that were delegated to the republics after 1966.[46] The Czech law, on the other hand, goes to great pains to assert the right of the central government to defend the federal constitution, reflecting Czech constitutional tradition that the central government is to exercise ultimate responsibility for fixing relations between various levels of government. In the realm of finances, control over the "material resources of the federation" was to rest exclusively with the federal government. No such power was given the federal authorities in Yugoslavia; on the contrary, the republics won their battle to limit federal tax revenues.

Apart from differences in the area of exclusive federal concern, it is evident that the Yugoslav and Czech laws differ in another important respect: the Czech law is a type of "emergent federalism" in which the principle of republic control and intervention in the federal government is present, but not consistently carried through. This is especially evident in respect to the crucial decision that deputies in the Chamber of Nations not be chosen by the republics, but elected directly. The "national delegations" that then vote on matters listed under Article 42 were not necessarily representing the views of their republics, although this could in practice have occurred. In the Yugoslav case, both practice up to 1971 and the laws themselves suggest that the republic members of the federal government be considered republic delegates, while the "coordinating principle" leaves absolutely no doubt concerning the need for republic approval of many matters in the economic and social realm.

Also, the Yugoslav laws make it difficult, if not impossible, for the federal administration to act outside of matters of exclusive concern of the federal government. Thus the central authorities are, in the last analysis, highly dependent on the republic bureaucracies. This is not the case in respect to the Czech law, although enabling legislation could give great powers to the republics, as apparently happened in the case of the law dealing with the Ministry of the Interior.

The question arises as to whether these laws created truly federal systems. In the Czech case one would be justified in answering with a qualified "no," keeping in mind that a great deal would have depended on the cohesiveness shown by the Slovak parliamentary deputies. The Yugoslav case is much more complicated. In the controversy that grew up following the publication of the amendments, it was obvious that opinion in Serbia felt the new system went too far in the direction of the devolution of powers, especially in respect to the economic powers of the federal and republic governments.* The opinion in Slovenia, on the other hand, was that the amendments, notwithstanding all their concessions to the republics, in fact perpetuated a unitary form of rule.[47]

The Yugoslav system defies easy classification because the division of powers between the republics and the federal government is not precisely spelled out; because of the extensive emergency powers that may be employed by the federal government; and because the extent of republic control over the central government foreseen in the coordinating principle is unprecendented for governments with

---

*The Assembly of the Student Federation of Belgrade University opposed the revisions on the grounds that they created a system of "dual sovereignty," that the Presidency was not responsible to any popularly elected body, and that a "common market" was being created instead of a unified market. The April 30 issue of Student, which gave a detailed account of the meeting, was banned by the public prosecutor, as was a similar publication of the University's Law Faculty—the highly respected Anali pravnog fakulteta.

as highly developed a central bureaucracy and government as exists in Yugoslavia. The elaborate provisions of the system for representation in the federal government and for vetoing the federal government's decisions, while they reveal a deep distrust of that government, also seem to assume that the central authorities will continue to play a dominant role. The danger in this attitude is, of course, that the republics will continue to block the federal government from taking effective action, while themselves not assuming the necessary initiative to fill the vacuum.

Similar observations, but in a milder vein, might be made concerning the Czech constitutional law. There is the same focus on controlling the activities of the existing bureaucracy in Prague, combined with a reluctance to consider the alternative of a real devolution of powers to the republics. The principle of "Prohibited Majorities," no less so than the coordinating principle of the Yugoslav system, springs out of similar problems and attitudes.

If these systems are not federal in the Western sense, there is, nevertheless, perhaps a way in which these systems reflect a link between Eastern European traditions and contemporary problems of federalism. The link with Eastern European attitudes is, we would submit, indisputable. Enough has been said on the attitudes of elites in the interwar period to make the parallel clear.* The 1971 Yugoslav amendments are a product of the same kind of thinking, tactically at least, that led to the Sporazum of 1939: to find a way of strengthening the central government—that is, ending deadlocks over policy—even at the cost of an ill-defined autonomy for the republics.

At the same time there is an element of calculated risk in the Yugoslav maneuver that reflects a quite different attitude among the Yugoslav Communists than among the prewar elites. There is an attitude of flexibility, of willingness to compromise, of hope that the old spirit of "bratstvo i jedinistvo" will prevail if national grievances are recognized and in part satisfied. The difficulty lies in reconciling this attitude with the need for a strong central government at a time

---

*It is open to debate, of course, whether the elites of the postwar period in Slovakia, Croatia, and Slovenia have acquired their nationalism and their strength through a process of social mobilization "from below," as the result of being infected by the intellectuals of the prewar period whose influence continued after the war, or because they were a product of the decentralizing movement that sent persons back to their republics after gaining some ambition as a result of serving in the federal bureaucracy. All of these processes could be at work at the same time.

THE NATIONAL QUESTION   163

when regionalism and particularistic tendencies abound. Out of this dilemma comes an effort to manipulate the structure of government to please everyone. Substantial concessions are granted in one amendment, curtailed in the next.

This prompts one to think of the approach taken by the Yugoslavs as "manipulative," and the system, loosely and descriptively rather than legally, as "manipulative federalism." The term has been used by one researcher in connection with the governments of Southeast Asia to describe a response to conditions of economic growth in which federal structures are modified in the direction of offering some concessions to regional interests in order to maintain unity, under the assumption that developmental forces will eventually reintegrate the society and the political system from below.[48]

The point is not to press for a new category of federalism. Rather, we are considering certain parallels in the approach to problems of unity and diversity in developing political systems in which centralized governments, facing strong regional pressures, choose not to overwhelm the local elites (in the manner of an Averescu or a Pribicevic) but to seek compromises in the expectation that, in the long run, if unity of the market and the economy generally is not endangered, integration can be achieved. Such thinking is in sharp contrast to the Eastern European tradition, at least that which is a legacy of the interwar period when pressing issues of national security did not permit central governments to take such a lenient attitude.

CONCLUSIONS

In our discussion so far we have not attempted to make an overall assessment of the national question, more particularly of the impact of the problem on future events in Eastern Europe. The task, by its very nature, would take us outside the scope of this study. In respect to the question that concerns us more directly—the impact of the national question on the nature of the political system—we may note, briefly, the fact that, outside Yugoslavia, the possibilities of such influence have been reduced in Czechoslovakia by the collapse of the reform movement, but perhaps improved somewhat in Romania by changes in policy towards the minorities in that country. In both cases it would seem unwise to try to predict the course of events. The situation in Yugoslavia is too complex and uncertain. In Romania a new period is only beginning, which may or may not lead to significant change. It would seem more useful, therefore, to turn to certain points covered in our earlier discussion, reexamining once more the ways in which the national question and the development of political systems have been linked in the postwar period.

One point concerns the idea that national differences may have promoted the growth of the concept of a "loyal opposition" in Yugoslavia, as well as compelling the Communists to accept some notion of constitutional restraint. The idea that federalism is a framework within which democracy can develop is not a new one, and has been defended by Carl Friedrich.[49] We will not attempt to reproduce his argument here, except to note that it puts great stress on the way in which democratic opposition groups can develop within the shelter provided by state or provincial governments that form part of a federal structure. If we were to accept this idea, we might look for the development in Yugoslavia—for example, in Slovenia—of a liberal Communist republic government, maintaining its independence under the protection provided by the federal system. While such a possibility is not to be ruled out entirely, our account suggests that this has not been the pattern up to now. Nor does this seem likely to occur in the near future, given the fact that the central government has reasserted at least partial control over state security.

Is there nevertheless validity in the notion that the Communists have been prone to accept constitutional restraints as part of the process of developing a federal system? The case for the development of constitutionalism in Yugoslavia has been stated recently by Winston M. Fisk,[50] who argues that Yugoslavia "seems in important and far-reaching respects to be becoming a Rechtsstaat." Fisk can cite, in support of his position, the growing role of the constitutional court and the increased importance of the Federal Assembly. The case would seem to be strengthened by the introduction of the new federal system, requiring a much greater degree of observance of the constitution than has hitherto been the case.

The notion that Yugoslavia is developing into a Rechtsstaat seems difficult to accept, however, especially when one examines the recent constitutional amendments and sees how poorly they lend themselves to judicial review. What may encourage recourse to the courts—in our view—is the inability of the republic elites to harmonize their views, with the resultant tendency to "de-politicize" issues by granting greater responsibilities to government experts, by setting up independent authorities (such as the managing body of the fund for assistance to underdeveloped areas), or by allowing the constitutional court to settle conflicts of jurisdiction between republics and the federal government. Constitutionalism may be promoted by the needs of a federal system, but it may also, in the peculiar conditions that have prevailed in Yugoslavia, be a device to fill the vacuum created by the absence of elite consensus.

This leads us to a final consideration—also one concerned with elite relations. In our earlier discussion we talked of the alliance of liberal and national forces in Yugoslavia, and compared it to that

which led to the Czech spring. Relationships among these groups in
Yugoslavia require some special comment because of the strong possibility that the national factor played a role in shaping the development of Titoism, not only during the struggle against Rankovic, but from
the very inception of this system. The argument suggests itself because
it has proven very difficult to justify, in economic terms, the decentralization of the economy undertaken in the early 1950s. All else being
equal, decentralization was not a logical choice for a country at such
a low level of economic development. The rupture of trade relations
with the Cominform bloc also weighed against decentralization of the
economy, at least until new markets and sources of raw materials
had been found.[51]

It is within the realm of legitimate speculation to suggest that
there may nevertheless have been a compelling reason for decentralization, at least from the point of view of the areas in which most industry was concentrated at the time, Croatia and Slovenia. This reason
would have been the incompetence of the newly formed central bureaucracy in Belgrade and the expectation that industry in Slovenia and
Croatia would probably better survive the emergency if freed from
controls imposed by the economic ministries in Belgrade. Such
pragmatic considerations for decentralization would have fitted well
into the anti-Stalinist ideology that emerged in Yugoslavia at the time.
This argument would help explain the enthusiasm for decentralization
among some persons who were not really revisionists or liberals.
Indeed, it is notable that the reforms in Yugoslavia began before
revisionism, or liberal Communism, ever made its appearance.

It is certainly doubtful that a parallel will ever be found in
Eastern Europe to the Yugoslav case, characterized as it was by the
deep influence of national considerations on political development.
The Czech situation today is in a state of suspended animation. Still
there may be occasions when the alliance between liberals and nationalists provides the impetus necessary to promote reform and change in
the Communist political systems. The Soviet Union has resisted
reform successfully up to now. If change were to come about in that
country, it would not be surprising to see it based on such a coalition.

NOTES

1. Let us strike a familiar chord by quoting from Macartney
on the national feeling of the Balkan peasant: "The state, to most of
them, was altogether alien. But what they did possess . . . was the
personal bond of their nationality. . . . A Serb had never felt that he
was a citizen of the Ottoman Empire; he was mere Rayah; cattle.
But he had known he was a Serb. Now, when the passive acceptance

of his status had changed into pride and active ambition, all his hopes were naturally concentrated, not upon his state, but upon his nationality." Carlile A. Macartney, National States and National Minorities (New York: Russell and Russell, 1968), p. 94.

    2. Eberhard Menzel, "Das Minderheitenrecht in Europe," Nordfrisk Institut, Band 2 (1967), pp. 37-56.

    3. Erwin Viefhaus, "Die Nationalitatenfrage in den ostmitteleuropäischen Nationalstaaten nach 1919," Siebenburgisches Archiv, Band 6 (1967), p. 148.

    4. Rudolf Brandsch, "Mr. Maniu and the Minorities," Manchester Guardian, November 28, 1929.

    5. See also Georg Gelike, "Polen," in Institut fur Ostrecht, Fragen des Mitteleuropäischen Minderheitenrechts (1967), p. 128. No data was given on the minorities in the census of 1950. Information on the Volksdeutsch and the Autochthons, although not necessarily reliable, was made available by the Poles.

    6. "Minorities in Eastern Europe," East Europe, VIII, 3 (March 1959), 3-14; ibid, VIII, 4 (April 1959), 3-12.

    7. Nova Makedonija, February 6, 1967, p. 3.

    8. For discussions of this, see "Minorities in Eastern Europe." Laws dealing with the rights of the minorities in Czechoslovakia date from this time, as does the formation of the Hungarian Autonomous Region. The Rumanian constitution of 1952 also included guarantees of minority rights, including the use of national languages by local officials. Separate schools were set up for the minorities (which helped to isolate them); these schools were later to be integrated with the schools of the predominant nationality throughout Eastern Europe, including Yugoslavia.

    9. This began in Romania as early as 1956 with the placing of Hungarians in sections of Romanian schools, and gained momentum with the exit of the Soviet troops from Romania in 1958. The Hungarian University in Cluj was opened to Romanians until, in 1965, it graduated 218 Romanians and only 39 Hungarians. In 1962 the Hungarian Autonomous Region was reorganized. By 1966 the use of Hungarian by officials was forbidden. See Ferenc Vali, "Transylvania and the Hungarian Minority," Journal of International Affairs, 20, 1 (1966), 32-44; Handbuch der europäischen Volksgruppen, 619-28. In Yugoslavia integration of the minority schools and dissolution of the Hungarian and Romanian cultural organizations began in 1955 and was completed several years thereafter. Pressure was put on the minorities in Czechoslovakia in the same period, especially in the case of the Germans. An article published in Zivot strany, No. 16 (1960), reflects a policy of openly proclaimed assimilation: "The number of those Germans or citizens of German origin who have mastered well and in many cases perfectly the Czech or Slovak languages and who are

completely growing together with the two nationalities of the republic, the Czechs and the Slovaks, is growing fast. Just because we are not bourgeois nationalists but proletarian internationalists our party and our government purposely support this process of complete living together and assimilation of the remaining Germans into the republic with the Czech or Slovak nation. . . . ." Translated in Radio Free Europe, Evaluation and Analysis Department, "Communism and Slovakia," November 17, 1960. Policy in this period was not, by and large, aimed at total assimilation, however, and became more liberal after several years: in Czechoslovakia, by 1963; Yugoslavia, 1959; and Romania, 1968.

10. Vojvodina is the most obvious case of a region with minority populations that has been economically neglected. Kosovo was badly neglected until the early 1960s, when she began to receive considerable aid. The Hungarian Autonomous Region was given some assistance in the 1950s, but since that time has fallen behind the rest of Romania in the rate of economic growth. On the problems of regional economic development, see David Turnock, "The Pattern of Industrialization in Romania," Annals of the American Association of Geographers, September 1970, pp. 540-59, and F. E. Ian Hamilton, Yugoslavia: Patterns of Economic Activity (New York: Praeger Publishers, 1968).

11. See, for example, D. A. Tomasic, "Nationality Problems and Partisan Yugoslavia," Journal of Central European Affairs, VI (July 1946), pp. 111-25.

12. Polish policy is described in Geilke, "Polen," p. 101. Geilke refers to the decree of June 6, 1946, punishing expressions of racial hatred that were applied to anti-Semitic demonstrators after the war. At the same time, the regime gave Jews the means to open small shops.

13. Ghita Ionescu, Communism in Romania: 1944-1962 (New York and London: Oxford University Press, 1964), pp. 118, 241.

14. Vali, "Transylvania and the Hungarian Minority," p. 38.

15. They were allowed to return to their villages at the end of the 1950s. See Handbuch der europäischen Volksgruppen, pp. 420-29.

16. For treatment of the Poles in Czechoslovakia, see Rudolf Urban, "Tschechoslowakei," in Fragen des Mitteleuropäischen Minderheitenrechts, pp. 244-51.

17. For discussions of the Hungarians' role in the protests in Transylvania in 1956, see Ionescu, Communism in Romania, p. 270; Vali, "Transylvania and the Hungarian Minority"; and Handbuch der europäischen Volksgruppen, pp. 619-28. A brief account of the reaction of the Hungarians in Czechoslovakia to the events of 1956 is contained in Hungarians in Czechoslovakia, Research Institute for Minority Studies on Hungarians Attached to Czechoslovakia and Carpatho-Ruthenia, Inc., 1959.

18. For the impact of Czech events on the Soviet Ukraine, see Grey Hodnett and Peter J. Potichnyj, The Ukraine and the Czechoslovak Crisis, Occasional Paper No. 6, Department of Political Sciences, Austrialian National University (Canberra, 1970).

19. This policy could first be seen in the case of the Yugoslav reassessment of minorities policy in 1959, following the outbreak of the dispute with the Soviet Union in 1958. The policy of "bridgebuilding" did not initially apply to the Albanians in Kosovo but was extended to them as Yugoslavia drew closer to Albania in the 1960s, and following the fall of Rankovic in 1966. In the Romanian case we have seen a shift in policy as a response to the 1968 events in Czechoslovakia, and a marked shift in policy during the past six months as a result of Soviet pressures. Radio Free Europe, Rumania/19, July 23, 1971, by R. J. King, is an invaluable summary of recent developments in respect to the minority problem in Romania.

20. Edvard Kardelj in Komunist, March 4, 1971.

21. Jan Pasiak, Riesenie slovenske j norodnostnej otkazky (1962), p. 39.

22. For accounts of the dispute, see Politika, July 31, 1969.

23. Borba, November 17-21, 1969.

24. We have referred earlier to the problems of the Albanians. The Macedonians became involved in a dispute with the government of Bosnia-Herzegovina over the nationality of Slav Moslems in Macedonia. The position of Macedonia was that all Slavs in Macedonia would be recorded in the census as Macedonian. See Nova Makedonija, December 24, 1970. The plan to build a new mausoleum for Njegos on Mt. Lovcen has pitted the Serbs against the Montenegrins and attracted international attention because of the damage it is feared will be done to the mountain. For a summary of the entire affair, see Le Monde, June 9, 1971.

25. See Anali pravnog fakulteta u Beogradu, I, 3-4 (1955) and Zbornik pravnog fakulteta u Zagrebu, V, 3-4 (1955).

26. Pasiak, Riesenie slovenskej narodnostnej otkazky, p. 39.

27. Viliam Siroky, Za socialisticku industrializaciu slovenska.

28. The share of investments in Slovakia, if we are to accept Viktor Pavlenda's data, remained remarkably constaint: 30.4 percent, 1948-55; 29.4 percent, 1956-60; 31.5 percent, 1961-64 and 33.1 percent, 1965-66. Such consistency would seem to reflect a political decision on the division of investment funds. Ekonomicke zaklady socialistickeho riesenia narodnostnej otkazy v Ceskoslovensku, Table 9, p. 393.

29. Kurt Wessely, "Wirtschaftliche und soziale Probleme der Slowakei seit dem ersten Weltkriege," Die Slowakei als Mitteleuropäisches Problem in Geschichte und Gegenwart (1965), pp. 199-233.

30. Juraj Kramer, "Die Auswirkungen der Slowakischen Frage auf die Partei- und innenpolitik der CSSR von 1944 bis 1968,"

Berichte des Bundesinstituts für Ostwissenschaftliche und Internationale Studien, No. 36 (1969), Part II, p. 5. Kramer cites the figure of 90,000 commuters from Slovakia to Moravia, and a total of 350,000 Slovaks in the Czech lands.

31. Pavol Turcaṅ and Viktor Pavlenda, Le Développement Économique de la Slovaquie Socialiste (Bratislava: Acádemie Slovaque des Sciences, 1963), Chapters 12 and 13. Implicit at the time, and explicit later, was the argument that although differences between wages and incomes were dropping in percentage terms, in absolute terms the difference was increasing. Thus, while the per capita difference in absolute terms in 1948 between Slovakia and the Czech lands was 2,507 crowns, in 1965 it was 3,792 crowns. Pravda, March 6, 1968. On the other hand, the larger families in Slovakia were one reason this per capita difference had arisen, and on a per worker basis, there was a narrowing of income.

32. Harry Schwartz, Prague's 200 Days (New York: Praeger Publishers, 1969), Chapter 3; Fritz Beer, Die Zukunft funktioniert noch nicht (1969), p. 252.

33. Beer, Die Zukunft funktioneert noch nicht, p. 247.

34. Robin A. Remington, ed., Winter in Prague: Documents on Czechoslovak Communism in Crisis (Cambridge, Mass.: MIT Press, 1969), pp. 14-15.

35. Kramer, "Die Auswirkungen der Slowakischen Frage . . .," p. 27, and Pravda, January 21, 1968.

36. Kramer, "Die Auswirkungen der Slowakischen Frage . . .," p. 14, and Rude pravo, April 4, 1968.

37. Remington, Winter in Prague . . ., p. 173, translated from Rude pravo, May 18, 1968.

38. The Action Program may be found in Remington, Winter in Prague, pp. 88-141.

39. For example, see the article by Marian Sklenka, "Federation—Where do We Stand?" Rolnicke novine, April 20, translated in RFE Czechoslovak Press Survey, No. 2062, April 29, 1968; M. Nadubinsky, "Confederation" in Smena, April 29, translated in RFE Czechoslovak Press Survey, No. 2066, May 9, 1968, and the demands for confederation made by Vojtech Mihalik and Marian Sklenka in Rolnicke novine in April, reported in RFE Czech Situation Report, No. 44, April 24, 1968.

40. An indication of the difficulties that might have occurred had things taken their normal course is suggested by the attempt of Husak to have the Slovak party congress held before the CPCS congress scheduled for the fall in order, apparently, to present the Czechs with a fait accompli in respect to the Slovak demands on the federal system. Differences over the character of the federation persisted after the invasion. Rude pravo on October 16 summarized the

differences as (a) over the enumeration of federal bodies; (b) the structure of parliament; and (c) the electoral system. On October 22 the committees of the National Assembly discussing the bill agreed that both chambers of the federal assembly (the Chamber of Nations; the Chamber of the People) should be directly elected. On October 24 an 11-man delegation of the Slovak National Council was sent to Prague to explain the Slovak position, and on October 26 new proposals were submitted by the government and both national councils providing for indirect election to the Chamber of Nations. British Embassy, Czech Press Review, Nos. 198, 202, 206, 968.

41. Translated in RFE Czech Press Survey, No. 2244, July 30, 1969.

42. RFE Czechoslovak Situation Report, No. 87, August 13, 1968.

43. See, for example, Kardelj in Komunist, March 4, 1971.

44. The amendments are to be found in Sluzbeni list No. 29, July 8, 1971. They total 23 in number (Amendments 20 through 42 of the 1963 constitution).

45. Published in Sbirka zakonu Ceskoslovenske socialisticke republiky, No. 41, November 4, 1968.

46. Amendment 14 to the 1963 constitution provided that the federation and the republics would share responsibility for state security; the federal apparatus in this field was subsequently reduced by 60 percent. It has been suggested that the new system, although reversing the intent behind the above amendments, will provide for considerable decentralization of the secret police apparatus, with coordination carried out by the Presidency's council on security matters. Other duties of the Ministry of the Interior—besides state security— will be entirely in republic hands. NIN, February 28, 1971, p. 11.

47. See the comments of Vladimir Krivic, President of the Constitutional Court of Slovenia in Politika, April 6, 1971.

48. Joseph Rudolph, "Nation Building and Federalism: India, Pakistan, Malaysia, and Nigeria" (University of Virginia, Ph.D. dissertation, 1971).

49. Carl Friedrich, "Federalism and Opposition," Government in Opposition, I, 3 (May 1966), 286-95.

50. Winston M. Fisk, "The Constitutional Movement in Yugoslavia," Slavic Review, XXX, 2 (June 1971), 277-97.

51. Deborah D. Milenkovitch, Plan and Market in Yugoslav Economic Thought (New Haven: Yale University Press, 1971), Ch. 7.

* * * * *

ANALYSES
1. Stephen Fischer-Galati

The problems contained in Prof. Shoup's study are very well presented. I would like to raise some corollary points that are not discussed in the paper because Prof. Shoup is chiefly concerned with Czechoslovakia and Yugoslavia.

My main argument is that there is in this study, as, in general, all discussion of the Eastern European minority question, a lack of definition and a general tendency to confuse one national minority with another. It is impossible to equate the position of the Croats in Yugoslavia or the Slovaks in Czechoslovakia with that of the Hungarians in Romania or of the Jews in Poland. We are confronted in each case with entirely different circumstances. In this respect, then, any broad discussion of national minorities has to be much more clearly defined.

My other point is against the fundamental assumption that all national minorities have certain basic political grievances against the establishment; in other words, the establishment is hated simply because it is of a different nationality and not because it is inherently oppressive. The assumption is that the Hungarians in Romania would be less opposed to the central Romanian government than they would be to the central Hungarian government just because one is Romanian and the other is Hungarian. This kind of assumption obviously needs rethinking.

One should really think in terms of the reasons for discontent in the prewar and in the postwar periods and also who it was directed against. It would seem that the discontent was directed against an establishment that did not satisfy the rudimentary demands of particular minorities. This is a rather obvious thesis. More important, who exploited the discontent? Prof. Shoup claims that the difficulties during the prewar period originated from the exploitation of the minority problem by fellow nationals in other countries and also by Nazi Germany, thus raising the question of external interference in the internal affairs of the countries involved. It seems to me that this position is quite tenable, but also that it is far more relevant in terms of events that occurred after World War II. At no time has there been greater exploitation of minority questions than now when the Soviet Union has deliberately reopened these questions in order to undermine the stability of "hostile" regimes such as the Romanian or the Yugoslav.

Stephen Fischer-Galati is Professor of History at the University of Colorado, Boulder.

Another important question is that of the political consciousness of national minorities before and after the war. I would tend to agree that there is a fundamental intrinsic prejudice, for instance, on the part of the Croats toward the Serbs and on the part of the Hungarians toward the Romanians. But the ultimate question is who leads these particular national groups? It is in the composition of the leadership that fundamental changes have occurred since World War II. Prof. Shoup underemphasizes, in fact hardly mentions, the position of the Church. Obviously religion was a crucial factor in the nationality question before World War II, and it has to a certain extent survived even after World War II. What about the bourgeoisie of which very little is known?

Another question, crucial to any consideration of minority questions before World War II is that of the Jews. Anti-Semitism seems to have played a critical role in diverting and focusing existing prejudices. Immediately after World War II there was no Jewish question; but now religious and Jewish questions cannot be totally disregarded in analyzing minority problems in Eastern Europe, even though there have been major changes in the leadership of minority groups. These are fundamental problems.

Another basic difference between the minority questions before and after World War II involves the nature of the antagonists. In Yugoslavia, for instance, the Communist leaders of Croatia and Serbia each claim the respective national historic legacies. The historic legacy claimed by a Croatian Communist who fought for the establishment of a Croatian republic is indeed very different from the historic legacy claimed by the Croatian religious bourgeois leadership of the interwar period. In today's internecine Yugoslav conflict we are dealing essentially with rivalries among Communists operating within the establishment and within the framework of the Croatian, or the Serbian, or the Macedonian Communist organizations. Obviously a centralized Yugoslav state is not a historical phenomenon; Yugoslavia was in a sense an unrealistic creation even in the interwar years, as the complex minority question has so amply demonstrated.

One final word specifically connected with a few questions raised by Prof. Shoup. I have great doubt that the more important national minorities had greater sympathy for the Communist cause immediately after World War II than they had for other causes. I think that some did, but not because the Communists identified themselves with the national minorities' interests, but because the Communists posed as reformers. The question of the impact of the nationality question on institutional development is relevant only in the case of Yugoslavia. I see no influence of any sort exerted by various national minorities on the development of Romanian institutions. Nor do I believe that the national minorities of the U.S.S.R. will exert a decisive influence on the decisions of the central Soviet authorities in the foreseeable future.

The final point stressed by Prof. Shoup at some length is that of whether liberalism is an important factor in nationality questions. He suggests that the Communist reformers, unlike the nationalists of yore, colluded with the minorities for the ostensible purpose of bringing about reforms within the framework of an essentially liberal state favorable to the interests of national minorities. I see no fundamental incompatibility between nationalism and liberalism.

Ultimately, one would have to rethink the position of the national minorities, their functions, and their political consciousness in any appraisal of the impact that they have had on the history of Eastern Europe. This, of course, was not the function of Prof. Shoup's study, but I think that the questions raised in my comments provide additional dimensions to the problems that he analyzed in his necessarily limited study of Yugoslavia and Czechoslovakia on a broader Eastern European basis.

2. Paul Shapiro

I was greatly relieved to find that Prof. Shoup had liberated me from the necessity of formulating my comments within the context of issues that have tended to dominate our discussions of nationalism in Eastern Europe—for example, "the national question and state security," "nationalism versus communism," or, for those more historically oriented, the behavior of "historical versus nonhistorical nations." For this act of liberation alone, his study merits praise as one promoting new perspectives in understanding East Central Europe. It is, in addition, so full of useful information and provocative ideas that Prof. Shoup can be doubly credited in this respect.

There are two ways to approach a study of this scope and caliber. I could discuss the points of Prof. Shoup's analysis that I thought were particularly valuable—his discussion of the causes and nature of the dynamism of Eastern European political systems; his Czech-Yugoslav comparison <u>over time</u> of the interrelationship of national and political issues; or his comments concerning the ways in which a nationalist-reformist alliance, by promoting decentralization and federalism, might indirectly promote the "elite restraint" and "tolerance of a loyal opposition" that are constituent parts of "liberalism." After which I could go on to discuss those ideas that I found difficult to

---

Paul Shapiro is a Ph.D. candidate in the Department of History at Columbia University, New York.

accept—the notions, for instance, that the national question is less
a social issue now than it was between the wars; or that interwar
Czechoslovakia developed truly democratic institutions and solved
its nationality problems to the extent that Prof. Shoup has implied;
or that current developments in Romania represent a trend that could
lead to liberalization by way of the steps outlined in the analytical
framework of the study under discussion.

Having outlined this approach, I will now adopt a more general
one and, looking to the further development of Prof. Shoup's ideas,
play the role of devil's advocate in a methodological sense. I will
do this partly because I find it hard to disagree with the overall thesis
of his study and partly because I think that my comments may help to
eliminate some of the ambiguities that Prof. Shoup himself acknowledges at various points in his presentation. Since my comments will
reinforce my disagreements about the Romanian case I will later
devote some remarks to this specific question.

When I decided that I basically agreed with Prof. Shoup's ideas
on possible reformist-nationalist alliances and their effects, I was
disturbed to find that he had nowhere made reference to the one body
of political-science methodology that seemed to me always to lurk just
below the surface of his argumentation and to be particularly well
suited to assuring its persuasiveness. I refer to interest-group
analysis. Since David Truman's pathfinding work in the field, The
Governmental Process,[1] the methodological tools of interest-group
analysis have been greatly refined. They have been applied to developing countries by Gabriel Almond and others, important for us since
Prof. Shoup tries to give his analysis meaning for developing nations
in general. And they have most recently been used to explain the
development of pluralism in Communist systems by Gordon Skilling
and Franklyn Griffiths.[2] I wonder whether we can depict the reformist-nationalist alliance as two intersecting sets of interest groups,
one set formed around the issue of nationalism versus centralism,
and the other around that of reformism versus conservatism? At
any point of intersection of these sets, the interests of a group from
the first set would coincide with those of a group from the second set,
and the two could be expected to act in support of one another even if
their positions on other questions differed greatly. Thus the 1968 alliance of Czech reformers and Slovak nationalists despite Slovak conservatism. Basically Prof. Shoup has described a situation examined
closely by some interest-group analysts and called a situation of "multiple lines of political cleavage," with society, or at least its politically
decisive leadership, dividing in different ways over different political
issues. Where only one fundamental issue exists, the minority opinion
group cannot gain support for its cause by appealing to those segments
of the majority whose interests might have coincided with those of

the minority on the basis of some other political issue. Where more than one fundamental issue exists, I think it can credibly seek this sort of support. On the basis of these comments we might say that nationalism has favored reformism in Eastern Europe by evolving into an alternate line—or issue—of political cleavage, a line that at some point (or points) intersects the line based on the most fundamental issue in the post-Stalin era, namely, reformism versus conservatism. Prof. Shoup has provided us with the preconditions for this evolution in his discussion of the factors at work in the postwar period that have tended to enhance the institutional impact of the national question.

While I suggest the use of interest-group methodology primarily because it may facilitate the broader application of Prof. Shoup's ideas—perhaps to Third World countries—I do so also because it has helped me to deal, although still not in an entirely satisfactory way, with the one problem that I initially felt gravely marred his analysis. This is the too easily made suggestion that reformism and/or decentralization somehow is the equivalent of liberalization or liberalism. I think that we have to guard against the assumption that reform in the Communist world is inevitably liberal or progressive. Prof. Shoup points out, on the basis of his Czech and Yugoslav case studies, that there exists a danger that the reformist-nationalist alliance, rather than leading to liberal reform, may lead instead to the reproduction of the abuses of the central bureaucracy at the republic (i.e., local) level in some, if not all, of the federal units of the decentralized-devoluted states. But, given his thesis of the nationalist-reformist alliance bringing about liberalism and constitutionalism, Prof. Shoup has trouble dealing with the actuality of this danger in any systematic way. I hope that I am being helpful when I suggest that the possibility of liberal trends developing through the mechanism that Prof. Shoup has described disappears completely if the institutional impact of the nationalism versus centralism line of cleavage overpowers that of the reformism versus conservatism line of cleavage; that is, if questions of reformism versus conservatism are decided on the basis of strictly national divisions. When this happens we are back at the point where only one political issue with institutional impact exists, now nationalism versus centralism instead of reformism versus conservatism as in the past. According to my frame of analysis, this would make the operation of Prof. Shoup's mechanism impossible. I suggest that this would be the case if, as Prof. Shoup suggests may happen, popular representation is eliminated in the Yugoslav Federal Assembly and replaced with closely controlled delegations from the republics acting as units.

Coming finally to Romania, I have to disagree with Prof. Shoup's remarks when he says that recent changes in policy toward the minorities can be viewed as having improved the possibility of the national question acquiring greater institutional impact. I think he has lost sight of the fact that in his own analysis of multinational states the national question played a role largely because the nationalities involved were given corporate or collective rights as nationalities. I do not think that the Romanian reforms to which he refers in any way go beyond the simple expansion of the personal rights of individual members of the country's minorities. The Romanian government still aims at the "assimilation" of the Hungarian minority, but, for the first time, in a positive and progressive sense, not in the sense in which the term "assimilation" is normally understood. The government has continued its attempts to demonstrate to the Hungarians that they really have no alternative to becoming a part of the Romanian state community. And insofar as they are given equal rights as citizens of the state—this, in fact, is the effect of current reforms—I think that the government is justified in doing this. It has consistently moved to reduce the potential political power of the Hungarian sector of the population as a collectivity, just the opposite of the situation that has developed in Yugoslavia. That increased individual rights for minority group members have accompanied these moves does not alter the fact that the intent is to reduce the political influence of the Hungarian minority as a unit. I think that Kenneth Jowitt has correctly evaluated the current Romanian policy as one calculated to create a "solidary society": one in which the various parts have similar levels of economic and social development, with differences allowed for and even supported rather than intimidated, as long as they are individual rather than collective—or structurally expressed—and cultural rather than political.[3] Because I accept this point of view I can see no indication that the national minorities of Romania are on their way to acquiring greater institutional impact.

3. Georg W. Strobel

Prof. Shoup's study proceeds from the traditional interpretation of minority policy and from the minority situation in a specific state. It includes terms that date back to the nineteenth century and are based on an understanding of minority rights and problems in the setting of post-World War I Europe as structured at Versailles. This terminology does not accommodate supraregional state blocs as they

---

Georg W. Strobel is a Professor at the University of Mainz and a staff member of Bundesinstitut für ostwissenschaftliche and internationale Studien, Cologne, Federal Republic of Germany.

have evolved especially in the socialist camp today with its ideological defense and economic network. In this framework, political, governmental, and party interests determine developments in the same manner as the interests of minorities or nationality groups do on the level of national states. The Sokolen in prewar Czechoslovakia and the Zbowid in postwar Poland are examples. This interplay of forces is of special interest outside the socialist camp in the clash of young nationalistic movements—strengthened rather than weakened by World War II—and the supposedly internationalist claims of the supraregional state bloc, which at closer examination proves to be clearly focused on the specific interests of one dominant state. This, of course, leads to tensions. This significant issue is mentioned in Prof. Shoup's study only in passing, in the last paragraph of his study, while I believe that it should have been its central point.

The primary example of Eastern European nationalism has unfortunately been given only marginal attention—the Ukrainians even before 1939 tried to achieve independence, in Poland, Czechoslovakia, Romania, and certainly in the Soviet Union where there were resistance movements and even armed risings. The Ukrainians and the Germans also illustrate the exploitation of ethnic minorities in Eastern Europe between 1930 and 1935. The Ukrainians and the Germans in Poland and Czechoslovakia around 1930 were repeatedly instigated by the Comintern and the Soviet Union to dissociate themselves from their host countries within the limits of their conceded autonomy, in order to weaken and undermine the viability of these countries, thereby precipitating the revolution.

Efforts toward the establishment of a nation state, on the other hand, were made by the bourgeois politicians of the Ukraine, who formed two Ukrainian governments-in-exile. The Carpatho-Ukraine in 1938 seemed on the verge of becoming a Ukrainian Piedmont after the two attempts at setting up a Ukrainian state in 1917-21 had failed. The Hungarians, however, extinguished all Ukrainian hopes and the First Vienna Arbitration was the final coup de grâce.

Little else seems to be known about Ukrainian developments. The Ukrainians from the southern Polish region of Bieszczady were not resettled because of their collaboration with the Germans, but the problem of German-Ukrainian collaboration is not a simple one. After 1942 the nationalist Ukrainian Resistance movement, the UPA, fought against the Germans as well as the Russians. They did not collaborate with the Germans as did elements of the right-wing Polish Resistance movement, the NSZ. The anti-Communist Ukrainian Resistance movement continued to exist after the war until 1950. The resettlement of the Lemken was a move designed to crush them, but not a punitive measure for the collaboration of Ukrainians with the Germans.

The Polish pacification program of 1947 was even more disastrous and inhumane than that conducted in the Ukrainian territories by the bourgeois Polish government. However, both actions were induced by Polish nationalism and were partially directed against the Ukrainian minority, who since 1956 have repeatedly called upon Kiev for help and received it, only to become even more suspect in the eyes of Polish nationalists. In these instances, nationalistic "feeling" spread beyond the territory of one state, affecting intrastate relations.

In describing the favorable aspects of the coexistence of minorities, Prof. Shoup makes no mention of what I consider the most striking political and socioeconomic example, namely that of the former German citizens who remained in Poland after 1945, the so-called autochthons whose ranks were divided by the resettlement of people from Poland's central and eastern regions taken over by the Soviet Union. The new settlers were at a culturally and materially lower state of development than the autochthons, especially with regard to agricultural technology. Their resettlement, therefore, required an adjustment of the underdeveloped Old Poles to the more developed former Germans, now New Poles, so that the new settlers from East and Central Poland had to pass through several decades of material and cultural development within a few years, with important consequences for Poland's socioeconomic structure.

The autochthons, or New Poles, also had a beneficial influence on Polish policy. In 1947 those Germans who were willing to sign declarations of loyalty to the Polish state were awarded Polish citizenship, but for years this group was regarded as an insufficiently Polonized minority distinctly different from the rest of the population. References to this group served to underline the historical claim to the Oder-Neisse territories. The Polish argument, on the other hand, was that the presence of a large number of Polish nationals in these territories was proof that only former Polish territories were taken over. In this way ethnic policy was used as an argument for a nationally oriented policy.

As I mentioned earlier, conflicts arising from nationalist movements have their effects not only in the internal affairs of states, but also in interstate relations. The example of Poland during recent years may serve to illustrate my point.

During the last 15 years, Poland has been shaken by a total of 5 periods of internal unrest—twice in the last 3 years, in March of 1968 and between December 1970 and April 1971. In all instances national considerations played a considerable role. Nationalism characterized the student riots of March 1968 that evolved from earlier manifestations of anti-Russian sentiment. In their wake attempts were made to counteract the Russophobia—hazardous in foreign policy—by finding a substitute target for hatred—the Jews.

THE NATIONAL QUESTION

These efforts required considerable nationalistic manipulation of Polish society. For example, the March riots were described as a plot of anti-Polish, antisocialist, and Zionist elements. At the same time, Jews were blamed for all of Poland's difficulties.

But in spite of these efforts, distrust and aversion toward Russians did not disappear and similar attitudes toward Germany were intensified. Public reactions assumed a nationalist character. GDR participation in the occupation of Czechoslovakia in August 1968 was interpreted as an indication of possible East German-Soviet cooperation against a reluctant Poland. The Moscow Treaty of August 12, 1970, conjured up the ghost of Rapallo even in newspapers and on television. Concern grew over a possible Paris-Bonn-Berlin-Moscow axis with an anti-Polish flavor. This nationalist assessment of the situation developed within the community of socialist states that, at least on paper, are committed to an international outlook.

Fear, mistrust, and nationalistic overcompensation could not be completely eliminated even by the Bonn-Warsaw Treaty of December 1970 that recognized the Oder-Neisse line as Poland's Western border. Yet the Polish party leadership expected a significant pacifying effect and therefore dared institute unpopular economic measures. It was these measures that led to the December crisis of 1970.

In this manner nationalist elements have had an impact in shaping Poland's policy with respect to internal and foreign affairs. The war veterans' organization Zbowid, whose leadership made special efforts to instigate anti-Semitism, became a basis of nationalism. Favored by dual membership, it presented itself as an alternative to the Party. In reaction, the Party tried, in 1968-69, to adjust by taking over some of Zbowid's nationalistic slogans.

Even Gomulka did not remain unaffected. Skilled defamation against his Jewish wife made his position seem less unassailable. The preeminence of the nationalist element was demonstrated by a 1967 poll that showed that 60 percent of all Party functionaries at the middle level declared that they would let national interests take precedence over the interests of the Party under any circumstances. Only 30 percent of those interviewed chose the Party and its interests.

As far as Poland is concerned, therefore, we can note that nationalism, instigated and favored by foreign-policy considerations and injected into interparty discussions, began to encroach upon the state and the party, thereby affecting Poland's position within the socialist camp. It would be fair to say that party- or state-oriented nationalism in the future will have a greater impact on the supraregional socialist bloc and on its institutions than nationalistic symbols embodied in the traditional minority problem. One might also speculate on the possible development of a variant of Fascism in these countries, given the behavior of the Zbowid group. Only Yugoslavia— which Prof. Shoup has dealt with extensively in his study—might be an exception. But Yugoslavia does not belong to the socialist camp in the strict sense. Consequently that country can not be of decisive significance for the part of Eastern Europe that is under the influence of the Soviet Union, a problem that Prof. Shoup unfortunately does not sufficiently consider. Admittedly, following Tito's death or resignation, the country will be interesting and tense politically, but without clear consequences for the socialist bloc in the sense of party or state nationalism.

Also, Prof. Shoup fails to give sufficient consideration to the following questions. How do Romania's national interests affect the COMECON concept of other socialist countries? Or, how have Poland's defensive and strategic concepts led to the development of certain regional groupings within the Warsaw Pact? The problems are real in this area. And there are many more like them: for instance, Dimitrov's proposals in 1948 to form a Balkan Pact—these influenced Soviet policy toward Yugoslavia; and, in this context, Bulgaria's leanings toward such a Balkan Pact in 1955; and the Bled military alliance.

It is impossible to describe these problems here in detail or point out their significance. However, an analysis of them could yield more important results than the problem of resettlement of Ukrainians in Bieszcady to Northern Poland or the behavior of a small group of Polish nationals in October of 1965. Their attitudes in August of 1968 might be more interesting since they lived in the territory assigned to Polish invasion troops.

4. Kenneth Jowitt

Many of the most critical issues currently facing East European elites are problems of integration. Integration refers "to a shifting relationship between various changing identities within the framework of a variety of possible political arrangements capable of coping with a specifiable range of stresses."[1] Viewed from this perspective, integration is a dynamic and complex process. The dynamism and complexity of integration is partially due to the fact that it often becomes a political issue in several related arenas at the same time. Currently, for Marxist-Leninist elites in Eastern Europe the question of integration is salient in at least four arenas: the national arena, the "Eastern European bloc," the European community as a whole,

---

Kenneth Jowitt is professor of Political Science at the University of California at Berkeley.

and what I would term the regime community, namely that unit comprised of ruling Marxist-Leninist parties.

Stated in this fashion, the question of changes in the political identity* of these regimes becomes a matter of ascertaining how the behavior of Eastern European leaders affects the character of integration in the four specified arenas. First, in the national arena one is interested in how decisions affect the relation between a given party and its domestic base. Second, in the bloc setting one focuses on how decisions affect and shape the pattern of relationships existing between and among different East European nations. Third, regime setting, here one is concerned with noting the types of relations that exist between and among ruling parties. It is of course conceivable that two bloc members may have relatively developed economic exchanges while their respective regime leaderships are much less positively engaged, due to differences in political-ideological orientations. Fourth, in the European setting one is interested in determining the extent and character of ties with communities and regimes outside the bloc. What I am suggesting is that from this perspective, one that relates issues and settings, the analysis of political change in Eastern Europe becomes more susceptible to systematic and discriminating analysis. Too often Western analysts, like their Marxist-Leninist counterparts, tend to see every conflict occurring within the area (Eastern Europe or Western societies) as an indication of systemic crisis, and these analysts are often unable to weigh such conflicts in terms of their relative significance for the political identity and capacity of these systems. This tendency is largely due to the absence of analytic frameworks that sensitize the observer to the complex and dynamic factors that are involved. Without such frameworks it is not too surprising that the Western observer of East European development is usually able to say nothing more, after a crisis, than that there are indeed major unresolved problems in these societies.

I would like to suggest some concepts that can contribute to creating a more unified and discriminating approach, one that links issues, problem areas, and settings more effectively. I have in mind the notions of membership groupings and identity references; there

---

*As used here, political identity will refer to the set of ideological, institutional, and policy commitments that characterize a given regime. Changes in political identity involve reformulations of the ideology, redefinition of the institutional format, and innovations in policy. One could, of course, elaborate on this in terms of the order of change: routine, significant, critical.

is nothing peculiar about these notions. Individuals as well as organizations define themselves partially in terms of the kinds of groups to which they belong, and partially in terms of the units or groups to which they aspire to belong; the two are not necessarily identical or compatible. In any case, I would suggest that each Eastern European leadership belongs to a number of different membership units and identifies itself as part of several groupings. For example, currently the Romanian party elite sees itself as an integral and defining element of the Romanian national community; that is fairly obvious. At the same time, it perceives itself as an integral part of what, in contrast to the national community, might be termed the regime community. It defines itself in good part as a member in ambivalent standing in the community made up of the 14 ruling Marxist-Leninist parties.* It is defined as, and in certain respects defines itself, as a member of the bloc of socialist nations in Eastern Europe. In addition, the Romanian leadership sees Romania today as a member of the European community and the Third World community of nations. I am suggesting two things. First, that the political identity of a given East European regime is not simply a function of domestic factors but of the interplay between exogenous and endogenous factors, of the relation between and compatibility of membership and identity commitments. Second, and more generally, I am suggesting that working with the notion of membership groupings and identity references can sensitize an analyst to a series of related questions directly concerning the issue of changes in and conflicts over the political identity of individual East European regimes.

Let me specify some of the questions that follow from this approach. First, which of these references and which of these membership groupings have the greatest weight for which regimes?

Another question in how broad is the set of references for different regimes? Bulgaria, for instance, simplifies its universe by, in effect, having a very constrained and homogeneous range of identity references. However, Romania's institutional-ideological-and-policy evolution will presumably be influenced by the fact that it currently defines itself in terms of a more complex set of commitments.

A third question could be how compatible are these various orientations? To what extent can these regimes square the circle, i.e., consider themselves Third World regimes for certain purposes

---

*The fact that the R.C.P identifies the 14 ruling parties as its major identity referent, whereas the Soviets and others, such as the Bulgarian, define the acceptance of Soviet hegemony as the effective criterion of membership, is itself a major political issue.

and Marxist-Leninist for others, both European nations and members of the "Soviet bloc"? In short, what conditions are necessary for changes in institutional character, policy, and ideology to proceed in such a fashion as to permit and facilitate the <u>adoption of multiple vs. exclusive identities on the part of East European regimes</u>?

A fourth area of investigation that is suggested by this framework concerns the relationship between regime heterogeneity-homogeneity and the range of institutional innovation within the Eastern European area. Regime heterogeneity, such as existed within Eastern Europe in the 1960s, reflected among other things the inability of the Soviets and their dependents to arrive at a consensus as to what the character of the interregime and intrabloc community should be. The 1960s were, and in certain respects the 1970s continue to be, a period in which the crucial identity question faced domestically (in the national arena) by each regime is to define what is meant by the leading role of the party, to specify the place and role the party is to occupy vis-à-vis social forces making a variety of recognition demands (political, social, and economic). In the international arena the parallel question has been what will be the character of interregime and intercommunity relations among Marxist-Leninist parties and nation-states,* or, stated operationally, what will be the position of the CPSU relative to other ruling parties. I would argue that the incidence of political heterogeneity within Eastern Europe—at one point including Gemulka, Dubcek, Kadar, and Ceausescu regimes—was a reflection of the dissensus over these issues. Dissensus within the regime community about the limits on innovation created a situation that in certain (not all) respects was favorable to significant changes in institutional format, policy definition, and ideological orientation—to significant political identity changes. One could also argue that Marxist-Leninist elites place a high premium on the maintenance of a regime-community, on a membership unit comprising the political elites who govern individual nation-states, and that the integrity of this unit is seen as essential to the maintenance of each regime's Leninist identity. If this is so, any weakening of the integrity of this community would

---

*Interregime relations take place between individuals acting in party roles whereas inter-(national) community relations take place between individuals acting in governmental roles. Interregime issues tend to be dealt with in a less bureaucratic setting and take the form of occasional public and private meetings of party leaders. Intercommunity issues tend to be dealt with in institutions of an on-going nature, whose meetings are ordered in a scheduled fashion (i.e., Comecon and the Warsaw Pact).

lead these elites to strive for (though not necessarily achieve) a mutually acceptable (though not necessarily conflict-free) understanding of what the nature of such a community would be and how it would relate to other membership and identity references (i.e., national or nonbloc membership groupings). In fact, such a development seems to have occurred within Eastern Europe and, with the exception of Albania, Yugoslavia, and Romania, there appears to be a greater degree of interregime homogeneity, for example between Gierek, Honecker, Kadar, and Husak. This is simultaneously a significant and relative development. I by no means wish to suggest that regimes in this area are now identical, or to deny the significant differences existing between Hungary and the Soviet Union economically, Hungary and Czechoslovakia politically, and potentially between Poland and the Soviet Union. However, I am arguing that Eastern Europe, in contrast to the late 1960s is presently a more consensual area; there is a greater degree of interregime congruence, and the consequence is that we are more likely to see, on the one hand, "deviant" regimes such as the Romanian forced to make hard identity choices as the slack in their bloc and regime settings is diminished. On the other hand, we are likely to see reformist measures applied to existing institutions that, while possibly significant, will not vary as widely from regime to regime as in the 1960s. This is not a static conclusion. In fact one must recognize the possibility of future dramatic changes precisely because one is aware that the identity of these regimes, including the Soviet, is increasingly related to the different ways in which they define the relative weight and character of the distinct but related settings within which they all operate: national, bloc, regime, and European. The task of managing and coordinating decisions concerning regime identity is becoming increasingly complex for each East European regime and for the various groupings of Marxist-Leninist parties; simultaneously the task of analyzing changing patterns of integration and emerging definitions of political life is becoming more challenging for students of East European developments.

5. Paul E. Zinner

The topic before us is a vital one in relation to Eastern Europe and in relation to politics and political development throughout the world. I would like to emphasize that point because I think that we tend to be very egocentric and parochial and tend to talk about

---

Paul E. Zinner is Professor of Political Science at the University of California at Davis.

our area only in its own context, as though it did not belong to this planet of ours. Professor Shoup took the nationality question and molded it in his own image, as we all tend to do, and discussed it in terms of national minorities and their impact in a nation-state situation, and limited himself largely to Yugoslavia and Czechoslovakia. The nationality question can be cast in a different way; it is not only an internal problem in the nation-state, but also an external one. Once moved to a higher level, that of international relations, the nationality question becomes an enormously interesting topic. In this regard, Eastern Europe perhaps lags in an evolutionary sense behind Western Europe, where some of the problems about national affiliation have been overcome and therefore a possibility has been created for integration.

In any event, I would like to observe that perhaps the methodological approach to the problem is less rigorous than is implied in the first few pages of the study. This is not surprising, because the author set himself a rather difficult task. The framework itself is somewhat loose.

Specifically, what are we talking about: the national question and its impact on political institutions, or something else—and what do we understand by the national question? Is it a question of the minority nationalities or is it also a question of the dominant nationalities? Unless one defines it, one moves back and forth from one level to another. One needs to talk about the nationality question in as broad a setting and framework as possible, even if that leads to confusion. Prof. Shoup fails to ask certain important questions concerning the relationship between nationalism and socialism, between nationalism and democracy, or nationalism and authoritarianism that might be of greater interest to political scientists than to historians. But historians too might be interested in these interrelationships and the product of these interrelationships.

I have to note that during the interwar period the impact of the nationality question on politics was fairly violent. I am not quite sure how to handle the Czechoslovak situation, because in that country the nationality question, to all intents and purposes, was solved internally; in effect, however, it was not solved at all, because the nationality question was instrumental in the dismemberment of the Czechoslovak state. What one might indicate is that nationalism in the interwar period had a strong connotation of collectivism as against individualism and that it had a strongly romantic flavor that clashed and was not really compatible with professed democratic humanist ideals.

In the interwar period Hungary did not have a national minority problem of any significance, yet its politics were dominated by the nationality question and this question had a predominant influence on shaping Hungarian political institutions and the Hungarian political process.

In the contemporary period the nationality situation is simplified to some extent in terms of the multiple national minority problems that exist. In effect it was only after World War II that the principle upon which the reconstitution of Central and Eastern Europe that was supposed to have taken place after World War I was more or less implemented. It is interesting that after World War I the principle of ethnic self-determination had no important place in the creation of new states and drawing of new boundaries. It was after World War II that this was done, and not in the Wilsonian spirit of 1918. The German minorities were simply kicked out of Poland and Czechoslovakia, for example, and thereby an enormous problem was resolved. But in other ways the issue has been complicated because what has been brought into focus is the very intricate relationship between nationalism and Communism. This issue is both theoretically and practically very difficult to come to grips with, not only for analysts but for practitioners, including the Communists themselves.

If we look at the post-World War II situation chronologically, we find that in 1945-48 the Communists did attempt to identify themselves with national aspirations, obviously for political purposes, to maximize their appeal to the people and to move with as much popular support in this period of pseudo-parliamentary development as possible. This was particularly true in Romania, where the Communists were not strongly entrenched, and in Hungary where they wished to erase the memories of the antinational past of the Bolsheviks. From 1948 to 1953, there followed a period of denationalization, a deliberate policy of suppression of the national self. The brutal Stalinist policy of organizational homogenization of the different national entities was not limited to the relationship that is often foremost in people's minds, namely between the Communist Party as the agent of denationalization and the people, but in effect was taking place within the Communist parties themselves where the national element, so called, was deliberately and systematically eliminated.

The eradication of bourgeois nationalist tendencies, or Titoism, to use Communist terminology, affected all parties, albeit in different degrees. Some of the victims survived and had their day before the court of history as it were: for example, Gomulka in Poland (who has had the misfortune of being disgraced twice) and Husak in Czechoslovakia (who may yet share Gomulka's fate). Other victims, of course, did not survive. Nationalism did have a profound impact on internal politics in Eastern Europe. Predictably the policies of denationalization had repercussions because they could not be continued indefinitely. The change that came about after Stalin's death in 1953 witnessed the reaffirmation of the national self and it was that assertiveness that was fundamental to the cataclysmic or near-cataclysmic developments of 1956.

There are other elements that intrude—humanism, reformism, liberalism, the aspirations for a humanist socialism. But the basic propellant in the developments of 1956 was the reassertion of the national self both within the populations and within the Communist Party. Kadar is a national Communist, as is Ceausescu. But, of course, there are significant differences between Hungary and Romania. Among others there are the questions of luck and of the perspicacity of the leaders in charge. The difference between the Romanian leadership and the Hungarian leadership is startling, but the important thing is that the nationalistic urge is not directed only against the regimes in power. It may be manifested by the regime itself (as in Romania) and to the extent to which the Communist elite can exploit national strivings it manages to create a situation of stability and to entrench itself in power both vis-à-vis its population and vis-à-vis the Soviet Union.

As political analysts we should pay a great deal of attention to the question of this internalization of political power, the creation of many national centers of power. This development in Eastern Europe is of paramount importance, and is outstanding in Romania today. In effect, what we are witnessing is a combination of Communism and nationalism leading to the creation of certain independent national bases of political power. This is of enormous importance for the future. It is the essence of polycentrism, which is meaningful only if there is a tangible power base underlying it.

To move on to Czechoslovakia specifically, in this respect, it is interesting to note the inability or unwillingness of the Communist leadership to harness the latent power of nationalism. It was not until 1968, as part of what is commonly called the Prague Spring, that nationalism reasserted itself in Slovakia. Slovak nationalism played an integral part in the developments that took place, mainly in toppling the Stalinist conservative leadership. The gradual rise of Slovak nationalism throughout the 1960s paralleled in a classic sense the development of national sentiment in the nineteenth century. It manifested itself in the publication of voluminous historical literature glorifying and romanticizing past achievements, especially the abortive Slovak uprising of 1944. It was this that served as the basis of Slovak claims within Czechoslovakia for equal status and for the establishment of a dual state. It was an amazingly interesting development, one in which the tools of historical analysis and the writing of history were used to stake out a national claim.

An interesting connection developed between Slovak national aspirations and aspirations in the Czech lands of a more humanist-democratic-individualist orientation. The politics of Czechoslovakia in that period cannot be understood without interrelating these two disparate trends that seemed to work toward a common end, up to a point. This was a strength; but it was also a weakness since there was no essential unity between the strivings of the Czechs and of the Slovaks. This provided the Soviet Union with an entering wedge at a crucial moment.

To conclude, in Romania we find a stark variant of nationalism in that the Romanian Communist Party leadership uses Romanian nationalism as a vehicle for stabilizing the internal situation and for creating a power base from which it is possible to oppose the Soviet Union. I see no evidence in Romania of catering to the Hungarian national minority in terms of any collective aspirations that it might have. In effect, the Hungarian minority is still very much opposed because it is a potentially disruptive element in Romania. It has sympathies with Hungary, and at the present time these sympathies could be exploited.

I would like to end on a note that may not fully relate to my previous comments. The opportunities are plentiful for a systematic study of relations between nationalism and communism, if not between nationalism and democracy and humanism in Eastern Europe. It is indeed desirable for those of us who claim to be practitioners of respectable academic disciplines to pay much closer attention to the ethnic determinants of politics. Somehow we have tended to overlook this, especially in political science, and it is high time to make amends for our neglect.

NOTES TO ANALYSES

Analysis 2

1. David Truman, The Governmental Process (New York: Alfred A. Knopf, 1951).
2. Gordon Skilling and Franklyn Griffiths, Interest Groups in Soviet Politics (Princeton, N.J.: the University Press, 1971).
3. Kenneth Jowitt, Revolutionary Breakthroughs and National Development: The Case of Romania (Berkeley, Calif.: University of California Press, 1971), pp. 281-82.

Analysis 4

1. Aristide R. Zolberg, "Patterns of National Integration," Journal of Modern African Studies, No. 4 (December 1967), pp. 451-52.

CHAPTER 6

TOWARD A SOCIALIST ECONOMIC INTEGRATION OF EASTERN EUROPE
Heinrich Machowski

Since 1969, the twentieth anniversary of the founding of COMECON, a debate about "socialist economic integration" has been going on in Eastern Europe. This particular terminology was first mentioned in mid-1970 in an official COMECON publication,[1] and the discussion at that time culminated in the "Complex program for the further deepening and streamlining of cooperation and for developing socialist economic integration among the member countries of COMECON" (hereafter referred to as the "complex program") that was unanimously passed by the member countries in late July 1971, after two years of preliminary work.[2] The complex program establishes a 15-20 year transition period, during which cooperation among Eastern European economies is to be strengthened and preparations made to proceed in the direction of integration.

This paper will attempt to outline the development perspectives of COMECON. There are no clear-cut, generally accepted methods for examining integration problems of socialist planned economies, such as those found in Eastern Europe.[3] That is both an advantage and a disadvantage, for a specific methodological approach must exist at the outset of such a study of COMECON. The basic problem of any international alliance, including any interregional economic community, is to find and formulate realistic goals for common policy. Accordingly, my analysis of Eastern European economic integration is based on three criteria:

1. Have COMECON member countries been able to decide upon a common system of economic policy goals for the transition period?

Heinrich Machowski is a staff member of the Deutsches Institut für Wirtschaftsforschung in Berlin, Federal Republic of Germany.

2. Which methods—"policies"—are to be used to achieve these common goals?

3. Is there an adequate administrative structure in the community to do justice to these goals and methods?

My approach is an institutional one, first because I engage in empirical economic research, and because a large part of research on Eastern Europe carried out in the Federal Republic of Germany follows this approach. Second, because highly qualified theoreticians will analyze this study, and they are much more competent than I to handle theoretical aspects.

GOALS OF INTEGRATION

The strategic goal of "socialist integration" is not defined in the complex program of 1971. A precise definition for the term "socialist economic integration" is likewise absent. Actually, integration is vaguely described as a "definite and systematically designed process of the international socialist division of labor" by Communist parties and governments of COMECON member countries. During this process a number of goals are to be achieved: increased economic growth, a higher standard of living, a higher degree of self-sufficiency for the community, increased defensive strength, and higher and more stable intrabloc trade. The main goal of the community for the next 15-20 years is stated to be a gradual leveling off of the socioeconomic performance levels of the participating countries. The COMECON members, however, have not yet been able to determine the real significance of this equalization goal; nor is anything said about which countries are relatively underdeveloped and therefore entitled to demand aid from partner countries (Outer Mongolia is an exception), or about the character of this aid.

This is not surprising in light of the present structural differences in COMECON. Structural differences of large magnitude exist between the member countries. The economic productive potential is distributed quite disproportionately: the Soviet Union currently produces 65 to 70 percent of the (estimated) GNP of the community. This establishes the economic and political hegemony of the Soviet Union. The political side of this hegemony could well hamper the integration process; for success in cooperation in COMECON unavoidably will lead to an accentuation of the leading position of the Soviet Union, regardless of the political intent of the Soviet leadership.[4]

Furthermore, there are tremendous differences in economic performance levels between the member countries as measured by overall productivity and standard of living, and in national economic structure as noted by statistical contributions to the GNP by sectors. In this regard, an important element in the consideration of integration in Eastern Europe is the fact that the leading political power in the community, the Soviet Union, has one of the less developed economies. These differences not only result in opposing economic policy aims, such as widely diverging national growth targets, but are also expressed in the differing production and consumption patterns of the people, in fact in their entire psychological attitude toward economic problems. The importance of this fact for integration policies has recently been recognized in connection with planned monetary and economic union in the EEC.[5]

Another important structural problem in COMECON is the difference in the importance of foreign trade for the individual countries. The smaller countries have an average degree of foreign trade dependence (exports in percent of national product) of between 40 percent (Hungary) and 20 percent (Poland).[6] These countries must accordingly pay attention to foreign trade and integration as an aspect of their economic policies. The opposite is true for the Soviet Union, where the export ratio is only about 5 percent. This means that the Soviet Union can carry out economic policy measures without worrying about the foreign-trade sector. Soviet representatives in COMECON agencies have, without regard for their partners, brought work to a standstill, sometimes out of complete disinterest or even ignorance. A good American example along this line is the "New Deal" of President Nixon, a program that takes account of key domestic political and economic considerations at the expense of traditional international economic principles and obligations.

In light of these structural problems in COMECON, the following question by R. Nyers, member of the Politbureau of the Hungarian Communist Party, is understandable, although politically it hardly deserves an answer: "In connection with the integration of the socialist countries, it may be asked whether it would be possible and sensible to integrate the COMECON countries with the aid of an onlooking Soviet Union, since even on its own the Soviet Union is a powerful, integrated economic unit, which needs further integration little or not at all."[7]

From this background information about structural disparities, it is clear that a common denominator cannot be found for the economic interests of the respective COMECON countries. There probably is not even a sense of common economic interests present in the member countries. In order to be able to further economic cooperation in COMECON under these conditions, integration goals had to be formulated in such a way that all countries, despite diverging points of interest, could accept them. The complex program goals already mentioned, for which unanimous agreement was reached, are therefore written in vague terms that often contradict one another. They do not establish guidelines for concrete, common economic policy measures. Rather, they can be interpreted as a statement of intentions for the direction to be taken and for the means whereby a leveling off of economies can be brought about in the integration process.

INTEGRATION METHODS

In the light of the variety of economic interests and the deeply rooted differences in goals, it was only possible for COMECON to agree upon those methods of integration that do not affect national sovereignty—thus the coordination of plans denoted in the complex program as the "main method of organizing cooperation and deepening the international division of labor." The member countries are asked to coordinate middle- and particularly long-term economic policy measures in the area of structural policy and in the development of science and technology. Agreements about specialization of industrial production are to follow as a second step. However, neither the specific areas of co-ordination of plans nor a method of coordination has been worked out. The complex program envisages that both these problems will be solved by the end of 1972. National governments are assured ample control, since only "interested" countries have to participate in the coordination of certain subject areas. This means that coordination in the economic policy in COMECON can be either bilateral or multilateral. Plan coordination, as an instrument of international economic cooperation, has been in practice since 1962,[8] but despite original aims this coordination has been limited to bilateral trade negotiations between COMECON countries. It shaped the first decisive bargaining round over the five-year bilateral trade agreement.[9] The government protocols on plan coordination for the period 1971-75, signed by the Soviet Union and other COMECON countries in the last half of 1970, are almost identical to the trade agreements signed later by the parties.[10] These six government documents were signed within a period of only six weeks and it can be assumed that parallel negotiations were carried out. It is possible therefore that a type of multilateral coordination of the planned balances in Soviet-COMECON trade for the period 1971-75 was achieved. But because of the contradictions and the vagueness of goals within COMECON, one can agree with the skeptics who see plan coordination retaining its present bilateral form in the near future and limiting itself to mutual trade.[11]

In addition to plan coordination, the complex program stipulates a new method of economic integration: <u>the common planning of specific</u>

A SOCIALIST ECONOMIC INTEGRATION

industries and production facilities. With respect to the above-mentioned conditions for maximum preservation of national sovereignty, this method for future cooperation is limited in three ways: (1) only the "interested" countries should take part; (2) the independent character of "internal planning" must be maintained (whatever that might mean); and (3) the corresponding production facilities and resources will remain in the possession of the respective countries.

Furthermore, the COMECON countries are obliged to carry out mutual consultations—the least intensive of the various integration methods—in all basic questions of economic policy. The stress lies on mutual reporting of important socioeconomic development problems as well as of goals, measures, and experiences of national performance.

ORGANIZATIONAL PROBLEMS OF INTEGRATION

Because of uncertainty about the future development of cooperation, no changes in the decision-making process of the COMECON community were proposed in the complex plan. The basic principles of COMECON, as established in the 1962 Council Charter, were in fact confirmed and stressed: "Socialist economic integration proceeds along the basis of complete free will and is not dependent upon the creation of supranational bodies. . . ." The existing organizational structure insures the member countries maximum influence at the community level.[12] Of the principal organs of COMECON, the Council, the Executive Committee, and the Standing Commissions (presently 21) have the power to make recommendations on economic cooperation within their spheres of activity. There is, however, no hierarchical structure; the Standing Commissions are not controlled by the Executive Committee or the Council, and therefore recommendations of all competent bodies are considered "recommendations of COMECON" and differ only in content. This means that the representatives of the member countries in the individual COMECON organs form an independent country delegation, with the single responsibility of representing their country in the particular organ. This organizational structure insures the maximum influence of the countries at all levels of decision-making, particularly since control over representatives in COMECON bodies is usually handled by a special government committee at the national level. Oddly enough, the Secretariat, the only principal Council organ in a position to formulate common interests for the community, is not even empowered to make recommendations. Its function within COMECON is that of an initiator.

The current form of decision-making is even more important for the dominance of national interests over community interests: all recommendations must be passed unanimously. The principle of unanimity, the decisive guarantee for national sovereignty, is a universal principle of the COMECON constitution, applying even to the special organizations of COMECON members—for instance, the International Bank for Economic Cooperation, Intermetal, Interchim, etc.—which are allowed to accept recommendations and make decisions within their respective spheres of activity. Only the statute of the International Investment Bank of COMECON includes the possibility of doing away with the unanimity principle. Although all Bank decisions concerning "fundamental questions" have to be passed unanimously, other questions need only a qualified majority.

The special organizations of COMECON have been established in those subareas of economic cooperation, where—at least for most members—the costs and benefits of a deepened coordination and cooperation can easily be estimated. The complex program particularly stresses the further expansion of existing organizations of this type and the founding of new ones. These include, for the most part, "international economic organizations," that, aside from coordinating activities, are to perform common economic functions (for instance, production, trade, and engineering). The participants in these organizations retain complete independence with regard to their assets and organizational and legal position; economically they are supposed to assume the shape of "international socialist concerns or companies."

What does the complex program say about the future development of economic relations among the COMECON countries within the described institutional framework? This point is touched on only briefly, with examples referring to intrabloc trade, movement of capital, and freedom of establishment; the movement of labor, another important area of interregional cooperation, receives no mention at all. Freedom of movement for goods, labor, and capital—within certain formal and material limitations—as well as certain freedom of establishment within the integrated economic area are the characterizing features of the present EEC.

INTRABLOC TRADE

Structural differences and conflicts of interests stemming from them among the countries in the COMECON area are of a long-term nature. Consequently, the institutional structure and the forms of cooperation within this community will change only gradually. This is particularly true of COMECON intrabloc trade, the main area of integration in Eastern Europe thus far. The complex program foresees an accelerated development of mutual trade, an upswing that is to be accomplished within the present organizational framework. State trade monopoly, national planning, and bilateral trade agreements will continue to serve as bases for intrabloc trade. Accordingly, the exchange of goods is not likely to be liberalized in the future, but will continue to be subject to the direct control of national officials through quotas on exports and imports, the allocation of foreign currency, etc. The establishment of a common market within the COMECON area is not planned for the transition period. Also lacking are the beginnings of a common trade policy toward the rest of the world or even the EEC. A relaxation of the system of strict controls is foreseen by the complex program in only one marginal area, the so-called liberalized exchange of commodities. Apparently the intention here is to follow up on the experience of Hungary and Czechoslovakia subsequent to their 1967 agreement on the partial liberalization of bilateral trade. Assuming this to be the case, intrabloc quota-free trade will be conducted along the following lines:

1. A list of free-trade goods will be compiled through multilateral negotiation; this list would be subject to revision, i.e., lengthening or shortening on a year-to-year basis.

2. Producers, consumers, and trading firms would be entitled to buy and sell these commodities freely on all markets within COMECON.

3. In principle, the prices of these goods would not be negotiated and set by agreements between the states, but rather negotiated by the buyers and the sellers.

4. Free trade would be permitted only in "soft" commodities, primarily manufactured consumer goods; its volume could amount to a maximum of some 2 to 3 percent of total intrabloc trade.[13]

It is very doubtful, in view of its limited volume, that the trade of quota-free commodities can be a source of impluses sufficiently strong to effect even a partial phasing out of strict bilateralism in trade within COMECON. The main obstacle to multilateral relations is presumably to be found in the prices prevailing in intrabloc trade—perhaps the most controversial problem in connection with economic cooperation in COMECON. In spite of the drawn-out and rather heated discussion on the revision of these prices—which cannot be gone into at length here[14]—the complex program still offers no solution. The present formula for price formation is the following: "prices prevailing on the world market, adjusted to eliminate the harmful effects of cyclic factors of the capitalistic market." This formula is to be adhered to in the "coming period"; by the end of 1972, however, "a complex study of problems in the perfection of foreign trade price system" is to be completed. One of the principal difficulties in this connection—indirectly, structural differences also play a part here—lies in finding a concept for foreign trade price reform that will not have balance of payments repercussions. The sought-after convertibility of national currencies in COMECON will be attainable only if this problem is solved.

CAPITAL MARKET

Convertibility of national currencies is the most important requisite for a successful functioning of a supraregional capital market; or, to use the language of the Political Economy of Socialism, "for the increased international implementation of fixed assets and circulating funds."[15] This is borne out by the experience so far of the International Investment Bank of the COMECON countries, or, more precisely, the peculiar credit mechanism of this bank. On the basis of members' contributions to the original bank capital, which are made 70 percent in transferable rubles (trb) and 30 percent in freely convertible currencies or gold, this bank provides loans for the financing of investment projects in the common interest. However, only loans in freely convertible currencies are useful for the acquisition of necessary capital goods on the world market. The trb, on the other hand, is not a currency unit, i.e., it does not represent independent purchasing power, but is rather a clearing unit existing only in its trade-recording capacity. Bank deposits of members in trb serve only to define lending in natura. In other words, the capital subscription of a member country represents an obligation to make deliveries up to the subscription amount of certain capital goods to a borrower as specified by the bank, above and beyond trade quotas set by the agreements existing between the countries involved. Since COMECON countries at present have hardly any "convertible" capital goods at their disposal apart from trade obligations, it is by no means surprising that the credit activity of the bank and the applications for credit to date have been extremely low, totalling 330 million trb or not quite 2 percent of the present export volume on intrabloc trade.[16]

FREEDOM OF ESTABLISHMENT

According to the complex program, interested member countries can "establish joint enterprises, with independent assets, under the conditions laid down by the law of the country of establishment for its own nationals, to operate on the basis of khosrascet (economic accountability) and liable to the extent of the enterprises' assets."

The question as to the legal form of this "international socialistic ownership of the means of production" remains unanswered, as does the one regarding the functioning of the joint enterprises; these problems are to be solved by the partners concerned. Poland and East Germany recently reached agreement on the construction of a cotton spinning mill in Poland to be jointly owned by both countries "in accordance with each country's contribution" and operated under joint management.[17] Apparently, however, no agreement has been reached on the exact legal form of the enterprise or on its organization, financing, and integration into the Polish planning system. A model for the solution to this problem might be provided by the Polish-Hungarian joint stock company "Haldex" that was founded in 1959 and located in Poland.[18] The representatives of Poland and East Germany have emphasized the "pioneering spirit" of their decision in the quest for "higher forms of economic integration," noting that "enterprises of this nature had not existed previously." It remains to be seen upon what bases the Polish-East German enterprise will be placed, and whether this experiment will provide the spark for the establishment of additional joint enterprises within COMECON, including those involving multilateral participation.

CONCLUSIONS

Sufficient clarity and agreement are yet to be achieved among COMECON member countries regarding the central goals to be followed over the course of the transition to economic integration. Differences of economic structure within the community have yet to be reduced to a tolerable level to permit a successful development in this direction. A further hindrance lies in the fact that, for lack of adequate empirical and statistical material, none of the COMECON countries is in a position to estimate, even approximately, the prospective gains or losses for its own economy from integration. Although COMECON has been in existence for 20 years, harmonization of the most important areas of economic statistics is still a goal for the future as set down by the complex program. There is agreement everywhere in Eastern Europe that the logical consequence of economic integration is increased prosperity for the countries involved through increased specialization of production, production on a larger scale, reduction of unit costs, increased productivity of labor, increased growth of GNP. Missing, however, is a clear methodical approach for checking and quantifying these effects.

A theory of socialist integration has yet to be developed by means of which the effects of integration on the economic development in the individual countries can be forecast. But then, there is no concept on customs union in the West that is satisfactory both theoretically and empirically.19 In the language of the Political Economy of Socialism the challenge is stated thus: " . . . an urgent task is the thorough study of the specifics of the mechanism of the economic laws of socialism in economic relations among socialist nations, in order that the conditions for their effectiveness can be perfected in accordance with a plan."20

Under these conditions, the rate of progress toward "socialist economic integration," and thus the length of the present transition period of COMECON, will be decisively dependent on the desire for political unity of the member countries.

NOTES

1. C. Communique of the 24th Council Session of Comecon in Warsaw, Pravda and Trybuna Ludu, May 15, 1970.
2. The German version of the complex program was printed in Neues Deutschland, August 7, 1971. Cf. also, "Der 'Rat für gegenseitige Wirtschaftshilfe' (RGW) in einer Übergangsphase" (The council for mutual economic assistance (CMEA) in a transition phase), Wochenbericht des DIW, No. 40 (1971), compiled by Heinrich Machowski.
3. Cf. John M. Montias, "Obstacles to the economic integration of Eastern Europe," Studies in Comparative Communism (July-October 1970), p. 38.
4. Author's own estimates (as to the methods of estimation cf.: Erich Klinkmüller and Heinrich Machowski, "Nationaleinkommen und Bruttosozialprodukt einiger RGW-Länder, der USA und der BR Deutschland," Osteuropa-Wirtschaft, No. 2, 1966, pp. 115 f.) and those of the ECE (cf. Economic Survey of Europe in 1969, Part 1 (New York 1970), pp. 5 ff. Cf. Erich Klinkmüller, "Similarities and differences of the economic integration in Western and Eastern Europe," Europa-Archiv, No. 16 (1966), p. 577.
5. Cf. Jörg Thalmann, "Structural differences in the EEC countries as an obstacle to monetary and economic union," Europa-Archiv, No. 21 (1970), pp. 781 ff.
6. These are Soviet estimates, the methodological basis of which is unknown. Cf. Mir socializma v cifrach i faktach 1968 (The world of socialism in figures and facts, 1968), (Moskva, 1969), p. 129. As to the estimated degree of foreign-trade dependence of Eastern European economies, cf. Heinrich Machowski, "The degree of integration of East German Foreign Trade in Comecon, 1971-1975" (paper submitted to the NASEES conference in London, April 23-25, 1971).

7. Quoted from Stefan Stolte, "Comecon at the crossroads?" Bulletin, No. 3 (1969), p. 28. (Original source: Nepszabadsag, January 23, 1969.)

8. Cf. Michael Kaser, Comecon (London, New York, Toronto: Oxford University Press, 1967), 2d ed., pp. 106 ff.

9. Cf. Pawel Bozyk, ed., Integracja ekonomiczna krajow socjalistycznych (Economic integration of socialist countries), (Warszawa 1970), p. 54 ff; and Tibor Kiss, International Division of Labour in Open Economies—with Special Regard to the CMEA (Budapest 1971), p. 176 ff.

10. Cf. "Die Entwicklung des sowjetischen Aussenhandels mit den RGW-Ländern in den Jahren 1971-1975" (The development of Soviet Comecon trade in the period 1971-1975), Wochenbericht des DIW, No. 48 (1970), compiled by Heinrich Machowski.

11. Kiss, International Division of Labour . . . , p. 185.

12. Cf. Heinrich Machowski, "Organisatorische Probleme der wirtschaftlichen Zusammenarbeit im 'Rat für gegenseitige Wirtschaftshilfe'" (Organizational problems connected with economic cooperation in Comecon), Vierteljahrshefte zur Wirtschaftsforschung, No. 4 (1970), pp. 279 ff.

13. Kiss, International Division of Labour . . . , p. 193.

14. Cf. Kaser, Comecon, pp. 176 ff.; Montias, "Obstacles to the economic integration . . . ," pp. 56 ff.; Peter Wiles, Communist International Economies (Oxford: 1968), pp. 210 ff.; and Heinrich Machowski, "Zur Preisbildung im RGW-Intrablockhandel: Das Beispiel der polnischen Steinkohle" (Pricing in Comecon intrabloc trade: the example of Polish coal), Osteuropa-Wirtschaft, No. 2 (1969), pp. 89 ff.

15. Günther Kohlmey and Gerhard Kraft, "Volkswirtschaftliche Akkumlationskraft und sozialistische Integration" (National economic accumulative power and socialist integration), Wirtschaftswissenschaft, No. 8 (1971), p. 1195.

16. Cf. "Mezdunarodnyj socialisticeskii kredit" (International socialistic credit), Ekonomiceskaja gazeta, No. 39 (1971), p. 21; and "Jaki start?" (How was it in the beginning?), Zyci gospodarcze, No. 31 (1971), pp. 1, 2.

17. Trybuna Ludu, October 25, 1971.

18. Cf. Heinrich Machowski, "Die polnisch-ungarische Aktiengesellschaft 'Haldex' zur Verwertung der Abraumhalden im oberschlesischen Steinkohlenbergbau" (The Polish-Hungarian joint stock company "Haldex"), Osteuropa-Wirtschaft, No. 2 (1965), pp. 117 ff.

19. Cf. Christian Watrin, "Was ist die EWG wert?" (What is the EEC worth?), Wirtschaftswoche, No. 31 (1970), pp. 35 ff.; and Fritz Franzmeyer, "Zur EWG-Erweiterung—Beitrittsprobleme unter

besonderer Berücksichtigung Grossbritanniens" (Problems of EEC expansion—problems of entrance with special regard to the UK), Vierteljahrshefte zur Wirtschaftsforschung, No. 3 (1970), pp. 209 ff.

20. Edelhard Göbler and Otto Weitkus, "Theoretische Probleme der sozialistischen ökonomischen Integration" (Theoretical problems of socialist economic integration), Einheit, No. 2 (1971), p. 196.

* * * * *

ANALYSES

1. Ivan Berend

Dr. Machowski has chosen an institutional approach in dealing with theoretical problems. According to Hegel, the phenomenon itself and the history of the phenomenon are one and the same thing. I have therefore chosen the historical approach and will attempt to show the different stages of the historical progress of COMECON.

During the first period, 1949-54, COMECON did not endeavor to bring about economic integration, either in the economic conceptual sense or the institutional sense. The COMECON baby was delivered in a mixed family: its father was politics and its mother economics. It was primarily a political answer to the American Marshall Plan, as well as to the new Eastern European situation following developments in Yugoslavia. It declared the political unity of the Eastern European socialist countries and recognized the division of the world into two camps. It showed the unity of the socialist camp without Yugoslavia and without the previously planned customs union. But COMECON was also a product of real economic needs: there was a need to assure raw materials, goods and markets on an intracamp basis in circumstances of Western and American embargo policy, discrimination, and boycott. That is, COMECON was not an organization for industrial cooperation and economic integration in a real sense. Nevertheless, the volume of trade doubled or trebled among socialist countries and a well-organized trade development was achieved during the first five-year-plan period.

The second period, 1954-62 was a period of great accomplishment. The drive toward industrial cooperation, standardization, and creation of new forms of division of labor took place during this time. It was a time of important joint undertakings. But these years also

---

Ivan Berend is Professor of Economic History at Karl Marx University of Economics, Budapest, and Secretary-General of the Hungarian Historical Association.

witnessed a new form of voluntarism. Khrushchev and his colleagues thought that economic problems could best be solved by political means. The first desired result of the change was political; namely, to compete more efficiently with advanced capitalist countries and catch up with them in a short time. However, there were main contradictions during these years, as seen on the one hand, in the new aims of modern integration and sophisticated division of labor, and, on the other hand, in the use of methods of overcentralized planning based on compulsory directives. This economic mechanism was geared to circumstances and aims of another historical period, when forced industrialization was used to achieve quantitative results in an autarkic way. It could not serve the very different targets of a period characterized by international economic cooperation. The continued use of this method resulted in several contradictions and, in spite of completely different strategic aims, it could have no greater integrating effect than the economic policy of the previous period. This became abundantly clear as early as 1962.

The third period, beginning with 1962, and running to the present, is the period of realism. During this period emphasis has been placed on taking important or relatively small practical steps without sensational long-run aims and slogans. The effort has been to find every reasonable solution to achieve greater efficiency and to solve the crucial economic problems of technological progress. In Hungary, for example, it was decided to solve the fuel problem and to achieve a modern structure of fuel consumption, also to establish cooperation between the chemical and bauxite-aluminum industries. A higher stage of economic maturity and recognition of needs has been reached, and there is now an awareness of optimum ideas, aims, and methods. During these transitional years we cannot avoid experimenting with different approaches to integration.

Some of the most important preconditions for further efficient economic integration are seen to be:

1. Real incentives that give an impetus to firms to cooperate with others. The problems are too complex and do not lend themselves to solution on a governmental level. There is a paragraph at the end of the Complex Program that promises a better use of real price and market incentives. Further progress depends partly on the realization of this aim.

2. Solution of the problem of the price system and development of a value-oriented price system. A by-product of this would be a solution of the currency and convertibility problems.

3. Establishment of real economic integration in the framework of COMECON is not possible on the basis of COMECON autarky. In this connection it is necessary to develop trade and economic cooperation with the advanced highly industrialized countries of the

West. A common joint solution of world monetary problems and the creation of a worldwide monetary system would be highly desirable.

The Complex Program represents a realistic effort and reflects a need for further progress in economic integration. In a historical perspective, this stage of COMECON is a transitory stage and a turning point in the process of integration. The realization of real integration will be for the next generation of economic historians to discuss.

2. William Diebold, Jr.

My approach to this problem is somewhat different from that of most people at this conference. I am not a specialist in Eastern Europe, although I am much concerned with Eastern European problems. I look at them, however, in the framework of international economic relations as a whole, of the structure and organization of the world economy. Therefore, for me, Eastern European relations are important not only per se but because the characteristics peculiar to their internal relations have a bearing both on the place of this group of countries in the world and on the relation of their experience to the process of integration going on in different ways in different parts of the world.

With this comparative approach one can look first at the different processes called "integration." In the now familiar Western European type of integration (the EEC and EFTA), a series of steps has been taken as a result of a deliberate decision. There is also a broader and looser type of integration that is taking place among the economies of all industrialized countries outside the socialist sphere; this is a process that is less a matter of clear-cut decision-making and setting of objectives and more one of lowering barriers, increasing mobility of all sorts, and a great deal of initiative and innovation coming from uncoordinated private activity. All these lead to a high degree of integration of national economies, not as a matter of choice but as a response to a set of processes. Given mobility and the relative openness of economies, technological change and the increase in the minimum size required for efficiency have implications for these countries not only of an engineering but also of a financial sort. Nevertheless, there is a great deal of resistance to these processes. Meanwhile, in the poor countries there is a limited kind of integration. Small on a regional basis, it is probably greater in relation to the

---

William Diebold, Jr., is a Senior Research Fellow at the Council on Foreign Relations, New York.

world market but there it tends to spell dependency, especially given the historical position with which these countries started.

How does COMECON fit into this framework? Clearly we should not go very far in using the model of Western European integration to give us any ideas, for the character of the latter has been very different in that it has been mainly a barrier-removing exercise. The broader-based integration movement of the industrialized nations as a whole is also not a very helpful model since it too includes a set of factors related to private initiative that are not applicable to the socialist countries. The first phase of COMECON activity had some relation to the efforts at integration made by developing countries that were trying to broaden their economic base and make for a more rational process of development. But in these cases the core of the problem is to find ways of coordinating plans so as to develop a rational and interrelated system. One expects this type of integration to be more difficult than that carried on in Western Europe because it is always more difficult for separate governments to cooperate in what might be called a positive way—that is to work together for the implementation of a concrete project—than to agree to remove barriers, hard as this is. Yet it is this "positive" direction in which Western European integration and industrial-world integration are moving. That is to say, although there remain important barriers to be removed, there is a clear recognition in Western Europe of the need for common policies in different fields such as energy; the encouragement of research, development, and science-based industries; and, in general, the shaping of industrial patterns. Not quite as far advanced, but clearly perceptible, are the same tendencies in the nonsocialist industrial world as a whole. All these kinds of cooperation require agreed positive action. Thus we may find greater similarities in the future among Western, Eastern, and less developed country integrations.

Nevertheless, for the present one should look at COMECON integration as sui generis. That entails rejecting the tendency to see COMECON as primarily an Eastern Common Market. The analogy is misleading, not only because the functions are so different but the structure as well; the EEC has no U.S.S.R. Many observers of the COMECON conclude that it does not provide much integration. Their criteria are implied in such judgments as that there is too much bilateralism and not enough multilateralism, too much rigidity and not enough flexibility, only a marginal impact on national policies and little real coordination of national plans.

What are the possibilities of change? In the minds of some, increased economic decentralization and greater use of market economy in the member states would make possible a truer economic integration. Clearly this view leans toward the Western European model and seems to leave aside the question of whether it would be harder or easier (or more or less important) to coordinate national plans if each economy were more decentralized.

I will leave it to others to judge if we can expect major moves toward decentralization and the enlargement of market sectors. One interesting question on which I have seen no comment concerns what happens to integration if reforms go much farther in one or two countries than in the others. Do subregionalisms develop, with more integration among a few countries than within the area as a whole? Is there a tendency for the same problems to develop within the group that exist in East-West economic relations, i.e., those arising from differences in systems?

A second possible source of change comes from the great interest in joint ventures, whether with Western countries or between COMECON countries. The present emphasis of such efforts, or of thinking about them, is not on integration, but might that not change in the future? The economic feasibility of some joint ventures might depend on having a market of a more than national size, or on putting together resources from several places, or simply on sharing the costs of the ever-larger units required by modern technology. Any such possibilities may become forces for integration. After all, American investment is said to have done much to integrate the Common Market and I hear Easterners praising joint ventures because they help break the rigidities of established ways of doing things.

My outside approach suggests one more set of questions; these concern the dynamics of COMECON integration. One motive for Western European integration was to obtain gains in economic welfare; another factor that sometimes operates is the political will to draw closer together. How strong are these forces in the COMECON countries? How much agreement is there on goals? When the aim is to obtain economic gains, can these best be had through COMECON integration or improved relations with the outside world? Do these two goals mutually support one another or is there some contradiction between emphasizing relations with Western Europe and with members of the COMECON? In the past, a good deal of the motivation for integration in Western Europe came from the need to solve problems within Western Europe, but outside forces were always important and not least the pressures coming from the United States. In the early stages American help and encouragement were important. Now the initiatives are entirely European, but an important influence on decisions is the wish to see European opinions carry greater weight in the world, not least in Washington. Is there any comparable process in Eastern Europe? Will the enlargement of the European Community cause the COMECON countries to draw closer together—or would that only happen if the Western European countries finally established common policies toward the East? If having the United States outside helped Western European integration, does it follow that having the U.S.S.R. inside COMECON hampers Eastern European integration? It would certainly affect its character and seems to have an important influence on people's views as to whether such integration is desirable.

3. John M. Montias

I will concentrate on the problem faced by a number of very small countries in Eastern Europe in trying to cooperate with a very large country, the Soviet Union.

First some remarks on sovereignty and autonomy. The parallel between the gradual abandonment of economic sovereignty in the EEC or Western Europe as a whole and in Eastern Europe can be too hastily drawn. One forgets too easily that within the COMECON countries autonomy in the conduct of the economy is virtually the only political sovereignty the leaders of these countries have. One may also forget that this economic autonomy was not won immediately after the war. From 1949-53 these countries had very little autonomy in the conduct of their economic affairs, and it was only after the death of Stalin that one could detect important policy innovations in the conduct of economic affairs. Hence, to give up any part of this sovereignty would be a very painful process. This is true of all Eastern European countries, with the exception of the German Democratic Republic, which feels it to be to its advantage to police the others, to act as the junior partner of the Soviet Union in bringing about a closer integration through directed coordination, i.e., through the gradual erosion of autonomy in economic affairs.

There are, as Dr. Machowski points out, three types of integration in COMECON.

First, directed coordination with or without the agreement of the individual countries concerned. This is the direction that Khrushchev wanted to press these countries into, and it is perhaps also the direction in which the Soviet Union would like to go today, but it is pursuing this policy more cautiously.

The second type is through coordination on the basis of voluntary agreements and it is the type of coordination that is going on in COMECON now.

The third is coordination through decentralized decisions and market processes. This is the type that several COMECON countries would like to move toward, including first Hungary, then Poland

---

John M. Montias is Professor of Economics at Yale University, New Haven, Conn.

and possibly Bulgaria. (Czechoslovakia, at this point, can only minimize initiatives.)

It is interesting to speculate as to what market-type reforms might mean for individual countries such as Poland and Hungary at a time when other members of COMECON, including the Soviet Union, have not decentralized their foreign trade operations at all. It is hard to imagine the extent to which the Soviet Union centralizes its foreign trade operations; it is only in the last two years, for instance, that the Soviet Union has agreed to have Eastern European nations exhibit their wares in cities other than Moscow. There is virtually no contact between the official foreign trade representatives of Poland and Hungary and the managers of Soviet enterprises; everything is conducted through the Ministry of Foreign Trade in Moscow. There is little prospect of regionalization of Soviet foreign trade, which might have been an avenue toward voluntary cooperation in COMECON and toward a less unbalanced division of powers in the organization. Proposals along this line have been resisted systematically by the Soviet Union.

The question is what happens when, as in Poland, two-thirds of the volume of the export trade is supposed to be made on the basis of decisions taken at the level of the associations? With the representatives of what Soviet organs are association officials going to negotiate? If with officials of the Ministry of Foreign Trade in Moscow, what progress will have been made toward decentralization? My own feeling is that the decentralizing measures taken in the Eastern European states can only have the effect of redirecting trade either toward other members of COMECON that carry on trade in a decentralized way or toward the West. Whether the Soviet Union will tolerate such a diversion is another matter.

Another important point relates to the economic policy of the Soviet Union with respect to the United States and Germany and its effect on the Eastern European members of COMECON. Maurice Stans has been in Moscow recently to conduct economic negotiations with the Soviet Union that may triple or quadruple trade in the next few years. I have been struck by the fact that the Soviet Union does not hesitate to engage in trade with the West when it feels that this is to its advantage. Yet it restrains other countries (such as Bulgaria in the mid-1960s) when they try to move too far too fast in that same direction. Is this going to mean that countries such as Czechoslovakia, the German Democratic Republic, and Hungary that all depend to some extent at least on the Soviet Union for their machinery-products markets are going to find difficulty in marketing their goods? Some Hungarian trade officials, when confronted with this problem, contend that this is not an insuperable problem, since Hungarian manufacturers can, and perhaps even should, be redirected toward some of the "harder," more competitive markets of the West. It was argued by a team of Czech economists, who published their findings in Nova Mysl two or three months before the Soviet invasion of Czechoslovakia in August 1968, that a similar reorientation of Czech exports of machinery products away from the soft markets of the East, toward the hard markets of the West, would be highly desirable since it would promote technical progress. The argument stated in this report was that, for years, exports of machinery and other manufactured products had been directed toward the Soviet Union and the less developed countries of COMECON without much challenge or effort and that this had led to a lack of initiative and innovation on the part of exporters. Imre Vajda, the late Hungarian economist, once wrote that an excessive concentration of exports of manufactured goods to "soft markets" had prevented the exporting countries from pursuing an intensive growth strategy. The extensive type of development practiced by the importers (e.g., the Soviet Union or Romania) was thus foisted on the exporter (Czechoslovakia or Hungary).

To shift the focus now to Western Europe, the changing role of the EEC and the entry of Great Britain into the Community would seem to be points worth considering in trying to make any kind of prediction about the future of COMECON. There is no question but that, in the past, the Eastern European countries have found the division between EFTA and EEC rather convenient. Poland found it possible, for example, to export its bacon to England. What will happen when Britain enters the EEC? Quite probably Denmark will have an advantage in exporting its pork products to Britain in a situation where all countries outside the new enlarged Community will have to pay customs duties. This is considered to be such a problem by the Poles that serious consideration is being given to deflecting resources from pork production to other agricultural activities.

There is one adverse circumstance that is likely to push the Eastern European countries toward the supine acceptance of directed coordination by a COMECON organ, with or without agreement of all parties affected by centralized measures. If the COMECON members cannot negotiate successfully with the expanded Community and can no longer export the raw materials and foodstuffs they can spare, as well as the manufactured products they have to sell, they will necessarily have to integrate more closely and submit themselves to increased direct coordination within the COMECON. In 1972 the EEC is scheduled to negotiate with COMECON on a united basis. This is not quite realistic because most of the agreements on exports for the next five years have been signed. But in 1976, when all these agreements will have lapsed, the EEC will deal as a bloc with COMECON and it will be interesting to speculate what the position of the smaller and weaker Eastern European countries will be within a bilateral situation of this sort.

One final remark involves the leveling off of economic development levels in Eastern Europe. We have been speculating about organizational or political aspects of COMECON affecting the future level or the rate of growth of trade in COMECON. We must not forget that, in addition to organizational and political obstacles to trade, there are also changes internal to the individual members that are taking place, which may have a decisive impact on trade. If the trend operating during the last 5 to 10 years, whereby the less developed countries of COMECON have been developing at a faster rate than the more developed ones, keeps up we may find that trade and coordination through voluntary agreements may continue to grow and may overcome some of the organizational obstacles that Dr. Machowski wrote about. During the last 20 years we have been hard put to make solid predictions about trends in COMECON because we have not been able to disentangle the effects on trade of changes in the level and structure of industry in each country from the effects of organizational changes that may hinder or promote development at a given stage of development and a given state of the country's environment. The econometric studies that are needed to sort out these different factors and to measure their individual effects have not yet been undertaken, at least on anything like the scale and depth that these problems merit. This is a field of enquiry where cooperation among Eastern and Western European scholars might well prove fruitful.

CHAPTER 7

EAST CENTRAL EUROPEAN STUDIES: THEIR PRESENT AND FUTURE

THE ROLE OF THE SOCIAL SCIENCES
by Peter C. Ludz

Scholars in the field of Communist studies have been reluctant to communicate and cooperate with social scientists; indeed they have been frequently criticized and have criticized themselves for insulating their subdiscipline from the rest of the social sciences. East Central European studies as one department within the subdiscipline of Communist-area studies have been included in this criticism.

In my following comments I shall refer to East Central European studies as Communist studies rather than to the general field of Eastern European area research—although the methodological problems encountered by Eastern European research that concentrates one pre-World War II developments seem to resemble those that are discussed here to a certain extent. "Communist studies" is an outgrowth of Russian-area studies and, as I use it, denotes all research work done in the West on countries ruled by Communist parties.[1] I know, of course, that the term "Communist studies" is a controversial one since it has frequently been used by anti-Communists for the purpose of discriminating against non-Western systems of rule. However, no alternative classification seems to be available as yet. In our context, the application of the term "Communist studies"

Peter C. Ludz is Professor of Political Science and Sociology at the University of Bielefeld, Federal Republic of Germany, and Visiting Senior Lecturer in Political Science, Columbia University, New York.

may thus be justified on the following grounds: for more than 20 years Eastern and Southeastern European countries—i.e., Poland, Czechoslovakia, the German Democratic Republic,* Bulgaria, Romania, Albania, and Yugoslavia—have been ruled by political elites who have defined their major principles as "Marxist-Leninist," "communist," or "socialist."** This self-understanding constitutes the differentia specifica between these systems and other social and political entities in the present and in the past.

The above-mentioned criticism and self-criticism of Communist studies in the East Central European field may be justified. However, our conference seems to prove the opposite, given the presence of specialists in the Eastern European field as well as of scholars representing various branches of the social sciences, i.e., sociology, political science, economics, and social philosophy. The series of subjects which we have been considering demonstrates that the subdiscipline is imbued with the vocabulary of at least the social sciences.

But despite the factual evidence we have produced, there exist some obstacles that stand in the way of area research and hamper effective cooperation with the rest of the social sciences. Let me refer to a few general problems:

1. In recent years political science, sociology, economics, and social psychology, i.e., the core social science disciplines, have gone through a period of successive "revolutions." This started with the expansion of the fields of study beyond the traditional limits in the United States and Europe. The expansion in scope also affected former concepts and approaches and helped to create new fields of interest and new approaches in traditional research.[2] Using some of the slogans in political science and sociology familiar to everyone present, "institutionalism" was followed by "behaviorism" which, in turn, lost ground to "systems analysis." Systems analysis, however, is at present undermined by what is called the "post-behavioral revolution"—although no one exactly knows what state of affairs that attractive label denotes. Even if we turn to the authorities in the field, we get a rather vague answer.[3] In other words, political science

---

*In the strict sense, the GDR cannot be called an Eastern European country. However, it may be treated as such in reference to the status ascribed to it by the mutual political and economic treaties in Eastern Europe and the Soviet Union.

**Russian studies are excluded here by definition of the scope of the Conference. All my remarks, however, can be applied to Russian studies as well.

and sociology have been changing so rapidly in recent years that there does not exist a commonly agreed upon stock of concepts and methods from which area research can borrow. Rather, the proliferation of existing schools is confusing to those students in the Eastern European field who look to sociology and political science for guidance. The situation is worsened by the time lag with which methodological and methodical "revolutions" spread from the core disciplines to the subdisciplines. Thus, scholars face a rather bewildering variety of approaches and pseudo-approaches.

2. In addition, the application of general social science concepts in Communist research is impeded by our ignorance of certain fundamental processes in the political and social systems under investigation. We are still unable to answer certain substantive questions. D. Richard Little in his chapter in F. J. Fleron's Communist Studies and the Social Sciences lists some of them: "How . . . are interests aggregated in Communist systems? To what extent has the socialization process invested Communist elites with political legitimacy? What regularized patterns of decision-making exist, and how are they affected by non-party organizations? What are the primary channels for informal communication within the political system?"[4]

3. Furthermore, many branches of political science, sociology and social psychology have developed methodologies and techniques of such a high level of sophistication that they cannot easily be utilized by scholars in the Eastern European field who are forced to base their research on relatively simple data.

4. Finally, Eastern European-area studies within the social sciences have as neighbors certain other subdisciplines, e.g., comparative politics and comparative sociology. Ever since Gordon Skilling called for a new discipline named "comparative Communist systems,"[5] the comparative study of political and social phenomena has increasingly become a field in its own right. Its concepts and categories require a high level of abstraction since its ultimate goal is to discover a theory of social development that can have universal application. Most categories and concepts used in comparative politics and comparative sociology can, indeed, be employed irrespective of geographic location, for they have been shaped for the conception of general regularities and irregularities rather than for the perception of specific differentiations. Eastern European studies, on the other hand, have been carried out on a different level of abstraction.

This short outline of the problems encountered by scholars in the Eastern European field when attempting to cooperate with their fellow social scientists points to the fact that the criticism referred to above has some basis in reality, to be discussed further.

There are two principal arguments that have rightly been advanced against all Communist and Eastern European studies. First, the subdiscipline suffers from conceptual underdevelopment. Although applying large-scale theoretical frameworks and ideal types, area studies have neglected the rules of theory-building by verification and falsification;[6] and research has often been conducted in less than precise categories and terms. In the same context it is argued that some concepts such as "totalitarianism" and "convergence" fall short of the requirements of present social science methodology, for they represent a theoretically uncontrolled mixture of political evaluation and historical and empirical facts.

Second, the subdiscipline is further blamed for not grasping the "reality" of the social and political systems it investigates. When speaking of "reality," the critics refer to two different methodological shortcomings of all Communist studies. (a) Scholarly activity has been concentrated on governmental institutions or political rule; the social system, or phenomena of social stratification, social groupings, and the network of social and political organizations as well as processes of social dynamics and change have been ignored. It is argued that careful attention should be given to the changing society as well as to the body politics. (b) Further, it is purported that Communist studies are stigmatized by the Cold War period that also gave them their raison d'être. An unaffected orientation toward specific facts characterized former research as well as a naive belief in the rightness of one's own, and the invalidity of the alien, political system. This more or less distorted perspective permitted an evaluation of the system investigated only on the basis of specific facts that, however, in the course of time became less representative of the system as a whole.

The critics, pointing to the lack of cooperation and communication between the area-study approach and the social sciences in general, add to the criticism a strong appeal for an alteration of this situation. They believe that compared to the outcomes of the traditional area approach in the Eastern European field, better research can be attained by cooperative efforts. In my view there is no doubt that this is a valid position. However, our criticism and our hopes should also lead us to reconsider and debate some of the basic problems of Eastern European studies in the light of the present state of the social sciences.

In the following pages I would like to add to that debate by posing a few rather simple questions and giving you my rather eclectic answers.

First question: What can we intend to achieve when investigating the countries of Eastern Europe? There are, to my mind, three approaches to research in the Communist field: the area or ethnocentric approach, the cross-national approach, and the cross-cultural approach. These approaches differ from one another in purpose and involve different methodological implications. In actual research, however, there exist various combinations of the three approaches; indeed most studies in the Eastern European field show a mixed pattern of the area, mainly of the cross-national and the cross-cultural approaches. The dilemma is that for a long time we have not been aware of the methodological consequences resulting from this fact.

To explain this further, I should first outline what in my view are the specifics of the three approaches just named. <u>The area or ethnocentric approach</u> attempts to explain and understand structures and processes in individual societies or sectors of those societies, such as particular institutions or economic processes. The intention is to grasp what is happening in a specific social entity and report on it as completely as possible. <u>The cross-national comparative approach</u> aims to understand and explain Communism as a cross-national movement and to construct some typology. Finally, <u>the cross-cultural comparative approach</u> attempts to understand and explain present-day Eastern European societies with regard to our own Western societies. The intention is either to discover some principles of dissimilarity (for instance, totalitarianism versus democratic rule) or to find converging concepts such as "industrialism," "bureaucratism," "technology," "modernization."

Irrespective of these differences in purpose and intention, we should keep in mind the cognitive presuppositions of all Eastern European research. Most studies in the Eastern European field have been, at least up to the present, conducted by people who not only live on the other side of the national borders of the countries under investigation, but rather are separated from the object of study by a cultural barrier. The fields of study do belong to a foreign country, indeed a country or a geographical region that exists more or less apart from our own world. Thus there are a couple of methodological questions that are unique in Eastern European research. We should first define our objectives: is our analysis of Eastern European systems or subsystems designed to give us a better understanding of alien social, political, cultural, and other structures as such? Do we have in mind what we in Germany call an "immanent" approach? Or is our purpose to obtain a better understanding of our own system? Or do we rather want to justify our own existing political and social structures in the light of the analysis of inimically conceived systems? To a certain degree, one can never jump over one's own fences. When trying to conceive of an alien system, this is one of the basic rules in present social science methodology. Our categories and our concepts define reality for us. In other words, the "immanent" understanding of an alien system is of limited scope. The intrusion of one's own conceptualization into a specific study, however, is varying and can be controlled. In the case of the three approaches just named, the area-study approach provides good possibilities for immanent research but only minor possibilities for methodological controls; the cross-cultural comparative approach, on the other hand, allows a higher degree of methodological control, but little scope for immanent research.

Present criticism of the area approach seems to disregard these differentiations. Area research should be rejected only when found to be distorted by uncritical and uncontrolled aspects of the cross-cultural analysis. In my view, we should not throw the area approach, per se, overboard. On the contrary, we should discard that fatal mixture of approaches that we find in Soviet and/or Communist studies conceived under the auspices of totalitarianism.

Nevertheless, one has to be aware that all Communist studies, area studies included, are comparative studies—comparative in a broad sense of the word. All research work done in the field more or less reflects what we have been thinking about our own society. Therefore our concept of totalitarianism has not only been invalidated by actual changes in the Soviet Union and Eastern European countries, but has also become irrelevant because of changes in the West. Democracy and freedom, which had served as guiding principles for the intellectual creators of the concept of totalitarianism, have become questionable. We in the West are posing many questions to ourselves and this allows us to throw a different light on developments in the East.[7]

Let me come to my second question: What are the data available and what are the methodological implications? The students of social and political systems of Eastern Europe can resort to three different kinds of data: first, to statistical data, a large amount of which is at their disposal now, and the flow is increasing rather than decreasing.[8] Second, a variety of sample survey data is available. These come from three sources: interviews with refugees, publications referring to empirical studies carried out by social scientists in Eastern Europe, and opinion polls organized in the West whereby Eastern European citizens visiting the West or Western diplomats assigned to Eastern European countries are interviewed. This body of data is also growing steadily.[9] Third, texts and documents, Eastern European official and unofficial publications, fiction and nonfiction, are widely available in the West.

The notable characteristic of all data available is that they are preformed. So far, the social and political scientist concentrating on Eastern European societies has had no control over his raw materials, much like the historian who can only conduct his research on the basis of documents handed down to him by previous generations. He is left to those resources that some people have found worthwhile to release to him. In addition, the data available permit analysis more on the macro (systems framework) or middle (theory of group behavior within systems) levels than on the micro level (theory of individual behavior).[10] Thus many concepts of modern political science and sociology are insufficient; they cannot be applied to Eastern European research because the data available do not measure up to the methodological standards. Other social science concepts and techniques prove to be highly valuable since they resort to specific data that are also available from Eastern European societies. This is true especially of statistical and sample-survey data, and indeed a great deal of today's social science studies are based on those materials. On the other hand, texts and documents are not very widely used by social scientists. They are indispensable, however, to the analysis of Eastern European societies, for in our study of these societies we have to take account of the ideological system, i.e., the codified self-portrait of the ruling groups, or as Milton Rokeach put it, the "belief system."[11]

To be more specific, the methodology required for an analysis of texts and documents could make use of three approaches. First, what I like to call the pragmatics and semantics of political language pioneered by Lasswell and Leites,[12] who have analyzed the vocabulary of totalitarian leaders by distinguishing semantic aspects from pragmatic ones, and have shown how language functions as an instrument of social control in the countries examined.[13] The second approach borrows from the philosophy and sociology of knowledge (Alfred Schutz and Karl Mannheim). The ideological dogma is examined under the auspices of the theory of ideology. Ideological statements are treated as social facts and thus made appropriate for comparative investigation.[14] A third approach was formulated by J. M. Bochenski, David Comey and others. We may call it the field analysis of ideology, particularly the precise research of the Marxist-Leninist epistemological, as well as the logical, system and its political and social functions.[15]

Despite the fact that the stock of data available for research in the Eastern European field has vastly increased and a variety of methods can now be used for analysis, two basic methodological problems persist, namely the need to separate reliable from unreliable data and to arrange the reliable data in a theoretical framework that is both valid and allows explanation, prediction, and, if necessary, comparison. The theoretical framework should not impose abstract categories upon empirical data; it should rather consist of a variety of micro- and middle-level-component theories, which may be arranged under some guiding principles.

For example, in my book, The Changing Party Elite in East Germany,[16] I attempted to determine forces of change and forces of inertia in East Germany by combining a systems concept composed of different middle-level theories, such as elite theory and the theory of organizations, with a historical approach (historical in the sense of contemporary history). The historical dimension is expressed in a number of detailed analyses and the construction of a framework is in terms of time periods. Kenneth Jowitt's recently published study on Romania[17] goes beyond my frame of reference. Jowitt seeks to advance his complex subject by theoretical and comparative investigations as well as by various case studies. He combines organizational and situational factors in the Romanian political system, i.e., ideology, elites, modes of accession to power, party structures, extent of social integration/disintegration, industrialization, and the level of development,[18] and relates these to his main concept, namely the nation-building process.

As can be shown by these examples, social sciences can help the area specialist. Social sciences in this framework include not only economics, political science, sociology, and psychology, but also history, especially contemporary and social history, and furthermore those disciplines that have added so much to the quality of methodological discussion, mainly the philosophy of science, the sociology of knowledge, and the theory of ideology. The correspondence of aspects, concepts, and methods from individual disciplines enables one to conduct comparative analyses with a specific political and social system. Various subsystems, such as the elite structure, the party's organizational structure, the ideological structure, can be related and compared with one another; they may be seen as context subsystems.

Let me turn to my third question: What seems desirable for the future? In their future cooperation, social scientists and Eastern European specialists should concentrate their efforts on what I would like to call multidimensional area and comparative research. Multidimensionality includes the application of different concepts and methods, or a methodological pluralism. This would give more solid ground to cross-national and cross-cultural comparative studies. Thus effective communication among scholars studying the various countries of Eastern Europe is highly desirable. Communication would be facilitated by a common use of the concepts and methods developed by the social sciences and by greater precision in describing the reality of the subject. In other words, I do not plead for highly sophisticated conceptualizations or unqualified and complete data, but for a continuous balancing of data and concepts against each other; I am fully aware of the difficulties involved, for the social sciences in general have not yet found a solution to the methodological problems posed by Eastern European research. While they have investigated in detail the behavior and attitudes of individuals and groups, they have not formulated methodologically satisfactory theories capable of explaining large-scale social phenomena. If, for example, we should seek an explanation for student unrest, we are left to rely on our perceptive faculties. There is no theory that offers a comprehensive explanation, at least so far.

All the above remarks are intended to demonstrate that cooperation between social scientists and area specialists can lead to a productive and a mutually beneficial relationship, and an additional impetus would be provided by the cooperation of social scientists from Eastern European countries. Some cross-cultural communication channels[19] and scientific projects[20] are in a budding stage and, once our political leaders renounce confrontation and aim at cooperation, we hope cross-cultural cooperation as well as interdisciplinary work will improve.

CONCLUSIONS

1. Criticism and evaluation of Communist studies in the West would be qualified if it is clearly indicated that specialists in the Eastern European field should endeavour to live up to the methodological standards set by social sciences. It should not be widened in such a way as to discriminate against area studies per se, since all comparative research has to rely on area research proper and vice versa.

2. The data available today for research on Eastern Europe require rigorous techniques. Social scientists today have at their disposal some techniques that undoubtedly can be useful for the specialist in the Eastern European field. Communication between social scientists and area specialists may also produce an awareness of methodological problems, especially on the part of the latter.

3. Eastern European studies, however, are characterized by an additional dimension that faces the area specialist with a problem, namely the evaluation of his findings. Evaluation is impossible if one does not know the contextual frameworks, the specificities of the areas under examination and the whole of which they are a part. The concepts developed in the social sciences should not be applied in a self-contained manner; they should be put to empirical tests.

4. Therefore, now as much as ever, serious studies in the Eastern European field require a body of precise knowledge. There should, however, be a genuine connection between factual knowledge and methodological knowledge.

5. The claim to combine factual research, methodological controls, and conceptualization in Eastern European studies includes a further requirement: that of team work in research. Area specialists and social science methodologists in the West should work together and, if possible, be joined by their colleagues in Eastern Europe.

Notes

1. Cf. Robert C. Tucker, "On the Comparative Study of Communism," Communist Studies and the Social Sciences, Frederic J. Fleron, Jr., ed. (Chicago: Rand McNally, 1966), p. 49.
2. Roger E. Kanet discusses these changes in his "Introduction" to The Behavioral Revolution and Communist Studies (New York: The Free Press; London: Collier Macmillan, 1971), pp. 1 ff.
3. For example, David Easton writes: "Post-behavioralism is both a movement, that is, an aggregate of people, and an intellectual tendency." Cf. David Easton, "The New Revolution in Political Science," The American Political Science Review, LXIII (December 1969), p. 1051.
4. D. Richard Little, "Communist Studies in a Comparative Framework: Some Unorthodox Proposals," Frederic J. Fleron, ed., Communist Studies and the Social Sciences (Chicago: Rand McNally, 1969), p. 101.
5. Cf. the discussions on the occasion of the "Symposium on Comparative Politics and Communist Systems," Slavic Review, XXVI (March 1967), pp. 3-28; reprinted in Fleron, Communist Studies . . . , pp. 188-214.
6. Cf. Fleron in his "Introduction" to Communist Studies . . . , pp. 8 ff.
7. Cf. Alfred G. Meyer's study on "Legitimacy of Power in East Central Europe," in this volume.
8. For further details, cf. Paul Shoup, "Comparing Communist Nations: Prospects for an Empirical Approach," in Fleron, Communist Studies . . . , pp. 72-73.
9. Ibid., pp. 73-74.
10. The distinction of macro, middle, and micro level theories is taken from Richard L. Merritt, Systematic Approaches to Comparative Politics (Chicago: Rand McNally, 1970), passim.
11. Milton Rokeach, in his The Open and Closed Mind (New York: Basic Books, 1960), p. 35, introduced this concept. For a discussion, cf. Ritz MacKelly and Frederic J. Fleron, Jr., "Motivation, Methodology, and Communist Ideology," in Kanet, The Behavioral Revolution . . . , pp. 53 ff. Like Kelly and Fleron (pp. 64 ff.), we disagree

with those who link ideology, values, or belief systems with political behavior and decision-making in a "'motive-belief' type of explanation" since this type of explanation is unacceptable on the basis of both our present knowledge in psychology and the data available for Eastern European research.

12. Cf. Harold D. Lasswell et al., Language of Politics: Studies in Quantitative Semantics (Cambridge, Mass.: Harvard University Press, 1966).

13. For the problems involved consult Walther Dieckmann, Sprache in der Politik: Einführung in die Pragmatik und Semantik der politischen Sprache (Heidelberg: Carl Winter, 1969).

14. Cf. my forthcoming book The Changing Party Elite in East Germany (Cambridge, Mass.: The MIT Press, 1972), which has been translated from the German Parteielite im Wandel (Köln-Opladen: Westdeutscher Verlag, 1968, 1970), 3d ed.

15. Cf. Joseph M. Bochenski, "Toward a Systematic Logic of Communist Ideology," Studies in Soviet Thought, IV, 3 (1964), 185 ff.; Joseph M. Bochenski, "The Three Components of Communist Ideology," Studies in Soviet Thought, II, 1 (1962), 7 ff.; David D. Comey, "Marxist-Leninist Ideology and Soviet Policy," Studies in Soviet Thought, II, 4 (1962) 301 ff.

16. Cf. note 14.

17. Kenneth Jowitt, Revolutionary Breakthroughs and National Development: The Case of Romania, 1944-1965 (Berkeley and Los Angeles: University of California Press, 1971). A variety of other studies—although displaying different levels of conceptualization—could be named here. In the field of elite research, cf. Part II, "Political Elites in the Soviet Union and Eastern Europe" in Kanet, The Behavioral Revolution . . . , which includes the already quoted study by Kelly and Fleron and further articles by Milton Lodge (pp. 79 ff.), Michael P. Gehlen and Michael McBride (pp. 103 ff.), Frederic J. Fleron, Jr. (pp. 125 ff.), Joel J. Schwartz and William R. Keech (pp. 151 ff.), and Carl Beck et al. (pp. 187 ff.).

18. Jowitt, Revolutionary Breakthroughs . . . , pp. 75-91.

19. Cf. the study by George W. Hoffmann, in this book, pp. 185-193.

20. A good example is provided by the time-budget studies carried out under the auspices of the UNESCO in the U.S., the U.S.S.R., Belgium, France, Bulgaria, Yugoslavia, Poland, Hungary, and West Germany. Cf. Erwin K. Scheuch, "Soziologie der Freizeit," Handbuch der empirischen Sozialforschung, René König, ed. (Stuttgart: Ernst Klett, 1969), Vol. II, pp. 735-833.

* * * * *

RESEARCH OPPORTUNITIES
by George W. Hoffman

I will concentrate specifically on the development of Eastern European studies in the United States and devote special attention to the future directions of university-level organizations that facilitate work in East Central and Southeastern Europe.[1] Obviously such a presentation by its very nature must be highly selective, and I therefore apologize for possible omissions and generalizations.

It is an obvious and now generally recognized fact that all countries in the area provide an excellent laboratory for an examination of the clash of divergent ideas and cultures in a particular geographic area. As the well-known Jelavich Survey made clear, "despite the extreme interests and importance of events in Eastern Europe, in both the past and the present, the area has not been adequately studied. In the opinion of most of those who aided in the project, the two major reasons for this neglect are the immensity of the language problem and the previous preoccupation with Soviet studies."[2] Let me add, at once, a point that the Survey itself made clear, "these hindrances are no longer the obstacles they once were."[3] Due to the initiative of numerous foresighted scholars and with the support of foundations, federal government, and universities, research and training funds were made available to numerous individuals on an ever-expanding basis. While work in the area for a long time was confined largely to students of language and history and to a very few individuals in the social sciences, their ranks were enlarged by those actively working in the area as part of their wartime experience, who in turn were able to interest an increasing number of students, although still in few fields of study. In addition, mention must be made of the contributions of World War II and postwar immigrants who, by their own research as well as by creating increasing interest in their original home, began training a new generation of North American citizens, and thus created demands for greater attention to the problems of East Central Europe and were directly or indirectly responsible for greatly increased scholarly output. The expansion of scholarly work in the area of East Central Europe, especially during the last 10 years, is a development of major significance. But it must also be recognized that the shortcomings are still numerous, and constantly emerging

---

George W. Hoffman is Professor of Geography at the University of Texas at Austin.

new problems will need the combined efforts of individual scholars, university administrators, foundations, government agencies, and scholarly societies.

The most important of these shortcomings is that relatively few scholars have been trained in the various social sciences (I am considering history as part of the humanities), and even within the social sciences there exists an imbalance among fields. For instance, it is often difficult to distinguish the Eastern European from the Russian specialist. Figures compiled for the Jelavich Survey, and the as yet incomplete Lambert Report[4] clearly indicate the scarcity of students trained in this area. To some extent, these scarcities and imbalances are also true for the Russian-Soviet field. In the field of East Central Europe they are not only shown in the imbalances among different scholarly fields, with anthropology, sociology, geography among the so-called underdeveloped subfields, but also by the lack of attention given to the non-Slavic people who play such an important role in this area. In part these difficulties are due to problems of academic organization and administration in our universities. Here I refer especially to the problems of finding a new home in existing language and literature departments and the well-known numbers game in terms of minimal enrollment in individual courses. The latter problem, unfortunately, is being intensified because of the squeeze on both instruction and research funds experienced by nearly all universities in the United States.

There are other deficiencies prevailing in the Eastern European field. In the past, considerable funds were channelled into the Russian-Soviet field, an obvious development when considering the political and economic problems of the Russian area. With an increasing number of Russian-Soviet specialists occupying university positions, opportunities for students trained as Eastern European specialists have not been plentiful, and the situation is not improving. There was a time when lack of qualified candidates discouraged the establishment of new positions. Therefore it is somewhat ironical that the changing priorities of national and state governments should cause such a serious setback affecting the establishment of new positions, or even at times abolishing recently established positions in institutions of higher education at a time when serious efforts are being made to train specialists in the expanding number of Eastern European fields.

Having cited just a few of the problems that the field faces, it is important to balance the picture by citing some positive achievements during the last few years, which are by no means unimportant. The increased interest in the area has made it possible to teach all Slavic and non-Slavic languages, though not always on a regular basis. The largest enrollment is found, based on Lambert's NDA Center

Survey, in Serbo-Croatian, followed by Polish, Czech, Modern Greek, Bulgarian, Hungarian, and Albanian, although these are overshadowed by those taking Russian. But we must quickly add that most students who now are working in Eastern European areas are taking Russian and an Eastern European language; while the latter is taught, for the most part, for only 2 years, Russian is regularly taught through the third and fourth year. Certainly a positive achievement is the greatly increased number of area-content courses taught in North American universities. The Jelavich Survey mentioned a figure of 20 universities having "committed themselves to the establishment of substantial progress of course offerings in the area."[5] This figure, according to all available evidence, has been further increased since the completion of this Survey. Special summer programs in the United States, overseas study tours, and overseas language institutes have become an accepted and vital part of Eastern European studies. Other hopeful signs for encouraging work in the area are the many exchange opportunities available. The list of shortcomings and achievements in the area in the United States certainly could be elaborated at will.

We have arrived at a crossroad in Eastern European studies in the United States. Scholars and administrators attending a recent meeting sponsored by the American Association for the Advancement of Slavic Studies (AAASS) made it clear "that at this juncture the circumstances—the needs and opportunities, the priorities and alternatives—have changed to such an extent that the successes and failures of a generation of graduate training now present challenges inviting prompt and decisive action."[6]

The increased number of specialists trained in the cultures of East Central European societies is reflected in both their scholarly output and the increasing number of publication outlets available to them. Close to twenty journals in North America and both Western and Eastern Europe accept contributions in English, German, or French. Of special importance are the outlets in Eastern European countries, opportunities that are unavailable to the Russian-Soviet specialists. The increased scholarly output can easily be ascertained by the number of papers listed at the annual meetings of the interdisciplinary AAASS and by the papers offered by scholars in their own professional societies. While in the beginning these scholarly contributions were largely descriptive in nature, based on primitive analytical tools available at that time, and all too frequently lacked a real interdisciplinary and comparative orientation, recent scholarly contributions indicate an awareness of the value of comparative, problem-oriented, and multidisciplinary research. Even though modern quantifiable data can much enhance research in certain problem-oriented studies, the often unreliable or insufficient data available in Eastern European countries make the experienced scholar aware of the pitfalls in relying too heavily on such data when using certain analytical techniques. Therefore more and more scholars have availed themselves of such nonquantifiable variables as national tradition, decision-making processes, political cultures, political dissent, and a whole range of problems dealing with the individual uprooted from his rural settings, to cite only a few examples.

Eastern European scholarship obviously must be part of the "mainstream" of theoretical and methodological scholarly research activities. Collaborative research efforts between major fields of study analyzing various aspects of the societies in Eastern Europe and of concern to both Soviet and Eastern European studies are essential and numerous. Problem-oriented comparative studies have appeared recently in the scholarly literature. A list of possible research projects is long and those actually undertaken are still in their infancy. One example of the type of studies we all agree are urgently needed is those dealing with the technological future of the various societies. These types of studies would stress the impact of technological advances on such topics as high-density living, available leisure, the impact of recreational developments, urban tension, to cite only a few. Again comparative and multidisciplinary analysis will be most effective in the study of problems such as these, for this could be combined with research in similar problems in Western European societies.

While I am fully aware of the need for certain sophisticated research endeavors, I also would be the first to agree that publications such as reference books and college textbooks containing large summary treatments and perhaps translations of important contributions are essential in the future for training in the field. The subcommittee on East Central and Southeast European Studies of the American Council of Learned Societies for years has given these possibilities special attention. Earlier in this study I raised the question of existing imbalances among the fields represented in Eastern European studies. While these imbalances still persist, as can be gathered from the data published in the available parts of the Lambert Report, I believe changes are evident based on the more than 100 abstracts so far submitted for the 1972 meetings of the AAASS. I had the good fortune, as program chairman, to do some analysis of these abstracts, which I hope, when the meetings are completed, can be published for use by the Society and its members. Imbalances in individual and scholarly research are an indication also of imbalances in the field due to the lack of direction or initiative by funding agencies in encouraging certain types of research. The latter is always a risky matter, although understandable in times of scarce resources. The program committee for the 1972 meeting of the AAASS has taken a step in this direction and all indications are that the initiative has been well received by the profession. The new Ford Foundation grant to the recently organized Joint Committee on Eastern Europe, as successor to the subcommittee mentioned earlier, gives the Joint Committee a mandate to set priorities for its field. At the same time, however, the committee recognized "that in order to formulate sound and practical policy guidelines it would require substantial advice and counsel from selected Eastern European experts in the various disciplines represented on the subcommittee."[7] The various reports published for the social sciences in the Jelavich Survey generally speak of the need to "promote conceptually and methodologically sound studies of contemporary political processes," encourage comparative analysis, assess analytically and forecast relevant problems, analyze the nature and motives of various policies, and, at the same time, caution the field of the danger of being swallowed up by Communist studies. In this way it attempted to consider both the traditional values in indigent societies in Eastern Europe and their individual contribution to the solving of problems and the study of contemporary processes. The greatly increased interaction among the social sciences in existing university centers, at specially organized meetings such as this, and at the meetings of the interdisciplinary AAASS, the appearance of new techniques in interviewing, the availability of increased data for comparative analysis, and, probably most important, the greater ease of travel, making first-hand observations in the individual countries of Eastern Europe possible, all have greatly increased research possibilities. Obviously, only the future will tell if these field-work opportunities have left their impact on the qualitative aspects of the research.

Nearly all of the basic training of future specialists in the area is accomplished in various undergraduate and graduate programs in American institutions of higher education. On the undergraduate level, training is largely discipline-oriented, though a few interdisciplinary programs do exist. Language training on the undergraduate level has greatly advanced in the last 25 years and students starting to specialize in the problems of the area can receive their basic language training at the undergraduate level. Ideally, all the basic background training both in language and in area disciplines should be completed before the interested student enters the graduate program. But inasmuch as a considerable number of graduate students delay their decisions because they lack the undergraduate work, many students enter their so-called specialized training at the graduate level inadequately prepared both in language and area content, and as a result their advanced area training must be supplemented by basic background courses. While this situation has greatly improved during the last few years, especially with the establishment of special summer programs on both the undergraduate and graduate levels, prospective area specialists entering advanced training often are in need of further language proficiency. It was for this reason that the Ford Foundation, some years ago, made available to the American Council of Learned Societies special funds for advanced summer language training, both within the United States and in Eastern European countries. With the traditional strict departmentalization in nearly all American universities and in the absence of interdisciplinary programs until World War II, it was an act of educational vision on the part of a few scholars and university administrators to initiate educational innovations in the form of Russian and Eastern European area programs, which were later accelerated by the National Defense Education Act in the late 1950s.

Philip Mosely, one of the pioneers in these programs, made clear the purpose when he stated that they were "to help people see a society, a system of power or an economy or all three interacting together as they do in real life, and to see them both in their interconnection and as a whole."[8] Much has been written in the meantime about the purposes and aims of these centers, and their accomplishments, and it is not necessary to repeat them here. It was the general opinion at the recently convened conference in Columbus, Ohio, that area programs, on the whole, had performed well with certain deficiencies. The all too often heard comment that these area programs were intended as a crash program must be strongly refuted; these programs were an educational innovation but are now a permanent part of our educational scene.

Two problems demanding changes have become quite obvious to all of us involved in both university-level area training and in the service of national committees. The recognition both of problems and of changes necessary will take much vision, understanding, and considerable diplomacy. Some problems are generally recognized but the solutions will not be easy to obtain. There has been a proliferation of programs, with most of them striving to be just like the other and of equal prestige, and most of them lack coherence and integration and are at best multidisciplinary but certainly not interdisciplinary. Let me briefly expand on these points.

Probably only 8 to 10 of the area programs in our field, perhaps even fewer, can be recognized as national resources, each possessing considerable strength for the field as a whole. But even these programs must aim at greater diversity rather than simply copying each other's offering; they should be known both for their functional specialization and their regional coverage. These programs, easily identified by a group of outstanding scholars and administrators, should receive every possible assistance; the outside funding of a large majority of area programs could easily be dropped without harming basic objectives. Concentration on a small number of key programs with secure financial basis would facilitate needed educational and structural changes in long-term planning activities. Such an assignment is nearly impossible to accomplish today in terms of the time available and other pressures.

Mention should also be made briefly here of the discussions initiated by the ACLS for strengthening Eastern European studies at universities. Basic to these discussions was the realization that the existing distribution of the intellectual and financial resources for Eastern European studies in the United States is a given fact. Therefore, it was suggested, as one type of program, that so-called faculty seminars should be established with one of the major centers taking a lead in scheduling such seminars during the academic year, with individual faculty members from nearby institutions of higher learning participating. The seminar initiated in Berkeley by Professor Gregory Grossman is thought of here as a model for this type of relationship. This and similar collaborative programs would contribute toward keeping participating faculty members from various institutions aware of major trends and opportunities in the field.

There are other possible programs, such as grants to outstanding existing centers for inviting regional specialists from smaller institutions of higher learning to spend one or two semesters. The fact remains that with the reduction of overall funds available during the next few years the proliferation existing in American area centers simply must be arrested if quality is not to suffer.

Finally, let me also say a few words about the content of area programs and their offerings. In the past it was generally agreed "that graduate and undergraduate students should be thoroughly prepared in a discipline, but at the same time they should be encouraged to choose widely among electives in the field given in other departments."[9] Little integration was evidenced in interdisciplinary seminars, with few exceptions, and there was a complete lack of comparative course offerings until very recently. Much has been changed during the last few years by theoretical or methodological updating of scholarly activities in nearly every discipline. It is now up to those guiding the disciplinary preparation of students, as well as area directors, to take these changes into account. In addition, area programs must become truly interdisciplinary. Comparative studies and area studies for example can learn much from each other's methodology, and some work has already started in integrating comparative Communist studies into Soviet area programs.[10] At this stage of our knowledge, very basic studies are still outstanding for many problems of the Eastern European area to be fully integrated into the most comparative analysis. Perhaps a beginning can be made by offering comparative courses in the traditional departments, but basic to the area approach in the future must be its comparative and interdisciplinary emphasis. This is still lacking even among the strongest area programs in the United States.

Notes

1. The term East Central Europe used at the Conference is used interchangeably with East Europe, Eastern Europe and the more and more accepted terms East Central and Southeast Europe, excluding the Soviet Union, but including Greece and the German Democratic Republic. For a discussion of this term used by geographers and many other social scientists in the United States see the chapter on "Geography," by George W. Hoffman in Charles Jelavich, ed., Language and Area Studies—East Central and Southeastern Europe: A Survey (Chicago and London: The University of Chicago Press, 1969), p. 199.

2. Jelavich, Language and Area Studies . . . , pp. x and xi (referred to in the text as "Survey").

3. Ibid., pp. xi-xii.

4. Ibid., appendices 1-12, pp. 36-45 and Richard D. Lambert, "Language and Area Studies Programs Review," November 1971 (abstracts of incomplete report).

5. Jelavich, Language and Area Studies . . . , p. 11.

6. Alexander Dallin, "Graduate Training: Soviet and East European Languages and Area Studies," Summary report presented to AAASS Conference, October 1971 (draft).

7. Minutes of the Subcommittee on East-Central and Southeast European Studies, SSRC-ACLS (May 1, 1971), p. 5.

8. Harold H. Fisher, ed., American Research on Russia (Bloomington; Ind.: the University Press, 1959), p. 10.

9. Jelavich, Language and Area Studies . . . , p. 17.

10. Helen Desfosses Cohn, "Symposium on Soviet Area Studies and Comparative Communist Studies. Part I: Soviet Area Studies," Newsletter on Comparative Studies of Communism, IV, 4 (August 1971), 24-26.

CHAPTER

8

**NORMALIZATION
OF RELATIONS BETWEEN
THE FEDERAL REPUBLIC OF GERMANY
AND EASTERN EUROPE**

ROUNDTABLE DISCUSSION   Moderated by Zbigniew Brzezinski
NUMBER ONE

PARTICIPANTS
1. Richard Löwenthal

    It is obvious that my topic would have no meaning without a prolonged state of anomaly in relations between the Federal Republic of Germany and Eastern Europe, even by the standards of the divided Europe and of the divided postwar world. In fact, there were for many years, and in many cases still are, no diplomatic relations between the Federal Republic of Germany and the other states of Eastern Europe, except the Soviet Union, even after the Western world had established such relations; and this, as the Marxist saying goes, was no accident. The reason was that beyond the general conflict between the Western world and the Soviet bloc, the Federal Republic had some special conflicts of its own, arising from the heritage of Hitler's war and Germany's defeat. I say Hitler's war and Germany's defeat because Germany, as a nation, had to pay for the consequences of Hitler's war.
    One of these consequences was the change in Germany's eastern frontier with Poland; another consequence was the partition of Germany as a nation. It was natural that the Federal Republic, having arisen some years after the war in the context of the Cold War and in the

---

Richard Löwenthal is Professor of International Relations at Free University, Berlin, Federal Republic of Germany

context of the Western Alliance, would strive for the restoration of the unity of the German nation in a single state and, if possible, for some adjustment of its frontier with Poland. This meant that for a number of years the Federal Republic was the one state in Europe that did not accept the territorial status quo, and indeed had an official policy of wishing to change it. The allies' formal commitment to reunification and to the provisional character of the German-Polish frontier ceased to represent this policy following their realization of the futility of any "rollback" attempts, leaving the Federal Republic as the only serious obstacle to a settlement based on the status quo in a situation of general desire for détente between East and West in the 1960s. The Federal Republic's rigid stance became increasingly more difficult to maintain and, given the growing internal and external pressures, change of policy became urgent.

The first set of reasons for this change in policy were realistic in nature. In the period immediately following the Cuban Missile Crisis in 1962, the Federal Republic became increasingly aware that its position had no serious support from its allies and tended to lead to self-isolation. At the same time, in the climate of the Vietnam war and of the American temporary near-paralysis in all areas except southeast Asia, it was becoming clear that the persistence of conflict with the Soviet bloc might even endanger state security.

Moreover, as the desire to change the status quo in favor of German unity became less and less realistic, the Federal Republic has increasingly recognized that it had an interest in maintaining a status quo in Berlin that could not be defended by conventional weapons and was only protected by nuclear deterrence in a situation of diminishing credibility of any kind of nuclear deterrence. Thus the realistic motivation for a change of policy toward Eastern Europe was compelling, for the Federal Republic could no longer afford to maintain special conflicts of its own with the Soviet bloc beyond that general conflict between the contrasting political and ideological systems in West and East.

The second motivation was a moral one. This was not merely a superstructure upon the realistic one; it was a consequence of a change of generation. The moral shock about what the German army and special forces had done in World War II came home to the majority of Germans only during the next generation. It probably is a normal phenomenon that great and profound moral conversions do not take place within one and the same generation and that the full impact of past deeds is felt only by the following generation, a generation that has not itself participated in the deeds yet feels the force of guilt. It should also be remembered that for many years one important factor in German domestic politics had been the leagues of expellees from the lands that had once been German and were now Polish, and that one of the stocks-in-trade of these leagues had, of course, been the very real injustice and suffering that their members had undergone in 1945. It took 20 years until a powerful organization, the German Evangelical Church, as opposed to isolated writers, publicists and professors, raised its voice in October 1965 to remind the Germans in the Federal Republic, in a memorandum, that the injustices done by the Poles to the Germans in 1944-45 had been preceded by the injustice done by the Germans to the Poles, and that what was needed was not a settling of accounts and mutual reproaches but a reconciliation in a Christian spirit. This action on the part of the Evangelical Church crystallized and put into focus a new national attitude that was getting stronger in the wake of the change of generations in Germany.

In addition to the realistic and the moral motivation, there was, thirdly, a national motivation. After all, one of the main reasons for the old rigid policy had been the desire to restore the unity of the German national state. This policy had come to a dead end, as evidenced by the very visible Berlin Wall. The new generation, doubtful that it would ever be possible to create German unity in a national state, considered it more important to maintain or restore normal human, economic, and cultural ties between the German people on both sides of the border, and came to accept the partition of the two states as a basis for imposing human contact by negotiation.

These have been the three main motivations for the change in policy initiated by the Government of the Great Coalition at the end of 1966. At that time there was still hope that by removing the bogey of German revanchism it would be possible to facilitate a measure of political change toward "liberalism" in Eastern Europe in general and in East Germany in particular. It was believed that as a result of an improvement of relations with Germany's eastern neighbors and of these internal changes it would be possible in the end to establish normal relations also with a somewhat changed, still Communist, but more humane, more liberal East German state.

This policy of "change by rapprochement," as the phrase went, had some initial success. Indeed the fear of Germany was diminished in Eastern Europe. But as the processes of change began to gather speed, the Soviet Union came to regard them as a danger to its own security and to its control of Eastern Europe, and, of course, the phase ended with Soviet intervention in Czechoslovakia. With that action, the first phase of the new German Eastern policy came to an end. The Federal Republic had to decide whether it should revert to its former rigidity, or whether it should scale down its goals and come to realize that since it could not bring about major changes in the East by its foreign policy, its ends would be best served by improvement of relations with states as they were, including the German Democratic Republic. The central point of this second phase of

Ostpolitik has then been the de facto acceptance of the status quo in Europe. Chancellor Brandt's policy is clearly committed to the liquidation of the remaining special conflicts between the Federal Republic and Eastern Europe, and to normalization of relations on that basis.

The treaties with Moscow and Warsaw have laid the groundwork for that normalization. They establish a recognition by the Federal Republic of the inviolability both of the German-Polish border and of the border between the two German states. They do not renounce the goal of reunification, but they accept the reality of the existence of the East German state. They seek a situation in which relations between the Federal Republic and the Soviet Union and the states of Eastern Europe will become as normal as the relations of any other Western power with the Soviet Union and the states of Eastern Europe, where the Federal Republic will no longer be regarded as the special enemy of the Soviet bloc.

This is a major shift when we consider that the central aims of the Soviet Union in its policy toward Europe had long been the consolidation and legitimization of its control of Eastern Europe, including the German Democratic Republic, on one side, and the dissolution of the NATO alliance, above all the alliance between Germany and the United States, removing the basis for the American presence in Western Europe, on the other. For a long time these two aims had been regarded by the Soviet Union as inseparable, and in a sense they were inseparable so long as one important member of the Western alliance was opposed to any legitimization of the status quo in Eastern Europe, and kept its allies in that line.

Only when the German Federal Republic announced its readiness to accept the status quo as a basis of diplomatic relations did the two main Soviet goals become separable.

This change was aided by the pressure of other international factors that caused the Soviet Union to separate these goals. One of these factors was the fact that, after the Soviet occupation of Czechoslovakia, Soviet propaganda for a dissolution of the military blocs in Europe lost all credibility. There was thus a new situation in which the Federal Republic of Germany was ready to normalize relations and the Soviet Union was ready to recognize the continued existence of the ties between the Federal Republic and the Atlantic Alliance. For its part, the Federal Republic was concerned with its own security and the security of West Berlin. Therefore, from the point of view of the Federal Republic, normalization of its relations with the Soviet bloc entailed as its corollary recognition by the Soviet Union and by the East German state of the special ties of West Berlin with the political, legal, economic, and financial institutions of the Federal Republic, including the right of the Federal Republic to negotiate on behalf of West Berlin. The Federal Republic set as a condition for the ratification of the Moscow treaty that there should be such an agreement on Berlin, which, of course, has been concluded in the course of the four-power negotiations. Together the Moscow and Warsaw treaties and the Berlin Agreement are likely to result in the stabilization of East-West relations in Europe, and thus offer a basis for more normal relations between the two German states.

It should be strongly emphasized that the above changes in policy have occurred in the framework of the Federal Republic's membership in the Western Alliance. They are not to be interpreted as representing a bid on the part of the Federal Republic for a special relationship with Eastern Europe, but rather a bid for a normal relationship. To that extent, the special importance of West German Ostpolitik will come to an end when the package of treaties is concluded. We can see that there are still further pieces to be included in this package; one of them is a treaty of normalization between the Federal Republic and the German Democratic Republic that would encompass not only technical items such as traffic, but also the normalization of legal relations and the abolition of laws that impinge on the internal affairs of one state by the other. Another is membership of the two German states in the United Nations with general consent; in other words, an opening of the door to the Western part of the international community for the East German state as well.

In conclusion, a word should be added about the contribution of this policy of normalization to the future of Europe in general and to Eastern Europe in particular. First, it is the belief of this author that normalization will facilitate change and loosen controls following a greater feeling of security in Eastern Europe; but these are possible consequences of normalization, not conditions for it. The Federal Republic has realized that change in the Eastern sphere, while desirable, is not a realistic objective of foreign policy and is not in its power to bring about. It is something that may come, if it comes at all, as a result of internal developments in the Eastern sphere.

Secondly, the tendency toward more normal relations between East and West will be reinforced at the point where the barriers were most difficult. There will be more traffic of goods, of men, of ideas, and of course of capital. These will bring about more contact between the systems. In that sense, the new normalization will also open the door to the Conference on the Security of Europe that the Soviets have wanted for some time, and that is likely to include discussion of forms of cooperation across this border, as well as negotiations about a multilateral renunciation of force in which, as we hope and indeed insist, there must be no exceptions for the application of force within any one bloc.

Finally, the feeling of greater security should make a mutual and balanced reduction of military forces on both sides somewhat easier, and this in turn would free resources on both sides for other purposes.

2. Pierre Hassner

Since we are at a conference on East Central Europe in general, we could start with two aspects of normalization in current European politics: normalization of relations between Germany and her Eastern neighbors, and normalization of relations between Germany and the Soviet bloc in the sense in which the term is used when talking about the Soviet Union's relations with Czechoslovakia. The question is, what is the relationship between these two normalizations: does normalization number one help or hinder normalization number two, or is one independent and without relation to two? My point of departure will be Prof. Löwenthal's comments on Berlin and on the realistic moral and national motivations of the Federal Republic's policy of normalization with Eastern Europe.

One could reformulate this by saying that everywhere there is agreement on and admiration for the moral aspect, but that questions could be raised about the realistic and the national ones in long-range terms. Normalization number one entails normalizing the consequences of World War II, especially with respect to Poland and the smaller Eastern European states; there the job has been very well done. Normalization number two involves normalization of the results of the Cold War and of the East-West ideological struggle, which in turn reveals the resiliency of a structural problem for the European continent, that of the superior power of the Soviet Union and, potentially, of Germany.

Here again, while I would accept Prof. Löwenthal's general formulation that the special conflicts of the Federal Republic first had to be eliminated, questions arise following statements emanating from official German sources, including the Chancellor himself, to the effect that Adenauer completed the reconciliation with the West and now reconciliation with the East should be completed; and also statements, such as the one used by Prof. Löwenthal, that Germany wants normal relations with Eastern Europe on a basis no more and

---

Pierre Hassner is a professor at the Centre d'Études des Relations Internationales, Foundation Nationale des Sciences Politiques, Paris.

no less than those that Britain, Italy, or France entertains with these countries. Both directions are legitimate as long as one remembers, first, that West is not East and that basically there cannot be the same reconciliation with the East as with the West. Secondly, no matter how normal these relations become, the problem remains that, just by virtue of its superior size and power, the consequences of an action taken by Germany are bound to be different from those following similar actions by another Western country.

My second remark is about the distinction Prof. Löwenthal has has made between the first, or the pre-Czechoslovakia, phase and the second phase of Ostpolitik. I would agree with him with some reservations, for he tends to sharpen the distinction a little too much and to attribute to German public opinion and government excessive ambitions during the pre-Czechoslovakia phase, and excessive modesty in goals today. The distinction is there and one can express it through the old adage that in order to change the status quo you must accept it. However, whereas the accent used to be on changing the status quo, now it is on accepting it and hoping for the best. Nevertheless, there are the dynamics of the situation. There was really no great proof on either side of having had the dissolution of the bloc in mind in the past. To be sure, the hope is even less now, but, at the same time, under the umbrella of the existing structure the game of the mutual relations of the two Germanys, of the two Europes, of the two types of society is going on, a game whose dynamics, whose uncertainties, Prof. Löwenthal tends somewhat to minimize.

On the German side there are two ambiguities. The first one is about the motivations of Ostpolitik. There is the optimistic rationale based on the notion that the structure is stable with the Soviet acceptance of the status quo; and the less optimistic one based on the proposition that it is not the Soviet Union that has changed so much, but rather that the United States has become less reliable, hence making the Soviet Union more dangerous and making an agreement with the latter imperative.

The second ambiguity is between the acceptance of division and the hope of reunification. We seem to be discarding our obsolete legalistic claims, but is it in order to accept our divisions or to overcome them? Whereas before, to use the French expression, "on en parlait toujours, on n'y pensait jamais," which amounted simply to accepting the status quo, today the unspoken hope may be that the dynamics of the process must lead toward a rapprochement and toward a greater imprint of the West on the East than vice versa. Nobody can predict the outcome, but there seems to be a realization on the Soviet side too that pragmatism—whereby in order to change a situation one has to start by accepting it—may be more productive than Khrushchev's frontal attack against the status quo. In other words, rather than launch a massive attack against the European Community, it is better to try to weaken it or slow down its progress in political and military affairs. Similarly, rather than try to bring about forcibly the separation of Berlin from Germany, of Germany from Europe, and of Europe from the United States, the best course of action might be to try, in the long range, to get a situation in which Berlin would in fact be as detached as possible from West Germany, West Germany from Western Europe, and Western Europe from the United States. Hence, now that the status quo seems to be accepted by everybody, the situation has become more interesting. Now real changes are likely to be made; we will be placing bets on processes that are beyond our control. The name of the game is Finland and, referring to the famous lady of Khartoum, the question now is who is going to Finlandize who, how, when, and to what extent?

3. Claus Soenksen

There is no separate German "Eastern" policy; there is a German peace policy resting on 3 important pillars. The first is the belief that Western Europe can only face its future tasks united; the second is the Atlantic Alliance that has preserved peace in Central Europe for 20 years; the third is the hope that 26 years after World War II reconciliation with our Eastern European neighbors can be effected. Our efforts to conclude treaties with the countries of Eastern Europe are a consequence of the treaties we concluded with the West in the 1950s and of the experience gained from the policy of confrontation in the 1960s. The efforts of the Federal Republic of Germany are a part of similar efforts being made by her partners and friends. Indeed, in some respects, by normalizing its relations with the countries of Eastern Europe the Federal Republic of Germany is doing now what its allies have done already. The Federal Republic respects present borders and recognizes the fact that there is a political West and a political East with widely different social systems. It has also come to realize that no matter how much it may hurt, the division of the German nation can be surmounted only when the division of Europe is successfully surmounted.

We have renounced neither reunification nor a freely negotiated peace treaty for Germany. Nonetheless, we do not wish to wait until such a peace treaty has been concluded in order to negotiate a settlement with the countries of Eastern Europe and to establish with them

---

Claus Soenksen is Counsellor, Embassy of the Federal Republic of Germany, Washington.

the basis for good neighborly relations. In the gradual process of widening cooperation between East and West we shall endeavor to establish a common foundation for the development of a lasting system. This plan is a long-term one; its purpose is not to bring about the disintegration of the Warsaw Pact by playing individual members against one another, but to loosen rigidity all around. It does not rely on sensational rates of change, for we are still conscious of the risks of too rapid development such as we experienced in the summer of 1968. The Berlin agreement, at the very heart of Germany, seems to have proved that this modesty of speed and demand can achieve substantial results.

Only by achieving a stable equilibrium vis-à-vis the Soviet Union will we be enabled to conduct negotiations over a long term, free from pressure and constraints. A major subject of such negotiations is the proposed conference for security and cooperation in Europe. Such a conference, in the Federal Republic's eyes, may be a step forward along the road to détente, and if carefully prepared it could lead to less confrontation and more cooperation between East and West in Central Europe. We consequently have been taking an active part in NATO's deliberations on this subject and are anxious to coordinate our policies closely with those of the United States.

The members of NATO have agreed that it must be the aim of the CES to insure a common understanding of basic rules for the coexistence of states, for East and West can coexist only if they proceed on the basis of a common understanding of fundamental concepts such as security, sovereignty, and noninterference in the internal affairs of other states.

The question of nonuse of force also belongs in this context as a political element of security. The conference on security and cooperation in Europe is not a substitute for a peace treaty for Germany. It should not affect the rights and responsibilities of the four powers with regard to Berlin or Germany as a whole, nor bring us into conflict with our political objective of working for a state of peace in Europe in which the German nation will recover its unity through free self-determination. We shall attend this conference on European security without illusions and we shall keep a watchful eye on the objectives pursued by the Soviet Union; but we shall also endeavor to consider the motives behind the attitude and actions of the other Eastern European states that may be officially presented.

We and the nations of Eastern Europe have our roots in the same rich cultural past and share the same apprehensions about the continuing division of Europe, which we consider to be an unnatural state of affairs. The hopes of which I have spoken should not be disappointed. But all parties must satisfy themselves that we do not intend to undermine their security and the security of the Soviet Union. Lasting success will not be possible unless our program for cooperation and détente allows for the security requirements of all concerned. Our policy does not merely consist of applauding others when they speak of peace; we seek an active role in easing tensions, to the end that peace may become more secure in Central Europe.

4. P. Andrzej Wojtowicz

First, let me emphasize that the points that I am going to present are my personal views. Second, I would like to share with you my belief that the Ostpolitik is not an act of goodwill on the part of the Federal Republic of Germany toward her Eastern partners. Third, my comments will concern themselves with Poland more as an object than a subject of this policy.

It should be remembered that it was Mr. Gomulka who, on May 17, 1969, proposed common talks with Bonn on normalization of relations in Europe through abandonment of the territorial claims of the Federal Republic of Germany. In shaping our own Western policies, we aim at the elimination of these political pollutants. The following are our guidelines: the necessity of creating additional contractual guarantees of geopolitical stabilization in Europe through the formal recognition of the Western frontier of Poland by the Federal Republic of Germany, and the desirability of creating practical frameworks for building up Europe as a continent less subjected to conflict than it was in the past. We face in Europe several kinds of established status quos, mainly geographical and sociopolitical, and we are in favor of maintaining them. There is also a military status quo, as well as an economic and a cultural one. However, in this case, we are against the present status, which took shape in the atmosphere of the Cold War in an impregnable and divided Europe. In inviting the Federal Republic of Germany to a dialogue with us, we saw the possibility of commencing the process of liquidation of anomalies in our mutual relations, and at the same time the possibility of creating a foundation for the development of normal cooperation based on the same principles that constituted the foundation for establishing our cooperative ventures with other countries of Western Europe. Quite frankly, in the case of the Federal Republic of Germany this was obviously not an easy process for us, particularly from the moral point of view, given the historical and political background of our relations. However, several factors were operative in bringing about this important change of policy. The

---

P. Andrzej Wojtowicz is First Secretary at the Embassy of The People's Republic of Poland, Washington.

example of our ally, the German Democratic Republic, which first took the initiative in breaking with the past by extending recognition to the Polish western frontier, played a decisive role. This created the psychological premise for the belief that normalization of relations with Germany was possible. We could notice important attitudinal changes in West German society, particularly among the younger generation; also, the composition and political character of Chancellor Brandt's team was not without importance, as well as his own personal contribution to the creation of a dialogue with Eastern Europe.

What are our expectations of the Brandt-Scheel Ostpolitik? I think there are two replies: one of a general character, and a more detailed one. The first would be an acceptance and respect for all European realities on the part of the Federal Republic of Germany; the second, the quickest possible ratification of the treaties pending with Warsaw and Moscow, the conclusion of a corresponding treaty with Czechoslovakia, normalization of relations with the German Democratic Republic, and official recognition of universally accepted norms of international law that would put an end to the present unfavorable relations between Poland and the Federal Republic of Germany and other socialist states. The result of these will be the further development of economic, scientific, and technological cooperation between the two countries. These elements may, in an essential way, contribute to the construction of foundations for the process of reconciliation between Poland and the Federal Republic of Germany; they also constitute the premises for creating a quid pro quo situation for the Federal Republic of Germany. Commentators, when speaking of Chancellor Brandt, have variously described him as a nihilist or as an extreme nationalist; we are rather inclined to see him as a realist who is actively engaged in enhancing the standing and furthering the interests of the Federal Republic of Germany, in a manner that does not necessarily collide with the vital interests of other states.

All of the above create a basis for expressing the hope that Europe will become a more secure and consolidated continent on the foundation of the coexistence of two different social and philosophical concepts. In this building process, we fully appreciate the contribution of many Western European countries. The process will not be an easy one, nor will it be very fast. Most important, however, is the direction of this process and its dynamism.

5. Harry Schwartz

First, I would like to join Mr. Wojtowicz in saying that any

───────────────

Harry Schwartz is an editorial writer for the New York Times.

resemblance between my views and those of my employer is purely coincidental. Until about the middle of M. Hassner's comments, I was getting a little worried because the discussion was proceeding as though there were a planet called East Central Europe, bounded on one side by Germany and on the other by the Soviet Union, with Poland in between, and that it was an isolated game. M. Hassner finally reassured me that there was more to this planet. I would like to elaborate upon a theme to which M. Hassner briefly alluded and try to offer an alternative hypothesis to the view that has been expressed both by Mr. Löwenthal and by Mr. Wojtowicz.

I would argue that what is happening in East Central Europe, namely the Federal Republic's attempted policy of rapprochement, is merely one part of a general worldwide accommodation to a basically new situation. The basically new situation is a new estimate of the reality of power relationships in the world. The Cold War that went on for almost all of the last 25 years had for one of its axioms that the United States was militarily superior to the Soviet Union and that, as Nikita Khruschev said in a speech about 11 years ago, the United States might or might not be a paper tiger, but it certainly had nuclear teeth and could use them. The events in East Central Europe are but a symptom of a broader movement in the world, with repercussions in the Middle East and Asia.

Internationally, the United States is now largely a has-been nation. It may not be a paper tiger but it certainly is an emasculated tiger. Short of an armed attack upon it, the United States, for many years to come, is not likely to fight for anybody, anywhere, because of the impact of Vietnam, racial divisions, the generation gap, and all the forces with which all of you who spend time on college campuses are familiar. The United States is today in a very real sense weaker than at any time in its modern history. While it still possesses great hardware capability, it has no moral will to use this capability for any purpose save as a response to direct attack upon its territory.

All over the world, therefore, and not only in the Federal Republic of Germany, nations are making adjustments to what they perceive to be the new balance of power, especially after Czechoslovakia and the implied threat to Poland a little less than a year ago. The Soviet Union demonstrated then that it had not only the hardware but the willingness to use this hardware with the enthusiastic support of its population. There are not going to be any rollbacks, whether in the middle of Europe or Korea, and certainly not in the middle of Vietnam. Indeed, the pervasive feeling in these divided countries and others is that they should consider themselves lucky if the roll does not go in the opposite direction. Mr. Brandt probably felt he had no choice but to engage in his present policy, which comes pretty close to unconditional capitulation. He has given up the historic demands of an entire generation of Germans in exchange for some promises on Berlin that may or may not be observed. After all, Czechoslovakia also received promises on the sanctity, integrity, and sovereignty of its government and its territory. In other words, what we have seen in the middle of Europe, in the fears that prompted Golda Meir's flight to Washington this week, and in the ferocious political battle now raging in Japan and other places, reflects a world in which our friends, in the face of what they fear is disintegration of the United States, are attempting, to the best of their ability, to make accommodations to the new unhappy balance of power and are praying very hard that the outcome will not be as ugly as they fear it might be in their most pessimistic moments.

6. Robert Bowie

I would like to confine myself to just two comments.

One of them has already been made by M. Hassner. I suppose I am simply rallying to his view of Ostpolitik. It would seem to me that the intentions or the hopes are not quite as clear-cut as Mr. Löwenthal has suggested. There is indeed an element of a mutual confidence game on both sides in connection with détente, with each side convinced that the time factor is working to its advantage and that the process of change operating on the other side will disintegrate it more rapidly. That probably is one component of German thinking and of the thinking of others who are urging the pursuit of a détente policy. Thus, in their thinking, the decision is not to perpetuate the status quo so that history will end there. More likely, they assume that the forces for change may operate more effectively over time in an atmosphere in which there is less fear and less confrontation. Conversely, it seems quite clear that the Soviet Union is interested in more than just getting the Eastern side nailed down, and is hoping it will gradually be able to disintegrate the cohesion of the Western side, perhaps head off progress toward European political integration, and probably weaken the relations among the allies in Europe and in the Atlantic grouping.

The other comment relates to Mr. Schwartz. A good many of our friends and others are certainly asking the question that he has answered, but it seems that they have been more cautious in reaching their conclusion. Therefore, if the situation is not quite as he describes it, it is one in which our national behavior and our attitudes are certainly raising the question in the minds of many people in Asia

---

Robert Bowie is Director of the Center for International Affairs at Harvard University, Cambridge, Mass.

and in Europe as to whether we are reliable and predictable. This is a fair question but the answer is not foreclosed. A good deal will probably depend on the manner in which we conduct ourselves over time, and they will be looking at the evidence as it develops. In other words, they are more open-minded about the answer to the question. The outcome cannot be predicted, but my natural optimism leads me to think that once we have left Vietnam behind us we may very well rally ourselves back into a posture that is more reassuring and more in keeping with our national character. That does not mean that we will return to the same stance as in the heyday of our excessive self-confidence, but as a people we seem somewhat inclined to go through rather sweeping ups and downs in outlook. In the early 1960s we were perhaps in an excessively "up" stage, thinking that the world was our oyster; currently we seem to be at a rather low, perhaps unnecessarily low, stage and are undercutting ourselves. Hopefully we will adjust this kind of thinking over a period of time.

CHAPTER 9

THE ROLE OF THE GERMAN DEMOCRATIC REPUBLIC WITHIN EASTERN EUROPE

ROUNDTABLE DISCUSSION Moderated by Robert G.
NUMBER TWO Livingston

PARTICIPANTS
1. Melvin Croan

By beginning with the question of the stability of the German Democratic Republic's sociopolitical system, we are, in fact, beginning with the single, crucial question of the stability, and ultimately of the viability, of the German Democratic Republic as a political entity. Before offering a few comments on this theme, let me issue the following general caveat. If experience in the whole area of East Central Europe in the postwar period has proved anything at all, it is that one cannot, dare not, try to talk about stability per se; certainly this is the lesson of developments in Czechoslovakia in 1967-68 and of developments in 1970 in Poland. Stability throughout the area has been quite elusive; it is challenged not only by domestic forces and processes that we on the outside can see only imperfectly, but also by changes in the international political system. The German Democratic Republic is particularly susceptible to these pressures because of its origin and development in the process of national division.

With that caveat we can proceed to the issue of domestic and sociopolitical stability. Here one can usefully distinguish three levels or three kinds of stability. In the first instance one may talk

---

Melvin Croan is Professor of Political Science at the University of Wisconsin, Madison.

about the consolidation of Party rule; secondly, one can refer to the
viability of a distinctive East German socioeconomic administrative
structure; and thirdly, one has to address oneself to the intractable
question of the emergence if not now, then possibly in the future, of
a separate East German national identity. Although these are three
distinct areas or levels of analysis, in practical terms they are
obviously intimately related.

For example, it made no sense to most of us even to speculate
about the emergence of a separate sense of national identity in the
Democratic Republic before there was a consolidation of Party rule
and an elaboration of distinctive social structures and administrative
practices. The three levels stand here in a kind of dynamic, reciprocal
relationship; one aspect of that relationship suggests a remarkable
measure of stability at the level of Party rule and of administrative
and social structures. But, any tampering with the sense of national
identity, or, to put it more concretely, reemergence of a powerful
sense of all-German nationalism, could seriously jeopardize the
stability of institutions and processes.

Very briefly on the first of these levels of domestic consolidation,
Party rule. If one looks at Party rule and its consolidation at two
levels, first of leadership, second of the relationship between the
Party and the population, one has to agree that a considerable degree
of stability has been attained. At the level of leadership, the transition
from Ulbricht to Honecker was remarkably smooth, and the consolidation of Honecker's power has been proceeding efficiently and
methodically. In the first instance, there have been inhibitions upon
Party factionalism that have existed from the outset because of a
shared fear of an open exposure of internal elite cleavages, a fear
that this might lead to the wrong kind of political activization of the
population; second, the basic purpose of political infighting within
the elite has always been to win support from Moscow. This point
was again proved, one feels it fair to say, in the most recent transition
of leadership. Given stable leadership and a smooth transition of
power, there has been a kind of acceptance of Party rule in the German
Democratic Republic that one is hard put to find to such a degree in
countries like Czechoslovakia or Poland. The Party has rooted
itself in the population in a way that might be characterized as being
distinctively German. One can speculate that this has something to
do with the collectivist traditions of this part of Germany, perhaps
even curiously enough with the historic role of the SPD as a party
of integration rather than as a party of representation. One can
speculate about the continuity of the authoritarian political culture
since 1933 in this part of Germany. One can fairly say that, with
a stable leadership, there has developed a good measure of Party
consolidation.

How much more impressive is the second level of achievement in the German Democratic Republic, namely, the development of new socioeconomic administrative structures and patterns. It has been forcefully argued by Ralf Dahrendorf that the German Democratic Republic represents one of two German roads to sociopolitical modernization, different from and antagonistic to that of the Federal Republic, but a break as complete as that of the Federal Republic with earlier German social structure and political culture. And to the extent to which careers are increasingly based on talent, that imparts an additional degree of social support. Within the limits of the ideological control and the political discipline exercised by the Party within the last decade, the GDR has emerged increasingly as a rational bureaucratic state, one whose economic performance, whose record of economic growth, by any standard, not least of all by the standard of the previous decade of the German Democratic Republic, has been impressive. This judgment is one that one has to stand by, despite some recent signs of economic stagnation, especially in chemical industries, and problems in the production of energy. One finds at this level of analysis, that the new Honecker regime has proceeded with a policy of pronounced economic realism based upon improving the standard of living in terms of scaling down economic objectives, especially the more grandiose objectives and enterprises of Comrade Ulbricht, "without any expectations of meeting planned goals through miracles," as Honecker put it during the last Party Congress.

This course in the economic realm does not suggest a downgrading of the leading role of the Party, for that has never been in any way seriously attacked internally. If anything, since Czechoslovakia, the leading role of the Party has been strengthened, and under Honecker continues to be. The problem in analyzing this crucial question of stability comes precisely when one tries to look at the question of national consciousness at the third level, because despite a grudging acceptance of the powers-that-be in the land, it would be at best premature to talk about anything even vaguely approximating the emergence of a sense of separate and distinctive East German nationality. In part, this ought not to be surprising, for we must remember that until very recently the Communist regime in the German Democratic Republic was itself quite ambivalent about the notion of the German nation. It claimed that the Democratic Republic embodied not a separate nation but a better part of the whole German nation and thereby laid claim to eventual reunification under the aegis of its own social and political institutions. What has been most striking in this context in the last few months has been the regime's new program of Abgrenzung, of "incapsulation," or, better yet, "delimitation" of the German Democratic Republic from the Federal

Republic of Germany. I will not go into many manifestations of this Abgrenzung program. Suffice it only to say that it has gone so far that one wonders whether the Honecker leadership does not next contemplate perhaps dropping the name "Deutsche" in the official designation of the state: "Deutsche Demokratische Republik."

The official program of Abgrenzung, far from being a tactical move subject to reversal, is the dialectical underpinning of the reluctant commitment of the German Democratic Republic leadership to go along with the Soviets in the détente in the German question that Ulbricht had so strenuously opposed and that may come to fruition soon in the signing of the inter-German agreement. There is the fear, clearly, on the part of the Honecker leadership that this kind of détente could reawaken all-German sentiments in the population and to that extent serve to undermine the consolidation of the German Democratic Republic as a separate political entity. Here is the crucial problem, namely that détente is viewed by the political elite in the Democratic Republic as potentially destabilizing; and objectively it probably is as long as European détente does not serve to undo entirely the East-West balance in Europe to the favor of the East.

The regime has grown accustomed to tension under the present leadership, as it had under Ulbricht, and probably still needs a degree of tension in the absence of a durable sense of national identity that it has not been able to manufacture in this relatively short period of time by methods that have been essentially those of compulsion. Small wonder, therefore, that, as Peter Bender has shown in his recent study of European security views of members of the Warsaw Treaty Organization, the German Democratic Republic should continue to champion security through confrontation with the West, to the virtual exclusion of more constructive proposals based on East-West détente and cooperation. For alone among the Eastern European elites, the German Democratic Republic leaders still fear for the very existence of their state.

Now all of this makes it very difficult to see how the German Democratic Republic can fit constructively into the politics of East-West détente. The most that can be said is that the ability of the German Democratic Republic to block East-West détente is now considerably less. It is considerably less in the immediate short run because of the differential leverage of a Honecker as opposed to an Ulbricht over the policies of the Kremlin. Over the intermediate run, the leverage that the German Democratic Republic may exercise in a kind of negative way is likely never again to be that which Ulbricht exerted relatively successfully until the last days of his active political leadership. This is due to a variety of considerations, not the least of which is that the economic leverage of the German Democratic Republic as a conduit for Western technology is bound to decline in direct proportion to the extent to which economic relations are cemented between the Soviet Union and the West, and more particularly the Soviet Union and the Federal Republic of Germany.

Nonetheless, one should never underestimate the role of one large overreaching factor: the degree of Soviet concern over the stability and viability of the Communist regime in the German Democratic Republic.

2. William E. Griffith

The most important point to be made about the future is that one must not have very many hopes or illusions about what will happen after the so-called normalization of relations between the Federal Republic and the Democratic Republic. The fact is that in population, area, economics, and, above all, with respect to the national question, the asymmetry between the two is so great that not much should be expected even after the development in East Germany, not of national consciousness but of a certain amount of state consciousness. The problem is that a period of détente in Europe, and particularly détente in the relations between Moscow and Bonn, runs the danger from the point of view of the leadership of the German Democratic Republic of interfering somewhat with the continuation of the sense of resignation on the part of the inhabitants of the Democratic Republic to the belief that there can be no change. On the other hand, we should also be aware that, as Khrushchev remarked, peaceful coexistence is the intensification of the class struggle by means other than interstate war, so that the so-called normalization of relations between East and West Germany and entry of both states into the United Nations, for example, will probably result in an intensification of their political struggle and on a world-wide basis, not just here on the East River.

All the above would indicate that there is no reason, objective or subjective, why the leadership of the German Democratic Republic, given their calculations that to a large degree coincide with those of the Russians, are likely to lower the priority that they have always given to the maintenance of security: security of their state and therefore of their alliance with the Russians. One can speculate what would have happened to them in 1953 had the Red Army not intervened, and well understand their motives.

William E. Griffith is Professor of Political Science at the Massachusetts Institute of Technology, Cambridge, Mass.

Therefore, objectively, they must be opposed to détente. On the other hand, they are dependent on the Soviet Union, and most of us would now agree that this dependency has been greatly increased by the probable removal of Ulbricht by the Russians following his attempts to sabotage Soviet policy with respect to the Federal Republic and the West.

For these reasons it would seem that the objective tendency of the German Democratic Republic to sabotage détente will always meet and will always be overcome by any contrary Soviet tendency that exists. Nevertheless, the Soviet tendency will not be to stop the political contest between East and West Germany, but more likely to transfer it to a more active era of coexistence in Europe and the world. It is true therefore that East German influence in Moscow is certainly less than it once was, because of its economic problems, because of the departure of Ulbricht, and essentially because the Soviet Union has again, as in 1953 and to some extent in 1956, drastically demonstrated its power and its will to use it. It follows that the Democratic Republic will continue to be an obstacle to détente and to meaningful negotiations on such European questions as security. It will differ in this respect to some extent from the Soviet Union and even more from some Eastern European states, notably Yugoslavia and Romania.

In spite of this tendency on its part, once the inter-German agreement has been signed, and the Moscow and Warsaw treaties and the Berlin agreement ratified, I see no reason for the West to continue to keep the Democratic Republic out of various international bodies, ranging from the world conference against pollution to the United Nations and the world organization of Dachshund breeders. The Federal Republic should, from the American and Western point of view, take the lead in including the Democratic Republic in such meetings, for there might be some advantage for it in helping to bring the Democratic Republic out of its isolation.

But the resources of the West, and particularly of the Federal Republic in this respect, are very limited, essentially because of the objective limitations on the leadership of the Democratic Republic to bring about détente. The main area where some improvement in relations might come about is likely to be in trade. The intensification of the Abgrenzungpolitik imposes rigid limits on any improvement of relations in the political and cultural fields.

All the more reason, therefore, for the Federal Republic to make it constantly clear that it is the Democratic Republic, with whatever degree of Soviet support it may have, that is in fact determined to isolate itself. On the other hand, of course, one has to place careful limits on Western attempts to drag the German Democratic Republic out of its isolation; they would be counterproductive if they were too obvious or too extreme, and there is no reason to use this as a weapon of political warfare in the short term.

I would argue that in the long term it is in the interest of the West, including that of the Federal Republic, that there be a gradual increase of contacts between West and East Germany insofar as it is compatible with the maintenance of stability on the part of East Germany. For the idea that there can be German national Communism in East Germany, seems to be, at least for our generation, a <u>contradictio verbis</u>. As for the withdrawal of the Red Army from Berlin and East Germany, only one Russian Czar attempted it. It was Peter III, a German, who was murdered a few months later by his guards.

3. Henry Krisch

I am going to talk about the GDR-Soviet relationship and to some extent the question of the GDR's stability. The way to think about the present and future of the German Democratic Republic in Eastern Europe is to begin with the notion that what we have been witnessing is the end of World War II in Europe. If the Nobel Peace Prize is given for, literally, peacemaking, then Willy Brandt certainly deserves it because his policy has settled the war, which may not be the same thing as making peace in Europe. This means that for both East and West Germany, the question of their future role within a German national framework in Europe and in the world has to be rethought, reformulated, and new policies have to be adopted.

A quick review of GDR-Soviet relations may be useful here. For most of the past two and one-half decades, the relationship of the German Democratic Republic with the Soviet Union has been bound up with the frozen but unresolved status of the German question. As a result, the German Democratic Republic has represented to the Soviet Union an instrument to employ in arriving at a settlement suitable to itself. In the very early phase, ending roughly in 1953-54, the German Democratic Republic represented a Soviet holding operation, enabling the Soviet Union to have some chips on the table in formulating future relations with the West. During the period 1953 to August 1961, the German Democratic Republic in effect joined the bloc, that is, it became one of a number of states in Eastern Europe that were to some degree subordinate, to some degree autonomous, different degrees pertaining in different countries. In the course of this process its leadership developed some sense of its own purposes,

---

Henry Krisch is Professor of History at the University of Connecticut, Storrs.

destinies, and interests. Finally, in the period since 1961 there has been what has already been described as a process of stabilization and consolidation of the regime. This has meant that for the Soviet Union, the ability to manipulate the German Democratic Republic as an instrument of policy in the German question has been steadily more qualified by the need to take into account the interests, desires, and the needs of the German Democratic Republic itself. One cannot look at GDR-Soviet relations in the last decade in any useful way other than that of a mutual relationship; but it is a mutual relationship in which one of the two partners has a number of overwhelming material advantages and has not hesitated to use them. Speaking on this topic last March, I carefully said that it would remain to be seen whether the German Democratic Republic's leeway was sufficient, and a few months later it turned out to have been insufficient. I quite agree with my fellow panelists that the dismissal and downfall of Ulbricht was in part a direct result of his disagreements with the Soviet Union on their policy with respect to the German question.

That means, however, that until roughly 1968-69 there was something that tied the East Germans and the Soviets together, namely an open German question that still had to be resolved and in which both partners could contribute some elements of their common interests. What has happened in the period since August 1968 is that the Soviet Union has arrived at a European and, therefore, also German settlement that is satisfactory to it, and has enforced this settlement against the interests and wishes of the German Democratic Republic.

I will not take the time now to go into various crisis points prior to 1968 in GDR-Soviet relations; there were a number during which the East Germans maneuvered for advantage in influencing Soviet policy. The occupation of Czechoslovakia provided the Soviet Union with the necessary basis for stability in Eastern Europe that has enabled it to opt for the stability of the whole European situation as it now exists. This has been partly due to the inability or unwillingness of anyone else to do anything about the Czech situation, thereby giving the Soviet Union reassurance about an acceptance of the situation in Eastern Europe on the part of Western powers and especially the other Allied occupation powers.

In this same period, beginning roughly with Gromyko's speech of May 1969 and going on to the present day, the German Democratic Republic has tried to add its own elements of policy input into the Soviet policy-making process. This has taken three main forms. One has been an effort to demonstrate to the Soviet Union and other Eastern European regimes that the interests of the Federal Republic are not compatible with Soviet objectives. Second, an attempt to make the Democratic Republic an essential and, indeed, innovating element in the Eastern bloc. Ulbricht's "developed economic system of socialism," a phase that was dropped just before the SED Eighth Party Congress, was a kind of ideological symbolism to express this notion. Finally, in the economic sphere, the German Democratic Republic has wanted to be the Germany of the Eastern bloc, i.e., to provide for the Eastern bloc, a technology-importing area, the materials that only it could supply thanks to its unique economic base. The Soviet Union did not follow the same line of reasoning on these three points, as is now clear. In a rather historic reversal of attitude both on the part of German Social Democrats and Soviet Bolsheviks, the Soviet Union ceased to see the Federal Republic, especially since September 1969, as much of a continued threat. They furthermore decided to deal with the "real" Germany, a tendency already present in the Eastern European states that prefer trade and technological relations with the Federal Republic rather than with the Democratic Republic. The outcome of this process of divergent interests was the dismissal of Ulbricht.

Where does this leave the German Democratic Republic at the present time? The Honecker leadership has made a kind of choice, or perhaps it would be better to say that it has accepted the notion that its destiny lies in East Central Europe. The Honecker regime feels that its part of Germany is not part of the same unit of analysis as West Germany, but part of the Eastern bloc. Whereas formerly the line of special relationship—technological, military, ideological— with the Soviet Union operated as a kind of covert pressure on the Soviet Union, since the advent of Honecker the attitude of subservience to the Soviet Union represents a capitulation of the leadership, not an assertion of its interests. Secondly, there is the policy of Abgrenzung, however one may wish to translate the term. This sometimes takes a rather shrill form, indicating that the East German leadership wishes the GDR to be an East Central European state and not a part of a German community.

I will now turn to the question of internal stability. If the German Democratic Republic is going to find its major role as a member of the Eastern European community of states, the question of the nature of this role arises. Although the leadership has made a clear decision, the content of this decision and what this will mean in policy terms is very much open to question, perhaps even in their own minds. For example, the economic role of the German Democratic Republic is likely to decline in relation to the other Eastern European countries. If Eastern Europe, as seems likely, experiences an upsurge of nationalism, this may involve some difficulty for any German state that wishes to play a role in this area.

Finally, because the German question has been settled and because economic and technical aid is now being sought by the U.S.S.R. from, for example, the Mack Truck Corporation and from West German industry, the German Democratic Republic is simply no longer as important to the Soviet Union as it once was; so also the Federal Republic, in terms of the German question, is no longer as important. This means that there will be a real need to define what German nationality and statehood mean. Here I will take a rather extreme stance, partly to set a standard for a hypothesis, by taking a much more sanguine view of the prospects for East German national or state consciousness than any of the other panelists. We have to adopt a comparative basis of analysis, and when we do so we find that the question of national identity is and has been a very fragile thing in all parts of the modern world. It is very hard to determine what it means today, for example, to be an Irishman, but historically this is easier to do than to determine what it means to be a German. There is at least one precedent in the German-speaking kulturwelt for the secession of an element of this separate national consciousness, and I refer here to the change in attitude between the first and second Austrian republics on the question of Anschluss. With due recognition of the differences between Austria and the German Democratic Republic, it is not inconceivable that, given sufficient time, people growing up in the German Democratic Republic and finding their roles and their careers in its institutions will find the object of political socialization to be the German Democratic Republic and not some larger cultural entity, just as is the case for German-speaking Swiss and Austrians. I bring all this up in terms of nationalism because, if the German Democratic Republic is going to play a long-range role in Eastern Europe, which is I think what the leadership at the moment is committed to do—and I quite agree with Melvin Croan that the impact of world and external events has forced the leadership into this role—then the leadership will have to foster a GDR nationalism as a deliberate policy. As the "Heroic Age" of the German question ends, the future development of the Germanies will be determined by such long-run considerations.

4. Peter C. Ludz

I would like to concentrate on three topics. First, the situation of the German Democratic Republic within Eastern Europe under the

---

Peter C. Ludz is Professor of Political Science and Sociology at the University of Bielefeld, Federal Republic of Germany, and Visiting Senior Lecturer in Political Science, Columbia University, New York.

new leadership of Erich Honecker; second, the changes in the evaluation of the East German model of modernization and development; third, the question of national consciousness and the lack of national identity in the GDR.

First, the new political situation from the point of view of the Eighth SED Congress in the summer of 1971. For reasons that I cannot discuss here,* the position of Honecker seemed much weaker at the time of the Congress than Ulbricht's had been in times past and, as a consequence, the political position of the German Democratic Republic vis-à-vis the Soviet Union has been shakier. During the period 1965-69 Ulbricht was at the peak of his power and enjoyed immense prestige. This enabled him to assume a relatively autonomous stance vis-à-vis the Soviet Union in certain areas of domestic and foreign affairs. Clearly Honecker does not enjoy this privilege and indeed owes his accession to power to the Soviet Union, whose nod of approval was absolutely essential to him.

In this context, a review of the 25th COMECON meeting in July 1971 may be in order. The proceedings of this meeting reveal a shift in the direction of the GDR's trade activities toward the Soviet Union and Eastern Europe. For example, for the period 1971-75 it is envisaged that up to 75 percent of the GDR's exports and imports will be with the Soviet Union and the Eastern European countries— as opposed to 70-72 percent in the past few years. This is only one indicator of the political reality of intensified relations between the GDR and the Soviet Union after Ulbricht's passing from the scene.

The second point is perhaps the most interesting one. It concerns the East German model of development and modernization that emerged in the 1960s. As far as I have understood it, the "new economic system" of 1963-64 gave the German Democratic Republic an enhanced position vis-à-vis the Soviet Union and the other Eastern European countries. This was made possible by some important achievements in the economic and educational fields during the period 1964-68. On the whole, this period witnessed a certain stabilization in the socioeconomic sphere. However, after 1968 the German Democratic Republic—not unlike many other Eastern European countries— encountered difficulties on the economic front, and today the real strength and stability of its socioeconomic structures are again open to question. When one reads the reports published by the SED Politbureau and the GDR Council of Ministers carefully, one cannot help thinking that many in the West have overestimated the durability of

---

*Cf. my article, "Continuity and Change Since Ulbricht" in Problems of Communism, March-April 1972.

the stability period and made the error of drawing conclusions as well as making projections on the basis of insufficient data. The East German model of modernization—e.g., in the fields of economics and education—can no longer be viewed as the only alternative to the Czech or the Hungarian models of development.

The third point concerns the question of a GDR national consciousness or national identity—a subject that does not lend itself readily to scientific treatment. Here we can refer to three observations. First, a certain nationalistic attitude, a self-awareness perhaps, vis-à-vis the Soviet Union, that one could observe in times past has disappeared with Ulbricht's passing from the scene. This holds especially for the SED itself. The general public seems to be quite conscious of the GDR's own achievements and is reluctant to attribute credit to the Soviet Union.

A further observation has to do with the internal situation in the German Democratic Republic. Despite a general awareness among those Germans living in the East that their country constitutes an entity apart from the unit in the West, a distinct national identity remains to be articulated.

Still another observation involves the SED's understanding of the idea of nationhood vis-à-vis the Federal Republic of Germany. Since the new Constitution of 1968 the German Democratic Republic has displayed an aggressive attitude with regard to questions of national consciousness. It has claimed to be the legitimate German state on grounds that it represents the historically progressive forces of the German nation, i.e., the peasants and workers of Germany. This somewhat reversed version of the Hallstein doctrine is an important factor to consider in any discussion of the national question.

From this point of view the German Democratic Republic shows no real interest in peaceful coexistence with the Federal Republic. The political leaders of the German Democratic Republic interpret "peaceful coexistence" as including both "cooperation" and "class struggle." Peaceful coexistence in terms of cooperation would include working jointly with the leaders of the Federal Republic of Germany on some selected sociopolitical and economic questions. Cooperative efforts in this respect will increase as long as the general political barometer, at least in Europe, indicates an atmosphere of détente. However, efforts in the direction of peaceful coexistence in terms of class struggle will also augment. The German Democratic Republic is not likely to drop its claim to be the sole representative of the progressive forces in German history. Indeed, its leaders have often indicated that for them the "class struggle" is not confined to state limits and that the borders between the Democratic Republic and the Federal Republic have separated states from each other but not members of the progressive classes. This argument gives the leaders of the German Democratic Republic an opportunity to fight for "historical progress" not only in their own country but also in the Federal Republic of Germany. That is precisely the reason why, in my opinion, the German Democratic Republic does not display a consistent and comprehensive interest in peaceful coexistence.

5. Philipp Schmidt-Schlegel

This seems to be an era of an ongoing process of recognizing realities. This process is by no means limited to the Federal Republic of Germany. It took the Soviet Union 20 years to recognize the reality of Berlin, our American friends took a little longer to recognize the reality of China, and we look forward now to the recognition of another reality, that of the European Community by the Soviet Union sometime in 1973 or 1974.

The recognition of realities on the part of the Federal Republic of Germany was an important milestone and a prerequisite for coming to a modus vivendi. Before examining some of the difficulties of a potential modus vivendi, it might be helpful to review briefly our attempt at bringing about a détente starting in 1963-64, and to examine the role played at that time, as well as later, by the German Democratic Republic in this détente policy.

It is a matter for the record that we were successful in establishing commercial missions in 1963-64 in all of the East Central European countries with the exception of Albania. This, of course, was not to the liking of the regime in the GDR, but it had to accept it since this policy accorded with the economic interest of the other East Central European countries. Our attempt at rapprochement with Moscow in 1964 failed because it came at the time of the downfall of Khrushchev, which might have been caused—at least partly—precisely by his agreement to such a rapprochement.

In 1966-67 we tried to establish diplomatic relations with East Central European countries and, of course, were only partially successful; we established diplomatic relations with Romania in 1967 and reestablished diplomatic relations with Yugoslavia in 1969. Our failure with other countries was due to strong GDR efforts, with heavy Soviet support, to block our diplomatic move. The GDR felt, and rightly, that our move was calculated to isolate it from the other Eastern European countries.

Philipp Schmidt-Schlegel is Deputy Consul General of the Federal Republic of Germany in New York.

Seen in that perspective, the decision by the Brandt-Scheel government to include the GDR in the policy of détente from the very beginning was a triumph of diplomacy that turned the policy into a grand design that included all of the three potential partners in détente in East Central Europe, namely the Soviet Union, the other East Central European countries, and the German Democratic Republic. A further felicitous move was to make the arrangements for the German summit meeting in Erfurt and in Kassel in early 1970 to coincide with the ongoing negotiations with Moscow and Warsaw. These summit meetings convinced the world and all the people in Eastern Europe, including the Soviet Union and, to a certain degree the GDR, that we meant business this time and wanted to come to a kind of modus vivendi with the GDR.

Chancellor Brandt presented Willi Stoph, the Chairman of the GDR Council of Ministers, 20 points of principles. A close look at these principles gives us an awareness of how long and tortuous is the road leading to a modus vivendi, which would later have to be followed by closer cooperation. May I just refer randomly to a few points. Point 17, one can readily judge, could well lead to a kind of modus vivendi and also to more concrete forms of cooperation; it refers mainly to the technical field of transportation, to traffic posts, telecommunications, etc. The question of information exchanges, of course, is a trickier problem. Point 15 concerns the reuniting of families; again, this should not be too difficult, given a modicum of political will on both sides. But then we have, under Point 14, the difficult problem of freedom of movement, also part of the Berlin agreement that will hopefully be signed soon. Finally, hidden in a subpoint of a principle, and associated with less controversial questions, is the essential subject of the definition of the basis of human rights. This, of course, is likely to be a knotty issue. We in the government of the Federal Republic feel strongly that the question of human rights should form part of a treaty that will regularize our relations with the Democratic Republic.

Trade is another major issue. The principle of trade is laid down under Point 18, where it is said rather briefly that commercial relations shall be further cultivated. Of course we had what was called an interzonal trade with the GDR in the past, financed to a large extent by us; this is now called inter-German trade. A close look reveals that it does not amount to very much: about one billion dollars altogether. We export more to the Democratic Republic than we import from it, but there was a jump in the period 1967-70 by 60 percent. This is a reliable indicator of the seriousness of intent on our part about détente, for we are well aware that our supply of machinery and industrial tools is a significant input in the process of economic growth in the Democratic Republic. Still, unfortunately, the GDR is not a full trading partner and lags in the industrial division of labor; this is largely due to the fact that it has not yet become fully competitive pricewise and qualitywise despite the fact that it is considered to be the most advanced industrial state in the Eastern bloc. Of course the difficulty is with the political and economic policy of the regime. Reference has been made during the conference to the policy of Abgrenzung, with various interpretations given to the term; e.g., delimitation policy or insulation policy, depending on the objectives of the translator. From the viewpoint of the regime, in the GDR it would be correct to translate it as "delimitation policy" rather than "insulation policy."

The breakdown of the Democratic Republic's trade with other countries is as follows: 75 percent is with the eastern bloc—42 percent with the Soviet Union—and 4 to 5 percent with the Federal Republic of Germany. Trade with the GDR represents no more than 1.5 percent and probably a little less, of all our trade, and we would be favorably disposed toward extending it. The regime in the GDR seems to be reluctant to increase the volume of trade with us, fearing that increased trade will bring with it a dependence on us.

The regime also feels compelled to fulfil its share in the Soviet economic plan—as announced recently by Mr. Kosygin in somewhat milder terms than his predecessor Mr. Khrushchev—to overtake the United States in the next three or four years. This will mean that the GDR, because of large deliveries of industrial equipment to the Soviet Union, will be further hindered in its efforts to diversify its commercial relations with the rest of the world, and particularly with the Federal Republic.

The question of relations of the GDR with other countries in East Central Europe should not be neglected. In order to make further progress in the field of industrial exchange, the GDR must try to establish close relationships with Poland and Czechoslovakia, and possibly also with Hungary. Czechoslovakia has a good working industry, Poland is in the midst of industrialization, and so is Hungary. The establishment of a division of labor in the industrial field between these three or four countries might well strengthen the position of the German Democratic Republic vis-à-vis Moscow. Of course China is another important area for the GDR to consider. China started playing a role on the world scene a few years ago. We know about its bridgehead in Albania, but it is also developing warm relations with Romania and Yugoslavia. It is perhaps not entirely coincidental that these three countries are precisely those within East Central Europe with which the German Democratic Republic has rather cool relations. These countries developed into a kind of Chinese-oriented bloc with a smaller volume of trade with the GDR than other Eastern European countries. China may well try to enhance its influence in Eastern

Europe through its membership in the United Nations and otherwise; this is likely to face the GDR with a few difficult decisions in the very near future, especially in view of its increasing dependence on the Soviet Union.

Therefore, with all of the above serving as background, in answer to the question raised whether the GDR can afford to extend its political relations with the Federal Republic, I would offer the following cautious and not very optimistic reply. Over the short term the GDR will not be able to make the political readjustment necessary, due to inherent weaknesses in its system and because of a continued dependence on the Soviet Union. A decision for increased cooperation with us can only follow a similar decision on the part of the Soviet Union. Should the Soviet Union be genuinely interested in a modus vivendi with the Federal Republic of Germany and, in particular, in close economic and technological cooperation, it certainly would not hesitate to make its wishes understood to the political leaders in the GDR, who would then act accordingly.

CHAPTER
10
SUMMATION
Marshall Shulman

It is impossible to summarize the discussion, and in place of a summation I would offer you a few general and personal impressions of the conference.

As experienced conférenciers, you all know that each conference has a life of its own. Sometimes it is not what is planned. Happily we are dealing with intractable human nature and a conference takes on a metaphysical life. It consists not only of studies that are presented, but also of the corridor conversations, the meals, the contacts, and an acquaintance with what is going on in other places. Sometimes it is only in retrospect that one is able to judge what the effects of a conference have been. I think this may be the case with our present conference.

The most significant impression I have is that the conference has registered a growing sense of community among the scholars who are working on the countries of East Central Europe; it marks, perhaps, a coming of age of the field of study in many different dimensions. I think it is the case, as someone has suggested, that there is now less of a tendency for studies on this part of the world to be treated as an offshoot of Soviet and Russian studies. There has been usefully highlighted the distinctive contribution that is being made and can be made to comparative studies generally by the studies of the countries in Eastern and Central Europe, and there has been highlighted in a very provocative way the movement toward the

---

Marshall Shulman is Professor of Political Science and Director of the Russian Institute at Columbia University, New York.

SUMMATION

integration of these studies into newer advances in the social sciences. There has also been a useful interplay between those who have been occupied with an area-study approach and those who come to this from the point of view of the disciplines.

It seems to me quite evidently useful that the conference included participants from Eastern Europe. We all would have preferred to have had more Eastern European scholars among us, for we feel that a closer contact between scholars from Eastern Europe and the West surely would be productive in a number of ways that have been illustrated in our discussions.

As a further impression, it seems to me useful to have had the participation of younger scholars and students in this conference. This has not ordinarily been the practice. It seems to me to have justified itself. It has brought fresh perspectives to our discussion and it encourages faith that this will contribute to the stimulation of their work and future development of the field of study.

Another observation is that the conference seems to have marked a step forward in the recognition of the Democratic Republic of Germany as a field of study. Heretofore it has really not had a place either in Eastern nor in Western European studies. The discussions have suggested that both the internal developments of the Democratic Republic and its external relations deserve and require inclusion in the study of East Central Europe. This can be a valuable source of insight into comparative sociological developments, studies of the nature of national consciousness, and models of industrialization, among others.

Finally, in relation to the practice and the study of international politics, the search for new perspectives in understanding East Central Europe, as the title of our conference suggests, has particular force at this moment in time. The conference has been dominated by a sense that a new period is beginning in European politics and that the shape of European alignments are clearly changing; they have plasticity and fluidity.

The subject area of our conference (however we define it in the interesting distinctions made by Professor Seton-Watson at the very outset of our discussions), East Central Europe, Eastern Europe, or Central Europe, is essentially the in-between lands between Western Europe and the Soviet Union. One of the central questions of this period, as it has been since World War II, is how to define the status of these lands in international politics. One tendency that was represented in the conference was to define their status in fairly traditional spheres-of-influence terms as part of a Soviet sphere of countries, as a necessary step toward the stabilization of Europe. Another tendency represented with equal force was in the opposite direction; it rejected the concept of spheres of influence, at least as that concept came to be defined in the period immediately following World War II. Perhaps as some suggested in the discussions, the underlying forces of history will answer that question in ways that we cannot now foresee, since it is a mark of this period that the upheavals to which our societies, both East and West, are subject are proceeding from causes that are but dimly understood toward directions that we cannot now perceive. But there would be some utility, I think, in making differentiations in our discussions between the "spheres" conception in the sense in which it applies to military security, and the quite different sense in which it applies to the political, cultural, and economic dimensions of international life. The conditions of modern technology make it impossible, in my opinion, to seal off parts of the world in impermeable spheres, whether the Soviet Union from Canada, or Western Europe from Eastern Europe. The conference suggests that if there is to be a period of stabilization that is to follow the present fluidity in international politics, it will not take the forms of the past. It will have to take account of the closer association between the various parts of the world, not their separation. This is reflected in the discussions we have had; we are encouraged to believe they will mark a step toward the maturation of the field of East Central European studies as part of the academic pursuit of knowledge. Maturation in this sense means that we are more than ever able to approach this field of knowledge in the way that scholarly investigation should be carried on everywhere, freed from the special inhibitions and deflections that resulted from the strong feelings generated by the war. Perhaps this conference marks our emergence from under the shadow of that period.

ABOUT THE EDITORS

SYLVA SINANIAN is Associate Director of the Center for Continuing Education at Columbia University. Prior to assuming her present duties she was a research associate at the Council on Foreign Relations and an Adlai Stevenson Fellow at the United Nations, representing the United States. She received her education at the University of California and at Columbia University.

ISTVAN DEAK is Professor of History and Director of the Institute on East Central Europe at Columbia University. He has been a visiting lecturer at the University of Maryland's Overseas Program in Germany and at Yale University, and has taught at Smith College and Rutgers University prior to his arrival at Columbia. He is the author of Weimar Germany's Left-Wing Intellectuals: A Political History of the Weltbuhne and Its Circle and is currently working on Louis Kossuth and the Hungarian Revolution of 1848-1849. He has also published numerous articles in professional journals. He was educated at the University of Budapest, the University of Paris, and Columbia University.

PETER C. LUDZ is Professor of Political Science and Sociology at the University of Bielefeld in the Federal Republic of Germany. Prior to his professorship at the University of Bielefeld he taught at the Free University of Berlin. He is the author of Party Elite in Transformation and The German Democratic Republic from the Sixties to the Seventies, in addition to numerous articles in professional journals. He received his education at the universities of Mainz, Munich, Paris, and Berlin.